PUBLIC GOODS AND PRIVATE COMMUNITIES

THE LOCKE INSTITUTE

Founded in 1989, The Locke Institute is an independent, non-partisan, educational and research organization. The Institute is named for John Locke (1632–1704), philosopher and political theorist, who based his theory of society on natural law which required that the ultimate source of political sovereignty was with the individual. Individuals are possessed of inalienable rights variously defined by Locke as 'life, health, liberty and possession', or, more directly, 'life, liberty and property'. It is the function of the state to uphold these rights since individuals would not enter into a political society unless they believed that it would protect their lives, liberties and properties.

The Locke Institute seeks to engender a greater understanding of the concept of natural rights, its implications for constitutional democracy and for economic organization in modern society. The Institute encourages high-quality research utilizing in particular modern theories of property rights, public choice, law and economics, and the new institutional economics as a basis for a more profound understanding of important and controversial issues in political economy. To this end, it commissions books, monographs, and shorter studies involving substantive scholarship written for a wider audience, organizes major conferences on fundamental topics in political economy, and supports independent research. The Institute maintains a publishing relationship with Edward Elgar, the international publisher in the social sciences.

In order to maintain independence, The Locke Institute accepts no government funding. Funding for the Institute is solicited from private foundations, corporations, and individuals. In additions, the Institute raises funds from the sale of publications and from conference fees. The Institute is incorporated in the State of Virginia, USA.

Officers of the Institute are listed above. Please direct all enquiries to the address given below.

5188 Dungannon Road • Fairfax, Virginia 22030, USA
(703) 385–5486

Public Goods and Private Communities

The Market Provision of Social Services

Fred Foldvary

Edward Elgar

Published by
Edward Elgar Publishing Limited
Gower House
Croft Road
Aldershot
Hants GU11 3HR
England

Edward Elgar Publishing Company
Old Post Road
Brookfield
Vermont 05036
USA

British Library Cataloguing in Publication Data
Foldvary, Fred
  Public Goods and Private Communities. –
  (John Locke Series)
  I. Title II. Series
  330.01

Library of Congress Cataloguing in Publication Data
Foldvary, Fred E., 1946–
    Public goods and private communities: the market provision of social
services/Fred Foldvary.
      p. cm. — (John Locke series in classical liberal political
economy)
    Includes bibliographical references and index.
    1. Public goods. 2. Social choice. 3. Community. 4. NIMBY
syndrome. 5. Land use—Government policy—United States—Citizen
participation—Case studies. I. Title. II. Series.
HB846.5.F64 1994
338.9—dc20   93–14224
                                                              CIP

ISBN 1 85278 951 4

Printed and Bound in Great Britain by
Hartnolls Limited, Bodmin, Cornwall.

Contents

Maps

Acknowledgments

This book is based on the dissertation of the same title, which I wrote for my doctorate in economics obtained at George Mason University in the summer of 1992. Many thanks to my dissertation committee members, Dr Richard Wagner, Dr Charles Rowley, Dr Tyler Cowen and Dr Henry Butler, for their help and guidance. I thank my wife, Janet, for her moral support and also her assistance in transferring the text to a new computer. I appreciate the financial support provided by the Center for Study of Public Choice, Center for the Study of Market Processes and the George Mason Graduate School during my graduate studies.

I also express my heartfelt gratitude to Spencer MacCallum, professors at George Mason University, my fellow graduate students, the secretaries at the economics department, the librarians at the Planned Community Archives at George Mason's Fenwick Library, David Smith at the Walt Disney Archives, Michael Curtis and Carolyn (Pat) Liberman of Arden, Jim Rader and Libby Strickland of the Fort Ellsworth Condominium, Allan Matthews of Reston, Sylvia Haefer of Long & Foster Realtors® at Reston, and to John Metcalf for his help on the Players Club at Sawgrass. I am grateful also to my parents and my sister for their encouragement.

I appreciate as well the assistance of many other people in Arden village, Fort Ellsworth Condominium, The Briarcrest Condominium, Reston Association, the Community Associations Institute and others who helped me with materials and interviews.

Many thanks also to the Locke Institute for their editorial support and assistance in the publication of the book. I am most pleased to be included in The John Locke Series of The Locke Institute. I am grateful again to Charles Rowley for his careful reading of the manuscript and valued suggestions. Of course, the responsibility for the contents of the book remain with the author, but the book would not have been what it is without the valued help of my friends and colleagues.

1   The fallacy of the market-failure argument

The market-failure proposition

Do public goods and services such as streets, parks and dams have to be provided by government? The prevailing view is that they do, because agents (persons and organizations) in a market process normally fail to provide them. According to this view, since people benefit from civic services whether they pay for them or not, many will be 'free riders', not paying for the services unless they are forced to. For that reason, many economists, as well as much of the public, think that only the government or public sector can provide the collective services that people in a community may desire.

The theme of this book is that this proposition is incorrect. The market-failure argument treats persons as atomistic agents living in ether rather than in three-dimensional space and in a context of institutions and history. Such an unreal etherial abstraction, conditional on premises which no real society has ever lived in, produces a theory that may be validly concluded from its premises, but is unsound – incorrect for real-world human existence. Once these real-world factors are introduced into public-goods theory, the market-failure argument not only falls, but is turned on its head: rather than benefiting from the public goods whether or not they pay for them, people must pay private agents for the public goods whether or not these agents provide the goods. This is because, when the value of space is affected by the goods, the economic rent generated by the goods will be collected by the owner of that space. The theory of market failure is likewise turned on its head, since the fact that the public does pay for the goods implies that a private agent can collect the payment in return for providing the goods, and that government imposes needless costs if it interferes with such an arrangement and substitutes other methods to pay for the goods.

Moreover, the provision of public goods by the so-called 'public sector' is itself subject to government failure. The theory of public choice, applying economic analysis to the choices and actions of agents in a political process, shows that specialized interests, including elected officials and those in bureaucracies, seek (among other goals) to transfer resources to themselves and their agencies at the expense of the general public and the taxpayers. The political sector fails to allocate resources the way that most of the public would desire.

The following three stories illustrate the arguments for market failure, government failure and the possibility of contractual success. Suppose, for all three stories, that there is a valley – call it Happy Valley – with 100 000 residents, through which runs a river apt to flood periodically. Almost all residents would like to have a dam built to protect them against the flooding. This is a classic, much used, example in public-choice and public-finance theory.

In the first story, the market fails. An entrepreneur (call him Pierre) sees a profitable opportunity in building the dam. Unfortunately, Pierre calculates that the cost of buying the land, including compensating the users of the site for the loss of homes, farms and wildlife, would exceed the estimated amount he could earn just from the water and recreation offered by the dam. But surely the good residents of Happy Valley would be willing to pay an annual charge to be protected from the flooding, enough to make the venture profitable? Pierre proceeds to ask each household to pledge $100 per year for the indefinite future for the benefits of the dam, which is less than the insurance they need to pay to be compensated for the risk. It is surely in the interest of each household to pay this amount, but, to his astonishment, Pierre finds that no one wishes to sign up! He asks an economist friend for an explanation.

The economist explains that the residents of Happy Valley would find the dam to be beneficial, but they also realize that, if one does not sign up and others do, the resident will benefit from the flood protection as much as the others. So why sign up? Let the others pay! 'But this is foolish,' replies Pierre, 'for I shall not build the dam if no one pays, and all will end up losers.' Yes, the economist replies, and this is the well-known 'prisoner's dilemma': each person has an incentive not to cooperate, even though all would gain if all cooperated relative to none cooperating. Perhaps if there were only a few residents, such as 20 or 30, they could all meet and agree to fund the dam, but with 100 000 residents the transactions costs of meeting or organizing are too high and the large numbers prevent a loss of individual status from the failure to cooperate. The incentive to be a free-rider is so strong that no agreement is reached. 'The market' fails to produce the dam. This, say many economics texts,[1] is why we need government to produce the public good. Government can force everyone to cooperate. This is not true cooperation, since the choice is made by government agents rather than by all the individual citizens, but it does get the dam built.

However, public choice theory would indicate that the second story, that of government provision, also lacks a happy (or optimal) ending. The valley has an elected legislature which has the authority on whether to build a dam, how big it shall be, how much to spend on it and how the funds are to be raised. Each legislator is elected every two years and depends on campaign funds to generate the publicity that induces people to vote for him, and legislators also obtain votes from those who receive benefits from the public treasury. Some farmers down the river approach the committee considering the dam and suggest that, if the dam were larger than what was currently proposed, they would be able to draw out water to irrigate their crops, which would increase production and benefit the community. Also, a utility company offers to build an electricity-generating facility if the dam were even larger, which would provide electricity at lower cost than that currently provided by a rival company; of course, the company would not bear the cost of the dam, since the public would benefit. This larger dam would flood more forest land, and an amendment to the legislation provides for building a road through the forest to facilitate the removal of the trees for lumber. The local timber company will pay $1 per tree and, although the cost of the road averages out at $1.47 per tree, it is defended as avoiding a waste of the trees.

Much of the downtown area is owned by two corporations, whose representatives invite the committee members on a fact-finding mission to Las Vegas to study Hoover Dam. The dam will provide a large boost to real estate values, eliminating the cost of flood insurance, which will increase real estate taxes, and the legislators agree to lower the property tax rate; this also will enable them to campaign with the message to home owners that the dam did not increase their property taxes. However, downtown businesses tenants will pay as much rent or more than previously, so there will be no net benefit to them or their customers from the lower tax rate.

Pierre the entrepreneur discreetly offers to make campaign contributions if he rather than his competitors obtains the dam contract. He offers to build a road around the dam, which coincidentally passes by property owned by one of the legislators. The legislators favoring the dam also garner support from other legislators by log-rolling: they offer to support a bill to require taxi permits to a key member of the legislature who has been campaigning among his colleagues for the protection of taxi firms from competition by immigrants. This increased cost of transportation and decrease in job availability is a hidden cost of the dam that few voters will realize has been imposed because of the dam. Also, the public employees have a strong union and are granted a rise to compensate them for the increase in taxes in return for supporting the project.

The legislature orders a cost–benefit analysis, but it uses a low interest rate and ignores the increase in city payroll, the rental value of the land, the rise in taxi fares and the marginal cost of the lost beauty of the canyon the river went through, which would not have been lost with the original, smaller, dam. Also, an Indian tribe which traditionally used part of the upper river for ceremonies and for swimming is listened to but not included in the loss calculations; they do not hold title to that land and cannot afford to invite the legislators to free trips to pleasure resorts. The council determines that the broader public interest outweighs the interest of the few recreational users of the upper river, and that the public interest also requires a big dam which would provide electric power and water to farmers. They decide to fund the dam with a sales tax increase and a surtax on incomes over $50 000 per year, with a deduction for investments (such as those made by the farmers) related to water usage (to promote energy conservation). Since only 35 per cent of the households have annual incomes over $50 000, the measure has the support of the majority of the voters, who are not able to calculate the total annual cost of the increase in the sales tax, if they think about it at all.

The land is acquired by eminent domain, its purchase financed by tax-free municipal bonds. The alternative investments that would have been made had funds not been shifted to building the excessive dam, and the jobs that would have been created had only the original, smaller, flood-control dam been built, will never be known – but the dam and its benefits will be trumpeted by the city officials and become known to all.

The dam does get built, but it is three times larger than what Pierre the entrepreneur originally proposed for flood control. Even those who do not pay the surtax end up paying more than what they would have paid for the original design. Tax revenues pay for a public good larger than the public at large desires, and much of the benefit flows to a few parties, such as the farmers, the electrical company and the dam builder. Electricity bills are a bit lower than before, but total taxes plus electricity bills are still much higher than they would have been with the original design, although many members of the public are convinced that they have benefited, since they do not know, and would not be able to calculate easily, the cost of the original proposal. Moreover, the farmers, utility company and Pierre had to spend considerable funds lobbying the legislators, taking them to dinner and re-sorts, and offering (discreetly) gifts and campaign contributions. The total amount of resources devoted to seeking these benefits, plus the net wealth lost by the taxpayers and residents as a whole, constitutes government fail-ure. The dam is overproduced, and some alternative goods that the people would have preferred fail to be produced.

Now comes the third story. This time, we recognize that Happy Valley occupies space whose value is affected by the dam. The potential increased rental value of the valley sites provides an opportunity for the entrepreneur that does not skew the relative costs to the members of the community. The entrepreneur does not need to make a contract with each household to pay for the flood protection if he already has title to the increased rent that the dam will induce. This can be accomplished in several ways.

First, Pierre can buy a site suitable for a dam and for a potential commu-nity, and then lease or sell the sites, subject to the provision that the site owners or lessees pay periodic fees for the services offered by the dam. The new residents would then only obtain the sites if the cost were worth it for each individual. The market succeeds. The developer or subsequent owner could also build a dam after the community is already established if he can collect the increased rent that the dam will generate, in addition to selling other services associated with the dam. The owner will have no incentive to build too large a dam or to fail to build one if it can generate profits. Redistribution does not take place because the entire site is under a unified ownership and governance.

Suppose, however, that the valley is already settled and not owned by an outside firm. The market-failure scenario assumes that the households are atomistic, each an independent, isolated unit. But human society has always lived in communities, so the premise of atomistic households is antihistorical; if it is meant to apply to real-world civic goods, its ignoring of institutions commits the error of begging the question. The real-world distinction is not community organization versus lack of organization, but what kind of governance or organization an enterprise or a community has, for example consensual governance versus imposed governance.

Suppose Happy Valley were developed by three firms which turned over the governance of the communities to three respective residential associations, each of which had a mutual contract among the site holders. Pierre the entrepreneur would not have to contract with 100 000 parties but only with three, and if the three had a mutual cooperative association among them for valley-wide affairs, he need only address the umbrella association. The term 'market' provision can obfuscate the essential issue, that of provision by consensual means, which can involve an enterprise and a civic association. If the benefits of the dam were perceived by all, or almost all residents, any uncooperative community that wanted to free-ride would suffer the resentment and economic backlash of the other two and be expelled from the umbrella organization, most likely suffering greater losses than its contribution to the dam. Pierre can therefore offer to build the dam in return for a portion of the increased land rent that the dam would induce, without the burden of large organizing costs. The communities will agree only if the anticipated land rent, net of payments to Pierre, is positive. A too expensive dam will not be built, and the benefits will flow to all the residents and be paid for in proportion to the economic benefits of the site holders as reflected by the increased market rent of their sites. An affirmative vote by the valley residents, or the community boards, is quite likely, and the market again succeeds.

One could ask whether the residential associations too would not experience political failure, as in the second story. This would be less likely if the developer or founder of the community included constitutional provisions (in the master deed and bylaws) limiting the powers of the associations. The funding of civic associations is typically limited to flat-rate fees or assessments based on the property or land value, rather than imposing arbitrary taxation. Also, the constitution can require a super-majority vote of the residents for major expenditures, preventing gross privilege seeking. Members of the associations can also sue the association and its board.

If the umbrella association becomes prone to wasteful expenditures, the constituent communities may secede and form an alternative association. Large community associations could also have secession clauses for their neighborhoods and villages. Hence constitutional safeguards can be built into community organizations, significantly reducing the likelihood of institutional failure. The major safeguard would be the contractual nature of the relationship between a prospective resident and the developer or subsequent community governance – each potential resident or site owner would sign an agreement acknowledging agreement with the rules before joining the community, and know that there are safeguards against the arbitrary confiscation of his site-specific investment.

Still, it is possible for a developer or residential association to fail, just as any human individual, organization or institution can fail. The issue of market failure is not whether some collective goods will fail to be produced or be overproduced; such occurrences constitute entrepreneurial rather than systematic market failure and are inevitable in a world of uncertainty, change and imperfect human nature. The market-failure argument is that market or consensual processes must generally fail to provide public or civic goods, and the third story shows how 'the market' need not fail.

The issue to be addressed is the feasibility of public-goods provision by private means. The market-failure proposition is framed as the following hypothesis: *The incentives for personal gain, which induce agents in a market economy to provide private goods, do not in general induce such agents to provide the collective goods that the people in the service domain effectively demand, because even when transaction costs are not an obstacle, there is no way to induce individual users to pay for a portion of the good so that the total amount of the good is paid for.*

The theory presented in the initial chapters shows how collective goods can be provided by agents in a market process, and the case studies described in the later chapters demonstrate how real-world communities are in fact providing for such goods in accord with the theory. The market-failure hypothesis is thus shown to be unsound in theory and rejected by the evidence. This theory and evidence also contrasts contractual provision with government-imposed provision, showing how government failure can be and is overcome by consensual community arrangements.

The deficiency in examples of privatization

Heretofore, much of the literature contesting the market-failure argument has focused on aspects of privatization, the provision of civic services by particular private firms. Examples of services that have been provided contractually include police and fire protection, streets and roads, lighthouses, education and recreation. These case studies show that the argument for market-failure must be qualified to account for the conditions under which some civic services can be provided by decentralized and voluntary means. But this still does not prove that community public services can in general be provided via market processes.

For example, a study by High and Ellig (1988) finds that, in Great Britain and the United States, *education* was widely provided privately before governments became involved and largely displaced it. Such historical examples demonstrate the possibility but not necessarily the general feasibility of comprehensive private education. For the latter, a theory is required regarding the private-good aspect of education and the circumstances under which voluntary community organizations provide it. Private *fire protection* has been described by N. Poole (1991) and R. Poole (1980). The Rural/Metro Corporation provides fire protection for Scottsdale, Arizona and 50 other communities. Much of the fire service in small communities is provided by volunteer groups or by private firms. But is there a theory of the way such service can be provided for communities of all sizes? For example, can there be competition among fire companies in the same region? *Private streets* exist in many communities, most notably in St. Louis, Missouri, as described in Chapter 13. The 'Streets of Laredo' is a traditional western song; today, one could compose a song of the 'private streets of Laredo', which during 1982–5 sold 150 blocks to private enterprises and organizations (Fitzgerald, 1988, pp. 163–4). But can streets in general be built and maintained by private agents, or are these special cases? Some private highways and bridges are financed using tolls. Early American turnpikes were built by voluntary civic groups and companies (Klein, 1990). Streets are also funded using parking meters and fees for parades. But again, is there a theory of general private-sector highway and bridge provision?

Lighthouses have been pointed to as an example of a public good requiring government provision (cf. Heilbroner and Thurow, 1987, pp. 168–9). Yet Ronald Coase (1974) described how, in Great Britain, lighthouses near harbors had been funded by fees for the use of the harbors. Coase explains how financing the lighthouses from general revenues would tend to reduce the efficiency of the administration of the service owing to increased costs of administration, while making it less responsive to the shippers. But what of lighthouses far away from harbors? It is well known that *recreation* is provided both by governments and by private firms. Volunteer organizations, 'friends of the zoo', often assist in operating and funding government-run zoos, museums and parks (R. Poole, 1980). Many corporate buildings include a 'public square' in their private land. But is government provision needed for cases such as city parks in residential neighborhoods, where private funding is not tied into other private use and where entrance fees are impractical? *Security*, or protection against crime, is provided by such privately funded goods as locks, fences, guards, patrols and alarms. There are more private security guards in the USA than full-time uniformed police officers (Neely, 1990, p. 51). But is it feasible for such private efforts completely to take the place of government police?

National defense is often used as an example *par excellence* of a public good requiring government provision. But, even in this case, private efforts can supplement government defense. Examples include shelters, stored food and water, gas masks, medicine, remote retreats, weapons and voluntary armies. Can there be a purely voluntary national or large-scale defense? *Law* is often regarded as in the domain of government, but it too has been provided by the private sector. The Law Merchant, a commercial and contractual law, was created independently of royal law in Europe. Merchants used their own courts to adjudicate disputes, enforced by ostracism (Benson, 1990). Many private mediation and arbitration services supplement government courts today, but can such private services provide a complete alternative to government law and courts? *Money* is today universally provided for by governments, often as a monopoly (even where foreign currencies are permitted, often the issuance of private, competing currency is not). As Carl Menger (1976 [1871]) and others have described, money and banking evolved through a spontaneous process by private transactions and only later become subject to state authority. More so than for many other goods now provided by government, the theory of private money and banking has been developed (for example, Selgin, 1988) to the degree that its feasibility has a firm theoretical foundation.

These examples illustrate how some civic goods have been provided for by private actors, but not that private provision is feasible regardless of time, place and culture. Empirical case studies disprove impossibility but do not demonstrate general feasibility. Earl Brubaker (1975) proposes a more comprehensive theory, arguing that non-production is a form of exclusion, enabling private production to take place. Prior contracting reduces the free-rider problem, but does not preclude the possibility of non-participation.[2] Moreover, the existence of a public bad or even the failure to produce a public good is itself a public item, hence non-production is not sufficient to prevent the existence of public goods in all cases. Almost all of these examples and their treatment in the literature consist of private agents providing public goods as a substitute for government provision. In most cases, a comprehensive theory of market-process provision is lacking. Such a theory requires a different approach, in which government itself is endogenous to the theory and the spatial aspect of most civic goods is recognized. Rather than taking the place of particular government services, one at a time, a comprehensive theory of the voluntary provision of collective goods requires a systematic and comprehensive treatment of various categories of public goods, including the public good of governance itself.

The concepts of 'public' and 'private'

The term 'public' in 'public goods' has a distinctly different meaning from its usage in 'public sector'. The term 'private' in 'private goods' also has a meaning distinct from its usage in 'private sector'. The concepts of the public sector (government) and the private sector (firms and households) will be examined in greater detail in Chapter 5. For now, the commonly known meanings regarding governments and private actors will suffice. However, the terminology that will be used here needs to be clarified.

The terms 'private sector' and 'market' have various connotations, but their essential characteristic with regards to public goods is that the process of provision is consensual. The following terms will be considered as synonyms for 'private' in the context of the 'private sector' for goods provision, processes and communities: *market, voluntary, consensual, contractual* and *multilateral.* The following terms will be treated as synonyms for 'public' in the context of the 'public sector' for goods provision, processes and communities: *sovereign, political, government, imposed* and *unilateral.*

Terms such as 'political' and 'government' could logically be used in the context of contractual communities, which also have governmental and political processes, but, to keep the terminology clear, the meaning of these terms will be confined to the more conventional usage of public-sector governance unless the context clearly specifies otherwise. The term 'governance' will be used generically for both public- and private-sector organizations. The terms 'unilateral' and 'multilateral' as used here refer to the relationship between the agency providing goods and the recipients of the goods. Voluntary governance among two or more persons consists of agreements among equal parties, hence it is literally many-sided or multilateral. The political process, the public-sector governance of today's countries, states and cities, may encompass many persons who agree to some particular rule, but not all who are subject to the rule make an explicit agreement to enact it (otherwise it would be classified as a market process); therefore the rule is unilateral and imposed with respect to any person subject to the rule who has not or would not agree to it.

With regard to the terms 'public' and 'private' in the context of goods, the literature has emphasized a distinction between 'pure' private and public goods and 'mixed' goods, but the designation of 'mixed' goods begs the question of what determines the elements of the mixture. A set composed of mixed elements implies that there is some distinction among the elements. A foundation for a theory of public goods is a clear specification between private and public goods.

Paul Samuelson's (1954) formulation of private versus public goods became a landmark in making the distinction clear in mathematical terms, although, as discussed below, the mathematics are not sufficient for a clear definition. The classification between the two types of goods is determined by the way individual consumption or use relates to the aggregate. For a private good y, aggregate consumption equals the sum of individual consumption:

$$y_j = \sum_{i=1}^{I} y_i^j \qquad (1.1)$$

where i refers to an individual consumer, I to the total number of consumers, and j to a good. The total amount consumed of good j is the sum of the consumption of the individuals.

For a public or collective good y, aggregate use equals individual use for each individual:

$$y_k = y_i^k (i = 1, \ldots, I) \qquad (1.2)$$

for some public good k. Samuelson (1969) makes it clear that the equation of personal use with the total amount of a public good for all individuals using it does not imply that all individuals derive the same utility from the good.

This distinction between private and public goods long precedes Samuelson, public goods being described by Ugo Mazzola (1958 [1890], p. 42) as characterized by 'indivisibility in use'. Emil Sax (1958 [1924], p. 183) stated that collective activities are those which extend to all members of a community equally, and that the benefits are indivisible. Antonio de Viti de Marco (1936, pp. 38–9) described total individual wants as the sum of the quantities, while a total collective want is the sum of qualities. He also stated that a public good corresponds to a collective want (p. 44). Samuelson (1983, p. xxii) himself states that his 1954 model is an application of Abram Bergson's work on the 'new welfare economics' to the theory of public goods. Samuelson had summarized Bergson's analysis in his *Foundations of Economic Analysis* (Samuelson, 1983 [1947]).

Samuelson's formulation has been criticized as ambiguous, since not all goods can be neatly categorized in one of the two equations. A deeper ambiguity lies in the meaning of good '*y*'. A 'good' can refer to some physical commodity or service, or else to some aspect, property, attribute or feature of a good. These qualities have been termed 'characteristics'. Kelvin Lancaster (1966) theorized that utility is directly derived from the characteristics of goods and hence only indirectly from the physical goods. As noted by Lancaster, previous utility theory implicitly recognized the characteristics approach. Menger (1976 [1871], p. 52), a founder of modern utility theory, stated as a prerequisite to goods character that a thing have properties that render it capable of satisfying a desire or need. Building on the work of Lancaster, Auld and Eden (1990) apply the characteristics approach to public goods: publicness and privateness are characteristics of goods rather than referring to categories of physical goods. The characteristics approach provides a solution to the problem of 'mixed' goods: the mix consists of the distinct public and private characteristics of some physical good. As recognized by Richard Auster (1977), these characteristics are themselves goods, so that we can still speak of public and private goods, keeping in mind that we are referring to the properties of physical goods.

Kenneth Goldin (1977) points out another problem with Samuelson's distinction. Abstract goods such as music cannot be categorized as public or private; they can be produced as public goods (a concert in a park) or as private goods (one's own tape player). But Goldin is referring to a different type of good than Samuelson. Samuelson implicitly refers to a physical good, whereas Goldin refers to a final abstract good, similar to the 'Z good' proposed by Gary Becker (1965). Stigler and Becker (1977) posit Z goods as the ultimate items entering a utility function. Z goods are produced as functions of time and intermediate physical commodities, the X goods. With Z-good theory, the Lancastrian characteristics as goods are not themselves ultimates but form bundles of properties making up an ultimate abstract Z good such as music. Characteristics are therefore intermediate between X and Z goods; they can thus be labelled with the intermediate letter, that is as 'Y goods' (hence the use of the letter *y* in the above Samuelson equations rather than *x* as Samuelson used it). Thus X goods are physical commodities (or services) with public and private characteristics, which are Y goods, and these characteristics are used to create abstract Z goods such as music or safety. Hence Goldin's criticism is met by the recognition of different types of goods, X goods being capable of mixed characteristics, Y goods being distinctly private or public, and Z goods having no inherent publicness or privateness.

However, defining the public/private distinction in terms of characteristics does not yet remove all the ambiguities in the concept of an economic 'good'. Another question arises: does the term refer to an existential good, one that actually exists, or does it refer to a potential good, or both? The more parsimonious choice is to define a good as an existential one, since we can determine the characteristics of hypothetical goods by imagining how they would be used once in existence. Hence a proposition such as 'producible public goods are necessarily excludable through the possibility of non-production' is not valid by the existential definition; excludability would only be determined by the use of the good once in existence. A final ambiguity lies in the persons using the goods, the term 'i' in the above equations. An individual 'i' can be a person actually using the good, or he can be someone not at present using it but who might use it, or both. Here, too, the existential interpretation will be used. The equations apply to persons actually using the goods.

The definition with regard to persons comes into play in the issue of rivalry. Public goods are generally regarded as non-rivalrous in the literature, but rivalry itself is multifaceted. There is 'quantity rivalry' in the consumption of private goods: the quantity consumed by one person cannot be consumed by another. This is different from 'quality rivalry', in which the utility obtained from a good decreases when others use it, even if there is no quantity rivalry. Characteristics subject to quality rivalry are private, the good being conceptually summed over the number of users. For example, a crowded swimming pool is less useful than a non-crowded one, even though the total quantity of water is the same in both cases; the surface area in which one can swim without being blocked might be one way to characterize this quality. A third type can be called 'marginal rivalry'; here the utility obtained from an X good diminishes with the addition of another user, even though there is no quality rivalry for those actually using the good. Quantity and quality rivalry are existential, and marginal rivalry is potential. Like potential goods and potential persons, potential rivalry does not enter into the existential definition of a public good.

Definitions of public and private

The above qualifications can now be summarized and formulated into a definition of public and private goods. A *'public good' is a characteristic of an existing phenomenon with a domain of impact containing at least two actual persons, such that the amount of the characteristic encountered by any individual in the domain is the entire amount of that characteristic.* A 'private good' is defined as any characteristic (of a phenomenon) that is not public. Hence public and private characteristics are defined as set complements.

'Collective goods' is a synonym for 'public goods', and 'severable goods' (those which can be severed or divided) will be used here as a synonym for 'private goods'. These synonyms can in some contexts eliminate the ambiguity and confusion in use of the terms 'private' and 'public'. In the economics literature, the term 'public goods' often refers to a particular subset of collective goods, those that are typically provided by governments. Here these will be called 'civic goods'. Much of the discussion in subsequent chapters refers to civic goods rather than public goods *per se*, since these are the subject of the discussions about public-goods provision.

Public goods have sometimes been associated with external effects. An externality or external effect consists of utility which comes from another person's acts. In practice, many externalities overlap with public goods, since they affect many persons. But if one person's acts affect only another person, this is an external effect without being a public good. Also, the characteristics of an externality can be both public and private; for example, the amount of polluted water entering a neighborhood is the sum of the amounts that is imposed on each household, making it private in quantity, although the toxicity of the pollution may be common to all, hence public. The use of a public good such as the sun does not necessarily involve externalities. Hence the definitions of public goods and externalities do not imply one another, and externalities *per se* will not be treated in this book, but are subsumed as public goods when they in practice overlap.

The taxonomy of public goods

Public goods can be divided into four categories on the basis of two features:[3] (1) potential congestion, or marginal cost in consumption for additional persons into the domain of the good for some population threshold, and (2) excludability from the domain. Goods which have a positive marginal cost of admitting persons in the domain can be termed 'congestible'.[4] A congestible public good is subject to marginal rivalry; that is, it has the ability to become crowded, but in general, or at the moment, it is not congested in fact. As discussed above, potential rivalry is not relevant to the determination of a public characteristic.[5] If the characteristic is subject to quality or quantity rivalry, or if the good is in fact congested or crowded at the moment of consideration, then it is not public. Hence congestible public goods are those which can become congested but are not congested at the moment of consideration.[6] The complement, those goods without a potential congestion cost, can be termed 'capacious': the domain has an unlimited capacity for the entry of extra individuals.

The other classification axis is excludability. Collective goods which are excludable (for which potential members can be prevented from using) will be referred to as 'excludable' goods, and non-excludable or 'global' goods will be the complement set, accessible to all. An important category of excludable goods, discussed in Chapter 3, is those which have an impact upon a certain territory in which an individual in the area can be found and moved. Excludable goods have also been called 'club' goods, but the adjective is ambiguous in English, since it could refer to goods produced by existing clubs, or to public goods which are subject to exclusion, however produced. Hence the more generic term 'excludable' will be used here. The following matrix illustrates the possibilities, with possible examples indicated:

	congestible	capacious	
	swimming pool	political association	excludable
	population growth	wildlife's existence	global

A swimming pool can exclude entrants, and each additional swimmer imposes a congestion cost on others. As discussed above, the classification of the pool characteristics as private or public depends on the relevant physical good and the domain of persons using it. The physical qualities of an entire pool, such as its size and temperature, are not congestible, whereas the usability of the pool, for example one's ability to swim laps, is congestible and, if the pool is crowded, this characteristic is characterized by quality rivalry; hence it is private. The category of public goods which are both excludable and congestible is an important one, since many so-called 'impure' public goods, including many typically provided by governments, fall into this category. It does not seem to have a commonly used name, and so we use the term 'clubhouse' goods, implying that they can be provided by a club and are located in a 'house' which can become crowded. A political association is excludable but might have no cost of admitting an additional member (a marginal member could well be a net benefit); hence it is capacious. Television transmission, which will be discussed in Chapter 3, is also made excludable through signal-scrambling devices, but has no marginal cost per user. An increasing world population creates the public bad of decreasing the availability of unused beaches and other natural sites on earth; those who wish to use these sites cannot be excluded from this bad, and its impact is global. (Increasing global population may also create public goods, such as an increased division of labor.) The utility obtained by lovers of wildlife from its very existence on earth is non-excludable. So long as the organisms exist, the utility gained by wildlife advocates cannot be excluded; the addition of another wildlife lover imposes no loss on the others. The wildlife itself, however, could conceivably be privately owned. An organization, for example, could be recognized as having title to a species of whale, and whales would then have a market price. Harvesting or damaging a particular whale would have a private characteristic in terms of the quantity of animals alive, but the existence of whales *per se* would still be a global public good for those who like whales.

Since both excludable and congestible characteristics, as defined here, can be public, it is not meaningful in this context to refer to public goods which are both capacious and global as 'polar' or 'pure', since all four cases are public. Holtermann (1972), making a distinction between the private utilization of a collective good and its public availability, states that variables in a consumption vector fall into one or the other Samuelson category, so that in that sense there are only pure public goods and pure private goods. Samuelson (1969) also indicates that he has moved towards a semantic preference for the two distinct types of goods. Instead of 'polar', public characteristics which are global and capacious can be called 'universal goods'. Of course, if the distinction is applied to physical commodities rather than characteristics, then a 'pure' public X good can be considered to be one which has no private characteristics.

The above taxonomy of public goods in the four classes is useful not only to clarify the terminology regarding public goods but to disaggregate the concept into classes which have different economic natures and thus different applications for public versus private provision. With public goods now defined and the different types analyzed, the question of market failure will now be examined. We have seen above that the market-failure argument is not fully countered by the existence of some contractually provided public goods. The theory of market failure will be analyzed so that the argument that market processes can provide for 'private' goods but not 'public' ones is shown to be false in general and not just for certain specific goods.

Notes

1. See, for example, Mansfield and Behravesh (1989, p. 551).
2. David Schmidtz (1991) reports on various experiments on the provision of public goods by voluntary payments. Even with money-back guarantees and a provision threshold, not everyone contributes.
3. Musgrave (1969) analyzes public goods on the basis of these two features, but uses rivalness versus non-rivalness rather than congestion or crowding as one feature.
4. Ellickson (1973) formulates crowding as the case in which a marginal user increases the resources required to maintain the quality of the public good.
5. Mishan (1969) states that any inference from Samuelson's equation (1.2) of a zero

marginal cost of sharing a public good is not warranted. Factor or social costs can rise with an increasing number of users, an external effect that can apply to public as well as private goods. Such external effects, he argues, should be excluded from the private/public distinction.

6.   Auster (1977) classifies public goods as either 'pure' or 'crowded'. Samuelson (1969, p. 118) provides the example of a crowded road as a 'public good – or rather, "public bad", type' of consumption externality. Sandmo (1989) points out that a public good such as a road can have private tie-in goods such as 'car use', which can be subject to congestion. Glazer and Niskanen (1991) present a model in which members of a community prefer to have a congested public facility, since wealthy members are induced to provide their own private-sector substitute, reducing the cost of the public-sector facility; hence voters may prefer congested public clubs.

2 The question of market failure

Free-riders

The problem of free-riders is the central issue in the market-failure argument. If a product is collectively consumed, how can we make sure that everyone using it will contribute to its cost in proportion to the value received? For excludable goods, one can charge admission into the domain of usage, so contractual provision is feasible. It is often not recognized that territorial goods are a class of excludable goods, and that most civic goods are territorial. There then remains the problem of non-excludable goods, which the literature on private provision has not dealt with in a comprehensive fashion. It will be shown in Chapter 7 that such goods are provided through tie-ins to excludable goods, and also through 'sympathy' as described by Adam Smith (1982 [1970]).

The normative rationale for the voluntary financing of public goods was posed by John Locke (1947 [1690], p. 193), who stated that 'it is fit every one who enjoys his share of the protection should pay out of his estate his proportion for the maintenance of it', but that the 'supreme power cannot take from any man part of his property without his own consent', since 'the preservation of property' is 'the end of government' (p. 191). The issue is thus how to protect property without the contradiction of negating such protection by confiscation. Locke left unanswered the question of how to induce a person to pay his share without taxation; that is, the taking of property.

The voluntary financing of a good is equivalent to the unanimous consent of the members of the community. Knut Wicksell (1958 [1896]) sought to implement unanimity by requiring that each item of government expenditure be linked to its financing. Though for large groups unanimity may be impractical for operating decisions, unanimity can be implemented at the constitutional level, that of the initial agreement on and subsequent changes to the basic rules of a community and the choice of joining or leaving a community. The rules can then include methods of raising revenues. However, while unanimity can be practical for the formation of new communities, it may not be feasible for changing the rules and membership of an existing community. The free-rider problem is then raised to the constitutional level, with individuals refusing to consent to an agreement either because they hope to gain from a good without paying for it or from honest differences of opinion.

17

Earl Brubaker (1975) argues that exclusion can be accomplished by non-provision. A good would only be produced if there were enough persons agreeing to pay for it. But the free-rider problem is still not overcome, since people may avoid signing in the hope that a sufficient number will. Davis and Hewlett (1977) point out that the reduction of a negative externality can be a public good subject to free-riding. Moreover, as in the case of unanimity, non-provision does not apply to goods already in existence, for example, public bads that people want to eliminate. Even deeper, the non-provision of a desired public good is itself a public bad, so that non-provision affects the type and amount of the public good but does not eliminate the publicness of the phenomenon.

As outlined in Chapter 1, the literature has provided many examples of public goods that have been provided through private and voluntary means. But the fact that free-riding was overcome in some particular cases or for some products does not imply that free-riding can be eliminated in general. The issue of free-riding requires a comprehensive theory that includes the elements of time, space and institutions, and will be set forth in subsequent chapters.

Demand revelation

If many people are using the same good, how can we possibly know how much each person really wants? For severable goods, like bread, demand is usually determined by the amounts obtained by purchasers, but for collective goods the amount must be decided jointly. People can give false information about how large a collective good they desire. Note that free-riding does not necessarily involve such a false signalling, since it could also be a case of the refusal to pay even when the desire for the good is honestly revealed.

Various schemes have been invented to induce persons to reveal their demands truthfully. William Vickrey (1961) formulated a way to reveal true demands by paying people the net surpluses of others due to the good. Edward Clarke (1971) proposed a tax that, as T. Nicolaus Tideman (1985, p. 182) expresses it, charges a citizen 'the net marginal cost to other citizens of including his or her preference in the determination of the decision'. Individuals state their offer schedules, which are added up vertically (with the cost on the vertical axis) to determine the aggregate demand schedule. An individual pays his expressed cost share plus a 'Clarke tax' equal to any loss of consumer surplus caused by his vote; that is, the change in result due to his vote. However, if there are a large number of voters, the chance that one vote will change the outcome is slim. The amount of money likely to be collected from an individual would be too insignificant to affect his expressed demand. As pointed out by Dennis Mueller (1979, p. 82), if income effects do matter, then 'the dominance property of honest preference revelation vanishes; strategizing becomes potentially attractive'.

Variants of the Clarke tax have been proposed, such as offering side payments and sequential rather than simultaneous voting. Aside from the questions of cost and incentives, these schemes are generally put forth, implicitly if not explicitly, as methods of determining demand for goods provided by a political rather than a market process. They are thus irrelevant to the question of voluntary provision, except as possible ways for contractual associations to make decisions. In practice, the Clarke schemes have not been adopted although, in many communities, some issues and candidates are voted on by means other than simple majority vote, mainly by requiring super-majorities, unanimity or proportional representation (as in Arden, discussed in Chapter 10).

The issue of Pareto optimality

The term 'efficiency' means a ratio of output to input. The adjective 'efficient' therefore refers to the efficiency of a given process relative to some norm; it can refer to a system that has the highest possible efficiency. In economics, efficiency has two meanings: (1) technical efficiency, the ratio of the volume (measured in terms of some unit of account) of the output of some process relative to the inputs (or costs) into that process, per unit of time; (2) Pareto efficiency, the situation in which no reallocation of resources either in production or exchange will increase someone's utility without decreasing the utility of at least one other person.

The term 'optimal' means the best or most favorable, given the exogenous environment of a system. An 'optimum' is a situation which is optimal. 'Optimal' in economics thus means the most efficient process of a system; the terms 'technically optimal' and '(most) technically efficient' are synonymous. 'Pareto-optimal' (or 'optimum') and 'Pareto-efficient' are related, 'efficiency' often being used for products and 'optimal' for the utility of persons. Pareto optimality is therefore related to unanimity; a Pareto-optimal situation is one in which there is no possible change that will not involve the objection of at least one person.

Samuelson (1954) described mathematically not only the distinction between severable and collective goods, but also their Pareto-efficient criteria. For collective goods, the marginal rate of transformation (the reduction in the production of one good when that of another is increased) equals the sum of the users' marginal rates of substitution (the amount of a good given up in order to obtain some amount of another good). The question posed by the Samuelson criteria is then whether these Pareto-efficiency conditions can be achieved via market processes. Samuelson's (1954, p. 388) answer is that *'no decentralized pricing system can serve to determine optimally these levels of collective consumption'* (italics in the original). By 'optimal', Samuelson means Pareto-optimal, explicitly referring to the Pareto-optimal utility frontier (p. 388). This statement of Samuelson (also expressed and repeated by others) will be termed here the 'optimality proposition'. As a reason, Samuelson points to demand revelation: it is in the selfish interest of each user to indicate less interest in the public good than he really has, to avoid payment for it. The implication is that the share of expenditure for each person can only be determined by that person's communicated expression of it.

But this premise does not logically follow purely from the definition of a collective good or from the Pareto-efficiency criterion. Several premises of Samuelson's logic are implied: (1) the public good is non-excludable; (2) the individuals providing or affected by the good are necessarily selfish in the narrow sense; (3) the public good is not provided as a by-product or tie-in to private goods or excludable public goods; (4) the transaction costs and any impossibility of obtaining the relevant information regarding utilities (in order to determine the demand and hence quantity to supply) are excluded from the production and hence of the rates of transformation among the goods. None of the first three premises are necessarily true in general, although they might well apply in some situations. The fourth premise, discussed below, is an arbitrary exclusion of a category of actual costs.

Regarding the first premise, a public good can be excludable by its nature or by its limited domain of users. As an example of the former, the public characteristics of a water supply are excludable by the nature of the severable supply of the quantity of the water. An example of the latter is a local public good, whose domain is limited to some geographical area. Relative to a larger region, the good, supplied separately by many local communities, is excludable. The optimality proposition presumes that the good in question is a global collective good, universally non-excludable. Few civic goods fit that category.

As indicated above, a system is 'efficient' relative to some norm or standard, and the realistic alternative to voluntary provision is imposed provision. If people will not reveal their true demands in a voluntary system, they will not do so under an imposed governance either, for even though they may suffer penalties for not telling the truth, the governors may have no means of determining what the truth is; prisoners may lie under duress or say what they feel their captors want them to say. Hence, if neither a unilateral nor a multilateral governance can be Pareto-optimal under the Samuelson conditions, a decentralized provision of collective goods is no less Pareto-optimal *a priori* than centralized provision. The market fails only relative to an unrealizable ideal system, not relative to governmental provision. Samuelson himself seems to acknowledge this, stating that even taxing according to a benefit theory does not solve the computational problem (1954, p. 389), given his premises. As Buchanan (1977, p. 215) notes, the ubiquity of market failure relative to an imaginary ideal renders the Pareto criterion of little value in classifying goods and services.

Even within this ideal, the utility conditions are problematical. A Pareto-optimal provision would depend on the total marginal utility obtained from the system, for example utility derived not only from the good but from the means of payment. The model by Erik Lindahl (1958 [1919]), in which the vertically added marginal valuations equal the price of the public good, presumes that the valuations are solely determined by one's marginal utility of the good. This implies that different persons pay different amounts if the marginal valuations differ, as they normally would. But if utility is also a function of the method of payment, and if those paying more than the mean would derive negative utility from the very fact of their above-average payment (perhaps due to egalitarian norms regarding such payments) and those paying less than the mean derive positive utility from their below-average payment, then the utility functions would need to include the method of finance and relative amounts paid by each person, resulting in equal payments if the utilities from the financing (perceived as unfair) overwhelm that derived from the good itself.

The importance of the method of finance does not always depend on such ethical considerations, but can be a function of competition. Public goods are often sold at a uniform price when there is a secondary market among the customers. Consider the example of a rare stamp, of which only 100 identical copies exist. Since the stamps can be resold, price discrimination is not feasible. If all were to be offered at an auction, they would tend to fetch a uniform price, even though various purchasers may have widely different marginal valuations for the ownership of their first stamp. (Typically, collectors desire only one example of a type of stamp. They would much rather obtain a different stamp than a second copy of the first stamp if the two cost the same.) Some collectors will enjoy a much greater consumer surplus than others. The situation is similar with the common goods associated with a condominium unit. Identical units will tend to sell in a fairly narrow price range, and the owners will have differing consumer surpluses. Purchasers of both stamps and condominium units would very likely consider it a gross injustice if they were somehow forced to pay different prices for the goods according to their personal utilities.

Francis Bator (1958) classifies various causes of market failure: ownership externalities (unpaid factors which do not have protected property rights), technical externalities due to indivisibilities or increasing returns, and public-good externalities that make price calculations inefficient. But since efficiency is relative to some standard, the Bator categories raise the question as to the standard by which markets fail to be efficient. These cases involve transaction costs (if not a governmental failure to establish legal property rights). These transaction costs prevent the bargaining that would eliminate divergences between collective and severable costs. But transaction costs are part of the costs or inputs of a production process, just as friction is a necessary element of the working of a machine. They must therefore be included in a real-world calculation of the marginal rates of transformation among goods, and therefore in the determination of the optimal conditions. Carl Dahlman (1979) compares transaction costs to transportation and set-up costs, which are not excludable from the costs of production, and therefore concludes that transaction costs do not create a deviation from an attainable optimum. With transaction costs included, Richard Wagner (1991a) points out that in the neoclassical paradigm, taking the viewpoint of a spectator observing the past, the world is necessarily Pareto-efficient because gains from trade do not remain unexploited. In contrast, in the Austrian-school paradigm that takes the viewpoint of a participant making conjectures about the future, there can be more efficient ways of acting. Hence optimality depends not on the type of goods produced but on the paradigm used by the analyst.

The determination of optimality also involves marketing, the distribution of income and other institutional factors, as pointed out by Tyler Cowen (1985). Hence marginal rates of transformation as well as marginal utilities need to take the cultural and institutional environment into account, and not simply depend on the types of physical commodities being produced. Another nail in the coffin of the optimality argument, that severable but not collective goods can be produced Pareto optimally, is the ubiquity of public characteristics, as recognized by Richard Auster (1977). Goods that are severable in quantity are typically collective in their various qualities. If two or more units of a quantity-severable good are produced with certain common quality characteristics, such as color, aroma, size, shape, beauty and texture, those qualities are subject to Samuelson's equation (1.2) as collective goods; there is no quality rivalry among the purchasers of the goods.

This argument can go even further, to the price of severable goods. Suppose there are 100 pencils of an identical type being sold in one location at the same price. That price is a public characteristic associated with the good. The price of oil, for example, is an important macroeconomic collective good. On the other hand, the Lindahl-type payments or contributions by individuals (based on differing marginal valuations) for a good *whose quantity consumption is collective* are private, severable characteristics associated with the good, the total cost being the sum of the individual payments.

Private goods have public payment characteristics, while public goods have private payment characteristics. Few goods, if any, can be purely private or public in all characteristics, except possibly for self-made and self-used goods, which could be private in all aspects.

Since the quality, let alone the price, of a good produced for more than one person is a collective characteristic, the inability of persons to obtain their subjective valuations of public goods is universal to all marketed goods. Since goods come as a set of many different types of qualities, and because there are limited sets of available quality mixtures, an impossibility theorem can be applied to obtaining the optimal amount of each quality. In practice, marginal valuations are second-best, equating marginal utilities subject to the qualities available in a market. As noted above, efficiency is relative to some norm. Jack Wiseman (1990) notes that the usual Pareto norm based on outcomes is too narrow; a more comprehensive norm would be based on processes, in which case a 'Wicksell-efficient' choice situation is one in which there is unanimous consent to a policy. Since people object to being made worse off, Pareto optimality is a subset of Wicksellian optimality.

To sum up, the optimality proposition, the argument that collective goods are inherently less optimally supplied than severable goods, is countered by its inapplicability to all collective goods, the failure of government provision to be any more optimal, the inclusion of transaction costs in production and thus in the marginal conditions, the universality of public characteristics, the inclusion of institutions, the choice of the efficiency norm and the dependence on the chosen paradigm. The failure of the optimality proposition refers to Pareto optimality; questions regarding technical efficiency can be meaningfully posed and answered. An entrepreneur creating a development wants to know the most profitable mixture and amounts of civic goods to produce. In the example of Chapter 1, he would want to determine how large a dam to build, and the answer would depend on the marginal revenues and costs of various sizes. Such issues regarding technical optimality or efficiency still preclude any universal assignment to collective goods of an optimality problem not also present with severable goods.

Towards a comprehensive theory of consensual provision

With the Pareto optimality aspect of market failure disposed of, the issues of free-riding and demand revelation remain. Theory often begins with taxonomy. A first step towards a comprehensive theory of the voluntary provision of collective goods is the disaggregation of public goods, as was begun in Chapter 1, with the categories concerning excludable and congestible goods and their set complements. Samuelson (1954, 1955) and others did not fully consider the fact that most civic goods are excludable. Exclusion may eliminate free riding, but it opens other questions, such as the following: (1) exclusion may be a matter of degree, and subject to costs; (2) the domain of exclusion may be so large, such as a continent, as to be irrelevant for provision; (3) exclusion *per se* may be irrelevant, for example for the elimination of a public bad whose effects are limited to some domain. Excludable goods themselves can be classified in various categories, an important one being those goods that affect a particular territory.

The diverse nature of public goods has a parallel with the nature of capital goods. In some contexts it may be useful to treat capital goods as homogeneous, as in contrasting them with labor. But the heterogeneity of capital goods is important in many applications, such as the Austrian theory of the business cycle. As Friedrich Hayek (1941, p. 6) stated, the 'stock of capital is not an amorphous mass but possesses a definite structure ... Its composition of essentially different items is much more important than its aggregate "quantity".' Ludwig Lachmann (1978 [1956], p. 2) further emphasized that the significant aspect is 'not physical heterogeneity but heterogeneity in use', and that the complementarity of capital is significant (p. 54).

Similarly, the different categories of collective goods and their heterogeneity in use are subject to different economic applications, and each major type of public good must be examined separately with respect to issues such as free-riding and demand revelation. The following chapter will focus on territorial public goods. The Samuelson model and much of the public-goods literature treat public goods as though they exist in ether rather than in three-dimensional space plus time. In disaggregating public goods, it is evident that, for territorial public goods, the market-failure argument does not hold.

3 Territorial collective goods

Human beings are land animals, creatures that live in three-dimensional space on the surface of the earth, a fact that is obvious to everyone except an economist writing about public goods. Much of the literature on public goods ignores the fact that most civic goods are provided within some bounded area and affect the demand for the use of that space. The goods become capitalized into site rents, *which turns the market-failure argument on its head*. Since users of territory cannot avoid paying rent, no one can sit, stand or ride free of charge. If the goods are provided by government and financed from taxes on production, it is the owners of land who get the free ride, not the consumers. But if the goods are provided consensually by the site owner (or by an association of title holders), there is no longer any free-rider. The users pay for what they get, and the site owner needs to deliver the goods to get paid.

The capitalization of collective goods

The literature on local public goods deals with civic goods that are available only in certain locations, such as a city. The literature on public goods does recognize such local goods as offering a way to overcome problems such as demand revelation, since in effect the goods are severable within a larger domain, among the communities of a state or country. But there is much more to territoriality than having polycentric communities.

Territorial collective goods are those whose significant impact or use is confined within some geographic territory, even if the territory is large, and where entry into and out of the territory can be controlled. Hence territorial goods are excludable. One could object that some territorial goods such as street lights are not exclusive since anyone may drive through the area and benefit from the lights. But this first of all presumes conventional institutions. A private area could well be closed off to through traffic. If there are no barriers, then, if the major beneficiaries are the residents or business in the area, the lights are exclusive for that usage, passers-by gaining an external benefit, though this benefit becomes mutual when people pass by one another's neighborhoods. If the situation is such that the main beneficiaries are passers-by who cannot be made to pay an entry fee (such as a bridge toll), then the good turns out not to be territorial after all, so the objection becomes mute.

Another objection can be made that some territorial goods may be non-rejectable. For example, suppose fire protection is provided to a territory, but there is one household which does not subscribe to the service. If that house catches fire, the service may put it out to prevent its neighbor from the fire. But such an objection begs the question of the precise nature of the fires. If most fires in that neighborhood do not in fact pose a danger to other houses because many are small fires, found early, or the houses are wide apart, then the service can be territorial. But if many of the fires do pose an external threat, the service is no longer excludable and hence not territorial, that is confined to the territory served. Logically, territorial goods are a subset of excludable goods so, if a good is not excludable by premise, then it is not territorial, muting such objections. What would likely happen in the case where most fires pose an external threat is that market processes would result in fire protection offered to contiguous neighborhood associations rather than to individual houses. Fire service would *become* a territorial good, or else one price paid for not being in a contiguous association would be a more expensive non-territorial fire protection service for those most risk-averse in the midst of an area not generally protected.

Most civic goods supplied by government are territorial. The territoriality can involve congestible tie-ins to the use of a non-congestible good. As Mason Gaffney (1968, p. 156) put it, 'one more pair of eyes gazing on the waterfall does not impair the beauty, but the owner of the eyes takes a campsite and road space, limited resources that have to be rationed'. Moreover, 'If Yosemite Falls truly met the criterion of a pure public good – no marginal cost – then one fall would serve the entire world. Obviously some factor has been omitted, and that is space. The falls serve a limited space, and access is rationed by control of the space, which generates rent.' National defense, sometimes considered a 'pure' public good, necessarily applies to the defense of a given territory; it would not be effective if it also defended the territory of the enemy. Other typical government-provided goods, such as police protection, parks, streets and recreation, are also territorially based.

'Capitalization' is the conversion of a stream of income, whether positive or negative, into capital assets. Income is capitalized into its present value, which is inversely proportional to the relevant discount or interest rate. Since the yield of an asset equals the interest rate times the principle, the principle or asset value equals the yield divided by the real interest rate. For land which is not increasing in value, the price equals the rent divided by the real interest rate: $p = r/i$. If there is a tax rate t on the land price p, the price of land is $p = r/(i+t)$. Rent r and its capitalized value p are economically equivalent in principle, and alterations to income, such as from taxes and subsidies, are capitalized into net changes to the present value.

Territorial goods are capitalized within their area of impact. To the extent that (1) the goods are valued positively by the residents and enterprises in the area, and (2) the benefits can only be obtained by being located in the area, they make the location more desirable, and this marginal increase in the demand to be located in that territory increases the ground rent that persons are willing to pay. Capitalization creates a variable in the utility functions of those located in the territory: ground rent. This rent is absent from models that treat public goods as a homogeneous aggregate. (Indeed, the capitalization of the utility of territorial public goods into ground rent and land value is typically absent from texts on microeconomics.) For example, Samuelson (1954, p. 387) assumes a set of collective consumption goods $(x_{n+1}, \ldots, x_{n+M})$, 'which all enjoy in common'. The benefits are not entirely 'in common' for territorial collective goods. The owners of sites benefit from the rent in addition to using the public good. This rent is not enjoyed in common, since it is obtained by the owner of each site. The ground rent is thus a severable good: the total rent equals the sum of the rents for each site. Even if an individual holder of a site title does not positively value a particular public good, the fact that others do creates a rent from which he benefits. Rent arises also, not just from a particular good, but from the availability of a range of goods. As Gaffney (1968, p. 158) states, 'people locate in cities to have many options; and they pay for it in land rent'. Also, 'Many elusive values such as the psychic value of security from flood, amenities, and etherial environmental enhancement are measurable in the premium that people bid for land near the fount of value' (p. 156).

A model of territorial rent

To bring the concept of the capitalization of collective goods into sharper focus, posit a model in which a territory T is divided into n sites of equal size and equal value. The sites have an annual rent of R_1. Now introduce G, a collective good which is supplied at no cost to those in T. (It could be a park funded externally, such as by a higher level of government.)

Good G is interpreted here as a flow of goods-value uniform within T during some time interval. The 'consumption' of G consists in obtaining utility from it during the interval, and it does not involve the destruction or using up of value by an individual user, as does the consumption of typical severable goods. If G can be provided to an additional user at no extra cost, other than possible congestion, then no value is destroyed by any individual user. The good is simultaneously created and used up (that is, consumed) in a particular time and territory independently of the number of persons located in that time and space.

A distinction between the availability (potential or stand-by use) of a good and its direct use is recognized by B.A. Weisbrod (1964), and S.E. Holtermann (1972) uses this distinction with regard to private and public goods, for example the use of an individual policeman being severable and the availability of a police force being collective. For many civic goods, such as police protection, the utility consists to a great extent in having the good available, in its very existence rather than in the direct use of it (indeed, one hopes not to have to suffer a direct use of the police to report a crime). The existence value along with the average expected direct-use value (for example of a park) for such usage generating positive utility are reflected together in the subjective valuation of the good per time interval.

Some individuals value G more intensely than others, and would pay more for a site in the location than others would. The supply of sites in a neighborhood with given borders is finite,[1] so in effect there is an auction market for the n sites. Given more than n individuals bidding for sites, the rent of the sites is determined by the bid of the $(n+1)$th bidder, since the nth bidder needs only to bid slightly more than the $(n+1)$th. Given a ranking of bids from highest to lowest, the nth highest bid would set the price for all n equivalent lots. Since they can be resold, price discrimination does not occur. Denote the rental price for the sites after the creation of G as R_2. The difference R_2 less R_1, denoted as R_d, is the rental increment caused by the presence of G. R_d therefore constitutes a revelation of the residents' preference for, or valuation of, G.

Samuelson (1958, p. 336) poses the following challenge: 'Try to devise a system of benefit taxation to make people pay for what they get and we discover that rational persons will hide their desires and consumer surpluses.' This challenge, this great difficulty in trying to divine people's demands, is resolved for the case of territorial goods: the demand is revealed by the marginal rent that people pay for being located in a site in order to use the good. A person may hide his identity in bidding for land, but the rent cannot be avoided.[2]

Though they are called 'rent' above and in the literature and by market participants, the site values generated by public goods are actually returns on capital goods. Suppose that a landlord plants a shade-providing tree by a tenant's house. The increase in rent generated by the tree is actually a return on the invested capital, just as the return on an additional room would be. If a city plants trees along a street, the increase in 'rent' along the street is likewise a yield on the 'capital employed' by the city, even though it is manifested as land rent.

In the voluntary-exchange model of public finance, taxes are voluntary payments in exchange for the value of services in the public economy. As Richard Musgrave (1939) noted, the pressure-group mechanism of democratic government results in unequal bargaining power, making voting an imperfect way to decide on a budget. The payment of rent in exchange for the services that induce the rent is a method of implementing the voluntary-exchange method without depending on voting. Even when a community association decides on a budget democratically, the rent is determined by market means, and the decision to accept the rent or to purchase land is a voluntary individual decision. Buchanan (1949) states that, in the individualistic theory of public finance, in which only individuals experience utility, ideally the fiscal process represents a *quid pro quo* between the provider and receivers, in accord with the benefit principle of public finance. Specific benefits are received by specific individuals. He notes that fiscal systems such as those in early 19th-century USA, which relied mainly on levies on property, tended to return to payers approximately the equivalent of their contribution (p. 502).

An illustration of how the territorial concept can enhance discussions on public goods is the debate on subscription television. Samuelson (1958) states that, since the marginal cost of providing the programming to an additional person is zero, this is a *prima facie* case for government subsidy. Minasian (1964) counters that such theory neglects institutional and technological considerations: that is, different systems of exclusion. Buchanan (1967) examines the provision of television by an entrepreneur who charges user prices, which is efficient if a sole provider can discriminate perfectly among users. Buchanan stresses the separation of public goods *per se* from problems of organization. This debate is carried out without reference to the effect of the transmission on the demand for sites in the area. If the service is provided at zero direct cost, then the availability of the television programs increases the desirability of being located there (relative to no transmissions) and thereby induces a marginal increase in land rent. If the induced rent is greater than the cost of the transmission, then all three participants in the debate could be reconciled by funding the service from the induced rent: there is a zero marginal cost for an additional user, an institution (site-rent collection) is set up to collect the funds, and the service can be efficiently operated by an entrepreneur who has title to the induced rent as well as the television transmission.

The question of size

A question now arises: does the rent depend on the size of a region? Would *G* be capitalized as rent for a local good but less so or not at all for a good which is in effect for a large area, such as a state or the United States? The issue is a particular application of the more general question of whether a phenomenon that exists in a micro application still remains in a macro setting, similar to the distinction between individual and market effects. Don Patinkin (1965, p. 11) points out the difference between individual and market conceptual experiments. For example, for price–quantity relationships in an economy-wide market, there can be no arbitrary change in price; price cannot be an independent variable as it is for an individual. The price of one product in an economy is determined in part by the prices of other goods.

Suppose that the US government offered perfect protection from all violence. This would still be a territorial good relative to areas which do not offer the good, such as Europe. An immigrant from Australia could settle either in Europe or in the USA. For him, the two locations are the same in utility except for the perfect protection. He would pay a premium to settle in the USA relative to settling in Europe. If instead of G being provided by the federal government, it was provided locally and by all locations, the effect would be the same. There would be a differential between the USA and the rest of the world. A region can be very large, but so long as the good G applies to the site and not to other sites, there will exist a differential rent.

A differential can exist within the same territory for the presence of G relative to its absence. G induces an increased marginal product of land regardless of the presence of other sites. This rent can be an absolute amount or proportional to the original rent R_1. In a closed economy, if G raises the productivity of all factors proportionally (by a certain percentage everywhere), it results in a proportionate increase in rent. But if G raises productivity by a certain fixed increment everywhere, then the effect would raise wages or rent or both by some uniform amount. Labor which had zero marginal productivity could now have a positive productivity, or possibly land which had no productivity would now be productive. Hence whether a ubiquitous public good induces a ubiquitous rent depends on how it affects differential productivity in labor and land.

The existence of a civic good can affect migration. Immigration into a territory may further stimulate rental increases as the population grows. Hence the total increase in rent caused by G includes both the direct effect of G and the effect of increased population. When an entrepreneur offers G, he may anticipate a certain population in the area affected, and his estimation of the rent will take both into account. In conclusion, territorial public goods can induce rent even if a territory is large, the rent being even greater if the good results in immigration.

Collective goods and tie-ins

The conceptual existence of a rent induced by the presence of a collective good raises the question of how one can determine that amount of rent due to the good among the other components of rent. A condominium unit, for example, can include the use of a swimming pool as a tie-in. How can one know the amount of the rent of the unit that is attributed to the swimming pool? One way to estimate the marginal demand for one tie-in is to do a market survey for properties with and without the tie-in. If there are similar condominiums with and without pools, the difference in rents or property values can be compared if there is no other significant difference in services.

As additional condominiums with pools are built, marginal residents will be willing to pay ever less for a pool (as the law of demand requires lower prices with increasing quantity) until the marginal rent just equals the marginal cost for a pool. Competition will tend to make the marginal rent from G equal to the marginal costs of producing G; hence, for collective goods which are available in multiple domains, one can estimate the rent induced by G from the monetary cost of producing G. For new collective goods, an entrepreneur must estimate the demand, but this is conceptually no different from estimating the demand for severable goods. However, the rents induced by various collective goods may not be additive, owing to complementarities. One can only calculate the rent from one G, relative to all other Gs. But if multiple goods such as swimming pools and tennis courts are common in some area, one may presume that each induces a rent not less than the costs.

The elimination of free rides

As mentioned above, the disaggregation of public goods into significant categories permits one to deal with their different economic effects. Territorial goods do not conform to many of the commonly made propositions about public goods. There are no free-riders of territorial public goods. People can be free guests in an area, and 'space thieves' (squatters) might trespass, but the rent is still paid by the user, who then may share the benefits with his guests or trespassers.

The marginal rent exists as economic rent regardless of how it is paid or who collects it. Therefore, *for territorial public goods, the usual free-rider argument is turned on its head*. Rather than the goods being used even if the users do not pay, the users pay a price for the goods even if the provider of the good does not collect the rent. For spatial goods, the free-riders are the owners of the sites if the goods are paid for by others, such as by taxes on labor or entrepreneurial profits.

A common argument regarding placing a price on a public good is that this discourages its 'consumption' by the marginal user. But for a territorial good G, the payment of marginal rent R_d for G imposes no price for the marginal user within the space, such as a resident of a house or employee in a firm. The price, as rent, pays only for the acquisition of marginal space. The use of G by a marginal user as a person is therefore not discouraged. Marginal rent R_d

constitutes a private good, conforming to Samuelson's (1954) equation (1.1). The total rent in a territory T equals the sum of the rents earned by the individual site owners. Hence territorial public goods have an inherent private-good characteristic in the rent received by the owners.

Free-riding is further eliminated by the capture by site rents of significant territorial externalities, which are themselves public goods. As Tideman (1990) notes, the internalization of spatial externalities is an application of marginal-cost pricing. Friedrich von Wieser (1967 [1927], p. 340), an early theorist of urban rent, stated that 'Urban rent is that part of the rental which is paid as a premium for the advantages of the better location', and these public-good advantages encompass the externalities present in the area. If a particular externality has a potentially relevant effect (cf. Buchanan and Stubblebine, 1962) on rent, then the social and private marginal rates of goods substitution are the same, since the social rate is manifested in the private rent that is bid for that location. Hence the presence of externalities need not be a 'market failure' (cf. Bator, 1958) if they are territorial.

Entrepreneurs who create communities will therefore find it in their interest to write constitutions which promote positive externalities and discourage negative ones. As Harold Demsetz (1964, p. 25) states, 'The enclosing of land into a single ownership entity which often undertakes to provide services usually provided by the government from tax revenues, such as streets, sidewalks, refuse collection, and even police protection, allows the owner to exclude those who refuse to pay rentals which cover the cost of these services.'

The benefits-maximizing provision of territorial goods

If the amount of a collective good G can vary, then, if an increase in G yields a greater increase in rent than the cost of G, it is rational for the owners of the sites to provide for an increase of G until its marginal cost equals the marginal rental increase. Joseph Stiglitz (1986, p. 574) notes that marginal rents represent marginal valuations by residents of community services, and 'As a result, a landowner-controlled community will provide an efficient level of public services.' This level is the technically (as opposed to Pareto) efficient amount of a collective good to provide in terms of maximizing the profits of an entrepreneur or the utility of a group of landowners providing it. Economizing agents will benefit from devoting resources to the good as compared with alternatives so long as the marginal rent exceeds the marginal monetary costs. The marginal rent provides not only a market price that can be charged for G but also the technically optimal quantity.

Given the existence of rent R_d, tenants who pay rent without owning any lots would benefit from an application of all the rent to the government rather than have any retained by the owners. However, rent R_d need not all be devoted to G; another option is the payment of a rent dividend to the residents (as has been done in Alaska), such as on a per-capita basis. The collected rent can also be saved in an endowment for future spending or distribution, as is done as well with the Alaska state oil revenues. Hence, with the option of rent dividends as an alternative to public works, in effect making the tenants co-owners, the technically optimal level of G, from both the viewpoints of the owners and tenants of sites, is the same, the level for which the marginal cost of the public good equals the marginal rent it yields.

The actual bids for sites may, of course, reflect goods other than G. Someone may choose to locate in a site because of proximity to work or to family, for example, and may be willing to pay for G even though he does not value it at that price because his consumer surplus from the site without G is greater than R_d. Nevertheless, the marginal site holder who values G at R_d determines the equilibrating amount. The inframarginal site holders then have either a consumer surplus or, if there for reasons other than G, a consumer 'deficit' with respect to G. Even for those who are located in the site for non-G reasons, the willingness to locate at a rental price R_2, with R_d included as a tie-in, implies that the site holder is equating his marginal rates of substitution between severable goods and the site. If the sites have a flexible size, then the holder will obtain the amount of space such that the rent R_2 on a marginal increment would just equal the marginal utility derived from that increment.

Samuelson's (1954, p. 389) statement that 'taxing according to a benefit theory of taxation can not at all solve the computational problem in the decentralized manner' does not hold for territorial goods. A tax proportional to and not greater than R_d is a benefit tax, since the rent reflects the benefit of the public good.

Public-goods illusion

Any product can be subject to illusions, the wrongful estimate by purchasers of the costs and benefits of the good. The perceived utility obtained from a collective good may be subject to illusion, possibly generating more rent than would be warranted by better information, but this is true for goods provided by taxation as well. There is less likely illusion from the payment side for goods funded from site rent than for those funded by a myriad of taxes.

In the case of territorial goods, systematic illusion can occur as a result of the wrongful evaluation of the goods, ignorance about public bads, the inability to estimate costs of creating a proposed capital good or maintaining an existing one, and uncertainty about future changes concerning the good and its provision. For most people, buying or renting real estate is an occasional event and there may be little prior experience to draw upon. Although general information can be obtained, there is typically no text available on what Hayek (1945, p. 522) called 'the knowledge of the particular circumstances of time and place'. The knowledge that one needs to be aware of such localized information is of little use if one does not know what to look for.

Some ignorance is also due to the hidden nature of many of the costs. When one buys a machine, the good qualities are clearly evident, but many of the bad qualities are opaque, not clearly visible. For example, whether a machine will function well in actual use and how long it will last can only be determined over time. Guarantees and warranties are therefore common. The public bads associated with a territory are likewise opaque, making themselves evident over time, but these are not normally insured against by warranties. Barking dogs, the frequency of burglaries and vandalism, noisy neighbors, unresponsive management, leaks, unfavorable rules discovered or added after moving in, all these may be difficult to discern beforehand, and there are so many possible negative variables that one may not think of all of them, and there may not be time to investigate them in any case when one is searching for a new community. One can estimate the totality of such bads from experience but, in a particular community, there can be a systematic bias for some time interval.

Whether systematic bias exists for the evaluation of civic goods overall is an empirical question. *A priori,* illusion cannot be ruled out as irrational, since perceived reality is interpreted by each individual. An interpretation depends on one's ideas and theories about the world, which might be erroneous or incomplete; rational ignorance precludes obtaining more knowledge than is personally beneficial, but how is one to know what is beneficial in the first place? Real estate agents and sellers typically emphasize the good qualities of the public goods, while the bad qualities are left to the buyer to determine for himself. As Debra Dean (1989a, p. 17) states, 'Potential buyers in RCA [Residential Community Association] communities are not always aware of the financial condition of the association, or of the condition of various common facilities. In such circumstances, they may be both surprised by special assessments and unable to pay them. This has the effect of increasing the cost of the home beyond what was expected.'

What may appear to be illusion can be a signal concerning quality. It is well known among real estate agents that first impressions matter, that the 'curb appeal' of property has a major impact on a prospective buyer. Clean, modern, well-kept appearances are not merely superficial illusions, but are signals as to the age, quality and care taken of the property. On the other hand, cosmetic effects such as new paint can hide defects, creating an illusion of quality where none exists. As one example of systematic illusion, Lawrence Friedman (1967) examined the persistence of odd digits, especially the number 9, in retail pricing. People know that 59¢ and 60¢ are only a penny apart, yet retailers know that the final digit, 9, presents the illusion of a significantly lower price.

The public-goods illusion for territorial goods, nevertheless, is likely to be substantially less than for civic goods funded by a complex tax structure. As noted by Buchanan and Wagner (1977), in typical government jurisdictions, individuals do not pay direct prices for government programs; they receive no monthly bill. Many taxes are not apparent. A complex tax structure with many indirect taxes is therefore subject to illusion on the funding side as well as the goods side. Complexity weakens the cost signals, and indirectness creates noise, since the tax is hidden in a price. Regulations that take the place of taxation compound the difficulty of calculating the imposed burdens. It is not worth the trouble for the typical taxpayer to obtain information about the various taxes and total amount, if it is available at all. But when civic goods are funded by rental payments there is much less fiscal illusion about the current costs. Moreover, the amount of illusion is reduced when many lots in an area are being sold or rented; many parties obtain various amounts of information that becomes reflected in the site rents and values of the neighborhood.

Theories of financing goods from rent

The theory that civic goods can be financed from land rent can be traced at least as far back as William Petty (1623–87). Vaggi (1987, p. 72) points out that when François Quesnay and the other Physiocrats referred to the net product, it was actually land rent, which they advocated using for public works as well as the private application of the net product for capital accumulation (p. 135). Henry George (1975 [1879]) proposed that public goods could be financed from economic land rent, making possible the abolition of other taxation. Léon Walras (1896)[3] wrote that land rent provides the means for funding a state. More recently, Gaffney (1970), Stiglitz (1977), Vickrey (1977) and Tideman (1985) have theorized on the feasibility and consequences of funding public goods from rent.

In a model by Stiglitz (1983), a community chooses the level of public goods that maximizes land rent. Individuals' income is a variable, and the result, under the restrictive conditions of the model, in which the goods are financed by payments based on land value, is that land-value maximization leads to an efficient level of supply of public goods. Stiglitz (1977, p. 278) also presents a model relating population, consumption, rent and public goods. As set forth in Atkinson and Stiglitz (1987 [1980]), the utility function is $U(G, X)$, where G is a collective and X a severable good. Output Y is a function of workers: $Y = f(N) = XN + G$. Since $X = (f(N)-G)/N$, the first-order condition implies that $G = f - Nf'$, which is output minus wage payments, workers being paid their marginal product. Hence 'the population that maximizes consumption *per capita* is such that rents equal public goods expenditure' (p. 525). This result was dubbed the 'Henry George theorem' (HGT) by Stiglitz (1977), since the rent is the 'single tax' that exactly finances G.

Vickrey (1977, 1990) has a similar conclusion, stating that, where cities compete on a world market, land rents aggregate to total inframarginal residues that reflect public goods. Efficiency requires that such rents fund decreasing-cost industries. Two essential elements of a city are transportation and the economies of scale in the city's activities. Hotelling (1938) had argued for marginal-cost pricing as a condition for an optimum of social welfare, with the deficits of decreasing-cost industries funded by taxation. Vickrey's GHV theorem (George/Hotelling/Vickrey) states that the land rents due to activities with economies of scale equal the subsidies required to enable the activities to sell their output at prices equal to their marginal cost.

Vickrey (1990, p. 1) notes, 'If transportation were costless, location would be unimportant and location rents could not arise, while if there were no economies of scale, production could take place on a small scale in hamlets and location rents would be negligibly small.' For goods having economies of scale, 'perhaps better termed economies of density of demand', optimal provision 'will usually require a subsidy'. Competition among communities induces 'location rents generated by the availability at marginal cost prices of goods and services produced under conditions of scale and density being just sufficient to finance the subsidies required to permit such pricing'.

Tideman (1985) states one set of sufficient and necessary conditions for the funding of public goods from the land rent due to the presence of the community: (1) perfect mobility; (2) a limited area affected by the goods; (3) the existence of persons outside the community who would value the goods as highly as those who receive them. These conditions, he states, are not perfectly satisfied, but offsetting this factor is the presence of the rent which would exist without public activities, which can also be tapped, as well as non-rent profits from public-goods provision.

The exact equating of G and rent in HGT is problematical. The HGT result is derived by 'taking a fixed value of G and then varying N to maximize X' (Atkinson and Stiglitz, 1987 [1980], p. 524). The equation of rent and G is a consequence of the derivative of G (with respect to N) being zero. But it is arbitrary to suppose that G is independent of population and the labor supply N. If the model is reformulated with G also a function of N, $Y = XN + G(N)$. Then:

$$X = \{f(N) - G(N)\}/N \tag{3.1}$$

$$\partial f/\partial N = X + \partial G/\partial N = \{f(N) - G(N))/N\} + \partial G/\partial N \tag{3.2}$$

$$G(N) = f(N) - Nf'(N) + \partial G/\partial N \tag{3.3}$$

R is the difference between total product Y and total wages:

$$R = f(N) - Nf'(N) \tag{3.4}$$

Hence

$$G(N) = R + \partial G/\partial N \tag{3.5}$$

Now there is an additional term $\partial G/\partial N$, so that rent does not exactly equal G unless $\partial G/\partial N$ is zero, which is not necessarily so.

Another problem is the assumption that the difference between total product and wages necessarily constitutes land rent as a residual. Since land rent is generated by the marginal product of land, R is determined independently and not merely as a surplus by (3.4). Equation (3.4) would be respecified as:

$$P = f(N) - Nf'(N), \tag{3.4a}$$

where P equals gross profits, which includes rent. Alternatively, G could include common expenditures and cash dividends to the residents or landowners in whichever mix is desired by the decision makers, and therefore can include severable goods funded by rent.

As theorized above, the technically optimal supply of G is such that the marginal cost of G equals the marginal rent induced by G, where the marginal rent is decreasing. In that case, G is a function of $\partial G/\partial R$, determined by the way marginal rent is affected by changes in G at various level of G. Furthermore, $\partial G/\partial R$ would itself be affected by the demand for G and the associated space, which would reasonably be a function of the population in the affected area, hence of labor supply N.

Let $Z = \partial G/\partial R$. Then $Y = f(N) = XN + G(Z(N))$, and the model is respecified as:

$$X = \{f(N) - G(Z(N))\}/N \tag{3.6}$$

$$\begin{aligned} f' &= X + (\partial G/\partial Z)(\partial Z/\partial N) \\ &= \{(f(N) - G(Z(N)))/N\} + (\partial G/\partial Z)(\partial Z/\partial N) \end{aligned} \tag{3.7}$$

$$G(Z(N)) = R + (\partial G/\partial Z) (\partial Z/\partial N) \qquad (3.8)$$

As N increases, one would typically expect the curve of G as a function of R to flatten. Hence $\partial G/\partial Z$ would be positive, but $\partial Z/\partial N$, the change in the slope of the curve with respect to increasing N, would be negative, the slope decreasing. Hence $(\partial G/\partial Z)(\partial Z/\partial N)$ would typically be negative, although not necessarily so; the actual sign would be an empirical matter. If negative, then $G < R$, and there is leftover rent. At any rate, $G = R$ only if $(\partial G/\partial Z)$ $(\partial Z/\partial N) = 0$, which is not given *a priori*.

Moreover, with optimal G produced where $\partial G/\partial R = 0$, one normally expects $R > G$. The following hypothetical cases illustrate why. In the tables, ΔG is the marginal cost of G, G is total G, ΔR is the marginal rent, R is total rent, and P is the profit $(R - G)$. In Case 1, as G is increased by equal increments (from 1 to 2 to 3, etc), ΔR is at first greater than the marginal cost of G; at first it increases and then it decreases with increasing G until it reaches 1, where it equals marginal cost G. After that level, marginal rent is 0.5, less than the marginal cost of 1.

Case 1

ΔG	G	ΔR	R	P
1	1	2	2	1
1	2	3	5	3
1	3	2	7	4
1	4	1	8	4
1	5	0.5	8.5	3.5

As marginal rent ΔR first increases and then decreases, an entrepreneur producing G would maximize profits as rent at a $G = 3$ or 4, with a profit P of 4, where ΔR equals ΔG. G is provided optimally, yet $R > G$, contrary to the Henry George theorem.

In Case 2, the cost of G again increases by equal increments, but now the marginal rent starts out at zero, below marginal cost.

Case 2

ΔG	G	ΔR	R	P
1	1	0	0	−1
1	2	0	0	−2
1	3	1	1	−2
1	4	2	3	−1
1	5	2	5	0
1	6	0	5	−1

Rent is not positive until G achieves some minimal amount, in this case 3. Marginal rent then becomes greater than marginal cost per increment of cost and total rent catches up with total cost at $G = 5$. Marginal rent then decreases, becoming less than marginal cost, so that P is maximized at $G = 5$ at zero, otherwise being negative. Here a community could provide itself with G optimally where $\Delta R = \Delta G$ and $R = G$, but have no rental profit after paying for G.

A Case 3 could be configured where $R < G$ at the rage where $\Delta R = \Delta G$ and ΔR is decreasing, in which case G would be provided at a loss and it would not be optimally funded by rent. Since, in Case 2, $R = G$ only as the result of the particular behavior of R as a function of G, and since Case 3 would not be provided by a profit-seeking agency, G would be provided by a combination of Cases 1 and 2, so that total R could be greater than G, contrary to what the Henry George theorem would suggest.

The technically optimal provision of G where $\Delta R = \Delta G$ could generate a profit for an entrepreneur providing G, providing an incentive for the market-process provision of collective goods. Many territorial goods generate much more rent than they cost. Studies of the impact of subways in New York City, for example, show that the landowners could have paid for the subway and still made a sizeable profit. The George Washington Bridge across the Hudson River increased New Jersey land values by six times the cost of the bridge (Tucker, 1958, p. 11).

Interestingly, Henry George himself thought that R would in general be greater than G. George (1975 [1879], p. 406) believed that 'the value of the land taken as a whole is sufficient to bear the entire expenses of government. In the better developed countries it is much more than sufficient.' In another passage (p. 456), he wrote, 'There would be a great and increasing surplus from the taxation of land values.' This revenue, he thought, 'could be applied to the common benefit', such as 'museums, libraries, gardens, lecture rooms, music and dancing halls, theaters, universities, technical schools, shooting galleries, play grounds, gymnasiums, etc'. Such goods as dancing halls and shooting galleries may not generate as much rent as their cost, but, to spend the surplus rent fully, some public consumption must be that which generates less rent than its cost. But some persons may prefer to spend the funds in different ways than for such common goods, and in order to equate marginal severable goods utility with that of collective goods, optimal consumption would require that the rent surplus from a collection of most of the ground rent be transferred to the residents as cash dividends, as Alaska has done with its severance fees on oil production. In the contractual production of collective goods, the surplus can be retained as profit, providing the stimulus as well as feasibility of voluntary provision.

The HGT and the proposition that there could be a rent surplus are at odds with the view taken by some that land rent is not sufficient to fund government expenses. But, first of all, the HGT does not limit the extent of revenues. Governments can also obtain funds from non-tax sources such as user fees and profits from government-owned enterprises. Secondly, the totality of land value and rent is substantial. Data published by the Board of Governors of the Federal Reserve System (1991) estimate US land value at $3.7 trillion, 23 per cent of domestic net worth. This figure is most likely an underestimate; a calculation by Cord (1991) put real property in the USA in 1986 at $10.8 trillion, close to that calculated by the Bureau of Economic Analysis for 1988 (Miles, 1990). Gaffney (1970, p. 181) estimates that 'land value today is at least half of real estate, and probably more', which would put the value of US land at an order of magnitude of $5 trillion. That estimate of land value does not include much of the economic rent that could be generated from oil leases, other extraction fees, the electro-magnetic spectrum, airline routes, satellite orbits and other types of spatial uses, plus the fact that present land value has negatively capitalized existing taxation. Much of the land rent in the USA is unreported and hidden behind other categories of income (Foldvary, 1989). Cord (1991) estimates the annual economic rent of land in the USA in 1986 at $680 billion, 20 per cent of national income; this estimate does not take into account any increase in productivity and therefore of land value that would follow the elimination of the taxation of productive effort.

Third, the HGT applies only to the funding of productive territorial public goods. Much government expenditure does not fit this category. Foreign aid, including military spending devoted to the defense of (or intervention in) foreign countries, does not increase domestic rent. Pure redistribution, taking funds from one set of persons and transferring them to another set, does not increase net rents: it can increase the land values of some recipients such as farmers, but the locations drained of net income would theoretically suffer a loss of land value. Special-interest spending due to lobbying and log-rolling is not likely to increase net rents. Severable goods, such as free publications, provided by government are also unlikely to increase rent. 'Wasted' spending (such as funds which a majority would prefer to spend voluntarily) does not increase net rent either. Hence the HGT does not imply that arbitrary levels of government spending can be financed entirely from site rents, but only that the territorial collective goods that are valued by persons in the area can be so funded. The HGT is therefore reduced to a tautology, irrefutable since only those public goods which generate at least sufficient rent to be funded by that rent count as the goods covered by the theory.

What allows funding from site rent to escape the confines of tautology is the existence of land rents beyond those due to public goods, for example those due to natural territorial advantages, population and commercial complementarities. Moreover, a broad definition of economic land includes the entire three-dimensional space around the earth. If the oceans and atmosphere were included, their use as a dump for pollutants would constitute a use of land, no less than the use of a surface dump. The annual value of such space as a dumping ground would be a land rent. If property rights to this water and air space were recognized, the owners could collect the rent by charging dumping fees, and these fees could feasibly replace all government revenues (in excess of the economic rent of other lands) that are currently obtained from taxes on income, consumption and capital goods, substituting dumping fees dollar for dollar for revenue now being raised by taxes.

Therefore, broadly conceived, land rent, in addition to fees and profits from government enterprises, can serve as a sufficient source of government revenue even for expenditures which do not generate surface rents, and can equally sufficiently serve as the source of funds for the consensual provision of civic goods by the owners of those sites. Hence the issue of the potential revenue from land rent depends in the final analysis on the definition of land and on the institutions, including property rights, which enable land rent to be collected.

The contractual provision of territorial goods

Adam Smith (1976 [1776], p. 341) stated that government revenue could be derived from 'some fund which peculiarly belongs to the sovereign' such as land. 'The rent of the crown lands constituted for a long time the greater part of the revenue of the ancient sovereigns of Europe' (p. 345). For the sovereign one can substitute a private owner, and the principle is the same.

The George/Stiglitz/Vickrey/Tideman models and theories refer to land rent as a source of revenues for collective goods provided by a political process, but the same analysis, modified as above to result in $R > G$, would apply to the provision of such goods by private entrepreneurs owning sites and offering public goods located in those sites. The theory of rent generated by and paying for territorial goods provides a theoretical foundation for the market provision of community civic goods. The ownership of sufficient territory so that the rent generated by the goods can be collected enables the owners to eliminate free-riders and determine the profit-maximizing level of collective goods to provide.

The use of rent for funding collective goods relates to the benefit principle of taxation, that the cost of government expenditures be allocated according to their benefits. Knut Wicksell (1958 [1896], p. 72) stated the benefit principle as 'the well-known principle between Value and Countervalue'. The benefit rule was posited as a condition of equilibrium and efficient allocation. Tax shares were to be determined 'according to subjective evaluation of public services' (Musgrave, 1959, p. 69). A tax, in this view, is a price paid for a collective good congruent with the demand for the good. The good is provided in exchange for the tax. M. Pantaleoni proposed that the revenue and expenditure sides of a government budget be determined together (Musgrave, 1959, p. 70), as did Wicksell (1958), who also argued in favor of unanimous and voluntary decisions, or approximately so if necessary. These economists believed that the benefit principle, the simultaneous revenue/ expenditure determination, the exchange relationship and the unanimity ideal could not be attained as a result of a market process (Musgrave, 1959, p. 70). But Adam Smith (1976 [1776], p. 350) inadvertently pointed to the way they could be achieved. In his first maxim of taxation, he wrote: 'The expense of government to the individuals of a great nation, is like the expense of management to the joint tenants of a great estate, who are all obliged to contribute in proportion to their respective interests in the estate.'

When a private agency owns the territory (estate) serviced by a territorial collective good, it can simultaneously provide the good and collect the rent generated by it, satisfying the conditions of simultaneity, benefit and voluntarism. The tenants of the 'estate' contribute to the collective good by their rental payment, which is only made if they choose to locate at that site. By locating there, a tenant reveals that the benefit of the goods associated with the site equal or exceed the rent. Wicksell (1958 [1896], p. 113) wrote that 'the general economic development of the community' increased the value of its land, and he proposed taxing such increases (p. 114). Consensual rent collection is an economic equivalent of government land-value taxation, except that the equilibrating agents operate by a market rather than a political process (the distinction between the two is discussed in Chapter 5).

Various means of payment of rentals

Rent need not be paid only as direct periodic payments. A taxonomy of rental payments includes: (1) direct rentals, payments by a tenant to an owner of a site; (2) admission fees (including cover charges and membership fees) paid to occupy a site for a certain time interval; (3) rental proxies, payments based on the amount of some activity such as gross receipts; (4) imputed rent of owners who own sites or of those to whom the sites are made available, buyers of sites in effect paying the present value of the rent at the beginning of an indefinite period of ownership.

Each of these methods can take diverse forms. For example, parking meters are a type of direct rental payment for the temporary occupation of street space. The fees paid to graze cattle on public lands are direct rentals, and the cattle owners also receive imputed rent if the fees are less than the full market rent. Students attending a university receive imputed rent if the institution is not required to pay rent or taxes for the site. In some shopping centers, stores pay rental proxies as a percentage of gross receipts, in addition to direct rentals, the receipts reflecting the territorial benefits and providing information regarding such benefits in a flexible and risk-sharing manner (somewhat like share-cropping). However, such an arrangement is facilitated by income and sales taxation, which provide a source for information on gross receipts, with enforcement provided by the government. Absent such taxation, it could be difficult to enforce the honest calculation of payments.

This chapter establishes the theory of rent as the basis for the private funding of territorial goods. A second element of private provision concerns governance: the agents providing the goods must also govern or manage their operation and distribution. Governance theory has been developed in the literature on industrial organization, which is discussed in Chapter 4.

Notes

1. The space T is determined by the surface area regardless of its material contents. Hence, if T includes a body of water, the area is not increased if the water is drained to make room for additional construction. The space is simply converted from one use to another. T also includes the usable three-dimensional space above and below the surface, so no extra land is created by adding an additional story to a building. The developed area of a neighborhood can expand within T, but the neighborhood T is defined here as the space within some arbitrary border, so that developing additional sites also does not increase the supply of land but merely converts the space from one usage to another.
2. Squatters do not pay rent but in that case, the economic rent is paid by the title holder as an opportunity cost. Squatters are free riders, but could in principle be expelled.
3. Book II, section 8. Gaffney (1982, p. 179) cites Walras on the taxation of land rent, noting that he was a 'thoroughgoing land taxer'.

4　Governance in industrial organization

Governance and markets are not opposites. Production may require a high level of governance within a firm. But governance is more relevant to the provision of collective goods than to their production. Provision refers to the selection of goods, method of funding and arrangement for production. The provision of collective goods by governments often involves their production by private agents. Economies of scale concerning production need not necessarily affect provision, since goods such as fire protection can be produced by a large firm serving many small providers.

Transaction costs and governance

Economists have found various reasons for why production requires organization within firms. R.H. Coase (1937), in analyzing the nature of the firm, found the distinguishing feature to be the 'supersession of the price mechanism' (p. 82), saving the costs of discovering prices (p. 83), whereby a factor is employed by contract and under the direction of the management. This rationale for a firm is more relevant to the production than to the provision of collective goods. Posit two firms, one a factory producing private goods and the other a landed estate producing public goods within the estate. The purchasers of the public goods are like the customers of the private goods, who could also have a contractual relationship with the producer, rather than like employees. The price mechanism is not suppressed; the tenants have leases with rental prices. Although their leases may specify that the lessees perform certain acts, this is incidental to their role as customers of the estate (for example, hotel guests are required to leave the key when leaving).

Instead of an owner/tenant relationship, public-goods provision may be effected by a partnership in various forms, such as cooperative, corporate or communal. In that case, the governance structure is not one of an owner and customers but of joint owners who delegate responsibility to a governing body. The members pay dues or assessments to the governing body operating on behalf of the association, so the price system is also not suppressed. In contrast, Steven Cheung (1983, p. 18) emphasized transaction costs in creating the firm, with equilibrium attained when the savings of transaction (pricing) costs equal at the margin the agency costs of a factor market, determining the extent of contract substitution for the price system. In this model, long-term landlord/tenant relationships are analogous to a firm, and short-term relationships, such as customers in a theater, are not. One could, for example, interpret a shopping mall with long-term leases as one firm, like a super department store. A civic association, with a contractual relationship between the members and the association, could also be interpreted as a firm.

The interpretation of a public-goods provider as a firm is given more substance by considering its governing principles. A behavioral premise in Oliver Williamson's (1975) model of industrial organization is 'self-interest with guile'. Agents can be (though need not always be) opportunistic, lacking candor or honesty. Opportunism combined with a small-numbers environment induces strategic behavior. Another premise in this model is 'bounded rationality', the limited capacity of the human mind to process information. 'Bounded cognition' may be a better term, since the rationality that is bounded is not the capacity of the mind for logical analysis but the efficiency of a system relative to what it would be with perfect cognitive abilities. These premises can be applied to the owner/tenant and member/association relationships of public-goods provision, with the added complication of a management firm hired to operate the facilities. This is a double principal–agent problem, a member/tenant having to deal with the governing board or owner as well as the manager, who in turn reports to the board or owner but deals with individual members/tenants as well.

In the Williamson (1985) model, economic organization is a function of contracting. Institutions economize on transactions costs. Asset specificity, the specialized use of assets not easily transferable to other uses, determines the contracting process. If there is little asset specificity, competitive market contracting is effective. With high asset specificity, governance within an organization is efficacious as agents economize on bounded cognition while protecting themselves against opportunism. Information impactedness, which occurs when the circumstances known to one party cannot be costlessly obtained by another, can be more easily overcome by internal organization.

The economizing on contracting costs, however, is not necessarily the keystone of governance or the need to have large firms and employees. Since 'employees' are free agents rather than slaves, for purposes of analysis they are actually independent contractors working under the continuous direction of the firm's management. Conceptually, the firm's capital goods can also be independently owned, and hired by the firm. To own an asset, a firm may borrow money and purchase it, contracting with the lender to make periodic payments. But, for security, the lender could retain a title or some claim to the asset, as banks do for secured loans, subject only to receiving the payments, while the firm retains control over the asset. This would be tantamount to renting out the asset under a long-term lease. Hence contracting is not necessarily eliminated. Governance is a type of contracting whereby the factors are subject to the long-term, continuous and flexible direction of the management. The contract may be with a firm's bondholders or share owners rather than a bank.

The need for large-sized firms may be primarily due to economies of scale rather than to an economizing of transaction costs. A single hunter can capture a deer, but to capture an elephant one may need a hunting party, even if there is no asset specificity, bounded cognition or opportunism. The need for a band of hunters and their tools creates a need for coordination, for governance, for a contract among the members of the team. The key feature of such a hunting firm is then the control over a sizeable amount of factors of production by one managing agent. The presence of variables such as asset specificity then affects the nature of the contracting. They also affect the size of the firm, but this may be secondary to the needs due to economies of scale. Note that, with more advanced technology, the elephant could be captured by one person, so that economies of scale are a function of technology as well as of the nature of the product.

Williamson (1979, 1985) regards the governance structure of transactions as the institutional framework for deciding about transactions as well as the contractual relationship itself. Three aspects he emphasizes are uncertainty, the frequency of recurrence and the degree of transaction-specific investments. Recurring, non-redeployable and idiosyncratic investments, along with asset specificity, require a unified governance with relational contracting; that is, some type of internal organization with vertical integration. Land, being fixed in place, and site-specific investments create the condition for this type of governance. Typically, tenants and members stay put for long time intervals. Residential associations fit this category and therefore require constitutions that protect mutual long-term interests. Rather than necessarily being vertically integrated, spatially oriented organizations are horizontally integrated within the territory, offering a multitude of services tied to the area. Territorial *provision* induces horizontal governance, as opposed to the vertical integration that asset-specific transactions can induce in the *production* of goods.

Williamson (1985, p. 78) states that, with vertical integration, a firm has no need to deal with inter-firm agreements. However, these agreements still exist. They are shifted to intrafirm politics and contracting, often implicit rather than overt. Opportunism exists within a firm as well, with individuals vying for favors, status and power. In a residential association, factions can compete for control of the board or for their favored goods. Williamson (1975) also states that internal organization precludes diverse claims on profits, but this proposition is not necessarily valid either, since various individuals, departments and interest groups may attempt to extract rents and perks, as well as interpreting contractual rights to obtain greater claims on income flows and assets.

Williamson (1991) states that the implicit contract law of internal organization is that of forbearance. Monitoring and auditing are more effectively accomplished within a firm (1975, p. 30). Disputes are normally resolved internally, and internal organization facilitates adaption. Harold Demsetz (1988) questions whether asset specificity increases transaction costs, since a contract can specify terms in detail, but Williamson recognizes this. To Williamson, successive adaption is important because of contingencies that cannot be predicted in an uncertain world. If agents were not opportunistic, a general clause in a contract could specify that adaptions be implemented without opposition. With opportunism, uncertainty and asset specificity, continuity matters and transactions require a governance structure with the capacity to resolve conflicts (1985, p. 79). But, as noted above, a contract could still leave the firm with effective control over an asset, subject to its making the payments for it. What the firm needs is control rather than title. Hence the directors of community associations are typically given wide powers by their governing documents, within fiscal constraints, even though title remains with the members. Demsetz (1988) adds that losses are greater with asset specificity when agreements fail, so this induces governance not directly related to transaction costs.

Complex contracts with a long duration induce a transaction-specific ongoing administrative type of contract (Williamson, 1985, p. 71). These are typical of landlord/tenant relationships in proprietary communities such as shopping centers and also of residential associations, which have complex governing documents of indefinite duration tied to real estate. These communities are characterized by unified governance. Another characteristic of such communities is the recurrent frequency of transactions. Residents or tenants use the same facilities day after day. Such recurrence, in addition to idiosyncratic investments, induces unified governance (p. 79).

An additional reason for the contractual protection of assets through governance is protection from sheer incompetence. This goes beyond the bounded cognition involved in being able to govern a large organization or anticipate all contingencies; there may be agents who are not opportunistic but are simply negligent, careless or unable to take care of their responsibilities. Contractual obligations enable a party to enforce an obligation through the courts or to recover damages. Contracts also protect the parties from differing post-contractual interpretations and interests even when there is no guile in the self-interest. As a reason for contractual governance, opportunism can be categorized under *human* failure of all types.

The choice of governance is affected by technology, transaction costs and economies of scale and scope. Site specificity, combined with a high cost of exit with current technology, and the economies of size that characterize many civic goods, induce a unified ownership of territory (or of the common elements of a territory) and an associated governance structure for contracts between either owners and tenants or the partners of an association. A board of directors is contractually obligated to safeguard the investment of the owners, whether of a corporation producing goods or an association providing goods. The charters and bylaws of associations constitute long-term contracts between the co-owners that safeguard continued governance.

Alchian and Demsetz (1972) note that, in a mutual-interest non-profit firm, there is more shirking than in a profit-making operation. In a corporation that issues transferable stock, the management is capitalized in the share price. The stocks of a corporation are analogous to the land values of a territorial association. In a community association, each member owns an individual lot whose value capitalizes community public goods, including its governance. Thus shirking or inefficiency becomes capitalized in lower land values, just as it is in lower share prices for stocks. A nominally non-profit non-stock corporation such as a residential association is in reality a profit-making organization with shares of land, profits and losses consisting of increases and decreases in the land values of the individual lots. The potential for such gains or losses constrains shirking.

Another aspect of governance concerns the technically optimal size of a firm with respect to the returns on investments. Williamson (1967) presents a model in which there are diminishing returns to increased size due to losses of control and information by top managers, a point made by many others, of course, as well. Decentralization within a firm reduces this loss of coordination and, as is discussed in Chapter 12, large residential associations such as Reston and Columbia are federated, local neighborhoods or villages having their own governance. Even with decentralization, bounded cognition imposes a limit to firm size, as Williamson and others have shown.

This limitation applies to top-down hierarchies, controlled by the top, but not necessarily to bottom-up organizations, alliances of organizations that are controlled by the organizations who join them voluntarily and renew their affiliation periodically. As analyzed by Allen Buchanan (1991, p. 37), there can be a 'strategic argument', a strong pragmatic ground in favor of including a secession clause in a political union. This argument would apply to any organizational union which does not have significant asset-specific investments. If any member organization may withdraw or secede from the alliance, the federal or umbrella organization's governors have an incentive to keep the alliance effective. The exit option also limits the feasibility of discriminatory redistribution, the unequal treatment of the members. Also, the functions of a federated league are limited to those which have economies of scope, scale and territory, otherwise they would be carried out by the constituent organizations. Hence it is possible to have an association of associations which covers a large territory, the union of the territories of the members, but whose functions are limited to those that the individual members would not carry out as effectively.

Related to secession is the possibility of takeover. Firms that operate inefficiently provide opportunities for entrepreneurs to buy them and profit by eliminating the waste. This creates what Henry Manne (1965) called the 'market for corporate control', as firms operated with greater efficiency take over those that are inefficiently managed. Not all takeovers or mergers are made to remove internal inefficiency; Dennis Mueller (1977) found that mergers do not necessarily increase stock values. Acquisitions may have other motives, such as long-term growth or increased market share, although these goals, too, would eventually increase profits or else subject the firm to a takeover. Takeovers are important in the production and provision of civic goods, as an ineffective developer may be replaced or an incompetent board of directors may be subject to removal. The case of Reston in Chapter 12 offers an example of the takeover of a residential development.

In a corporation, shareholders have the ultimate authority over the firm and typically vote both for the board of directors and on major policy issues. In cooperatives and non-stock corporations, the voting is typically by membership rather than the amount of stock held. In democratic governance, when an issue involves more than two possible choices, it is possible to have non-transitive preferences, so that choice A might be preferred over B, and B over C, yet C might be chosen over A owing to the particular preference pattern of the membership. In the literature, this intransitivity is regarded as implying a possibility of cycling through the possible choices, for example from A to B to C to A. But cycling implies choices over time, and choices at different times are not the same choices. Since utility is subjective, it is revealed only at the moment of effective choice, such as when an exchange takes place. An exchange taking place at a later moment does not necessarily use the same utility function or the same values for the function variables. Indeed, the previous choice will alter the world of the chooser, giving the second choice a different utility function or different values. Hence intransitivity does not imply cycling, but only the arbitrariness of each choice, making it dependent on the voting agenda. A choice may preclude choosing among the other alternatives. Such arbitrariness of choice is normatively neutral; its consequences depend on the specific factors peculiar to each situation. Cycling, of course, does take place, but it may occur in reaction to previous, unsatisfactory choices and to changing utility variables in addition to being caused by the arbitrariness of choice itself. Members may also deliberately choose to cycle, for example to give several options a chance or to permit a variety of persons to hold various positions.

In an uncertain world, with bounded cognition and limited knowledge, and with utility subject to change, a choice made by an individual also may be arbitrary to some degree, so arbitrariness is a characteristic of choice in general rather than being peculiar to the intransitivity of democratic governance, which may be more arbitrary in degree but not in kind. In summary, theories of industrial organization indicate that territorial public goods are produced by firm-like organizations with complex governance structures and long-term contractual relationships, rather than by one-at-a-time atomistic market transactions, owing to economies of scale and the site specificity within the territory. The arbitrariness of democratic governance is not intrinsically different from that of governance by one person, though it may well differ in degree. Organizations are limited in size because of the costs of information and control, but this does not preclude alliances of organizations that cover large areas for collective goods having large economies of territory.

Organization and spontaneous order

The theory of transaction costs accounts for the governance seen in the provision of territorial public goods, but there are also governance structures which evolve through spontaneous processes rather than being the result of deliberate design. Even governance which is designed cannot be completely controlled from a central director, but also has spontaneous action. F.A. Hayek (1945) pointed out that the data of an economy (or 'catallaxy') are not given to a single mind, but are dispersed as localized knowledge. Governance can organize a firm, but not an economy. The question is not whether there is planning or organization, but at what level and by whom. Even within firms, the decentralized knowledge about the 'circumstances of time and place' (p. 522) prevents the central director from controlling all the processes and decisions.

The type of product being made also affects the degree to which a constructivist approach, that is, one which deliberately designs an organization, will work. As Hayek (1979 [1952]) stated, engineering problems may be solved by design, but an engineering approach cannot be applied to a process that involves human beings without thwarting the desires of the people or causing unintended consequences. Hence, even if transaction costs can be reduced by designing a social club, the members will have their own ideas of what they desire and how to run the organization, which cannot be anticipated since this knowledge is lacking *a priori*.

As Hayek (1967) also noted, many institutions and practices evolved as a result of the unintended consequences of human action, being neither constructed nor 'natural' (independent of action). As institutions evolve, those that are less effective tend to be eliminated. It should be noted, however, that 'effective' institutions are not necessarily benign; they merely survive. This Hayekian theory applies to real estate residential developments. The physical infrastructure can be designed by one firm, but the social organizations of the community evolve from previous cultural affiliations and the individual interests of the residents, and cannot be effectively designed by a social engineer.

Since governance is an inherent part of private enterprise, we need to examine the distinction between public-sector and private-sector governance, the topic of the next chapter.

5 Imposed versus consensual governance

What exactly is a 'market economy', and what is the difference between the private and public sectors? Terms like these are common knowledge and seldom defined but, when we examine them closely, what seemed from afar to be a clear meaning can turn fuzzy when looked at under a logical microscope. In this chapter, these terms will be 'unfuzzed', so that the terms and distinctions can have clear and distinct meanings. The definitions developed here are not just words but derivations of the significance of the terms.

The meaning of 'market'

As Jack High (1985) has indicated, some normative standard is required to distinguish 'market' processes from non-market, governmental acts. Such a norm or ethic would need to be rational and universal in order to apply to economic theory independently of culture, time and place. This ethic would provide a means of distinguishing voluntary from imposed governance; indeed, it would determine what it means for an act to be 'voluntary'. The term 'voluntary' is often employed without being defined, the definition left to common usage, but for a deeper understanding of market or voluntary provision an explicit elucidation is required.

The term 'voluntary' derives from the Latin word 'voluntas', meaning 'will', but in the context of governance the term refers not to the arbitrary will of any individual but to the wills of all the members of a society, since an act expressing the will of one person may be against the will or desire of another. If all acts for which at least one person objects are classed as involuntary, then almost all acts would be classified as imposed. The question is thus the delineation of the set of acts that are classified as 'voluntary', the opposite being 'coercive' or 'imposed'.

While a thorough examination of ethical theory is beyond the scope of this book, a brief exposition of one approach to a rational and universal ethic will be presented here in order to ground the discussion on a non-arbitrary meaning of 'voluntary', and, hence, 'market'. This ethic was called a 'law of nature' by John Locke (1947 [1690], p. 123):

> The state of nature has a law of nature to govern it which obliges every one; and reason, which is that law, teaches all mankind who will but consult it that, being all equal and independent, no one ought to harm another in his life, health, liberty, or possessions.

This formulation of natural law, or a universal ethic, by Locke states that the ethic is to be derived by using reason. The premises for a rational derivation are to be found in the 'state of nature' (which contains the natural law). Such a state of nature has been interpreted to be a society without a state or government, and perhaps that is what Locke himself meant, but, since all human communities have always had some sort of *governance*, a realistic meaning of the 'state of nature' for a rational ethic cannot be an ahistorical absence of government, but the actual biological nature of human beings, that is, human nature *per se*. 'Without government' thus can be interpreted to mean 'without any particular cultural or historical *forms* of government', or human nature prior to culture. Hence natural law, or the universal ethic, must logically be derived from human nature and must be independent of any cultural or personal ethical views, values, beliefs, biases or attitudes.

In the passage cited above, Locke supplies two premises based on human nature: equality and independence. 'Equality' means in this context that human beings are biologically equal in the qualities that make one human: the capacity to reason, make choices and control one's acts. This capacity is different both from levels of intelligence (the quality of cognitive abilities) and from the actual exercise of the capacity (due to the influence of emotions, drugs, ideas and so on). Equality implies that there is no objective rationale for one set of human beings to be morally superior to another set, hence to make one set masters and another set slaves. 'Independence' means that the thinking, feeling and acting of each individual is entirely internal to that individual, but it does not deny any social or economic dependence of persons on other persons. Independence also implies that each individual person reacts to phenomena with a feeling that they are pleasing, displeasing or indifferent to himself, so that each person has a subjective view of what is good and bad for himself.

The Lockean premises of equality and independence imply that all ethical judgements (of good and evil) ultimately derive from the subjective views of individuals, otherwise the premises are contradicted. If some external moral 'good' is imposed on an individual, he is no longer independent in determining what acts he feels are 'good' (that is, beneficial or agreeable) for himself; moreover, if others determine what is 'good' for the individual, he is no longer equal with respect to them. The subjective origin of moral sentiments implies that, in the derived universal ethic, an act is judged to be a benefit to another person, and therefore a moral good, if and only if the recipient deems it agreeable or beneficial. Furthermore, an act which does not affect any other person cannot be judged as evil if the person doing the act does not consider it evil. Hence, using the premises, we can logically derive non-arbitrary rules for a universal ethic even though the derived values for good and evil originate in subjective personal values.

The key category of acts in determining 'voluntary' acts is that which affects others and for which at least one other deems it to be disagreeable. Such acts, which will be referred to as 'injuries', can be divided into two types: (1) those whose disagreeable effects are the result of the recipient's personal views and values; (2) those which do not entirely depend on such views for their effect. The first type of act can be called an 'offense' and the second a 'harm'. In the case of harm, if the effect is not due entirely to the internal disposition and predilections of the recipient, it must also be due to some entity that originates outside the person and enters into his domain against his will; that is, it is an invasion of his domain.

The first type is, by definition, non-invasive. A person is offended by what he observes or knows, but the bad feeling is due to his state of mind alone. Perhaps he does not like the beliefs of his neighbor or the rituals that someone practices; someone with different beliefs would not be dismayed. A harm involves some unwelcome invasion, such as the physical entry of a bullet into one's body, or the theft of some item in his domain, or the taking hold of your body so that you are no longer able to move where you desire. Since the recipient deems it to be disagreeable, the universal ethic, having no other source of moral values but those of individuals, must also assign to the act the value of 'evil' or 'wrong' (the two being synonymous). The fact that the perpetrator may like the act of theft does not neutralize the evil that the recipient feels, which makes the act evil. The existence of any one person's sentiment that an invasive act is unwelcomed is sufficient to assign to it a value of evil; otherwise, the equality and independence of the victim would be nullified. The practical consequence is that, no matter how much good an act may do, if it involves any evil, the good does not cancel out the evil.

Harm is further qualified as being direct, actual and significant. The responsibility for harm lies with the person directly responsible for the act. For example, if X sells a hammer to Y, not knowing that Y will use it to smash a window, X has not committed the harm. Actual harm is distinguished from hypothetical harm; someone carrying a hammer might smash a window, but no harm is committed until the act is actually done. However, a clear and present danger, or a threat, is an actual harm; for example, if someone turns on a time-bomb, actual harm has been committed even if the explosion has not yet occurred, since a train of events that results in harm is itself harmful. The requirement that harm be significant means that minor commonplace invasions, such as speech which enters the ears of someone nearby, are not harmful.

Harm generally constitutes some type of theft and involves force or fraud. Fraud is coercive in inducing someone to give up property on the basis of false information when the person would not be willing to do so if the true information were known; hence the false information is an invasion, an unwelcome entering. But what of a non-invasive offense that a recipient also deems to be evil? By his personal ethical view, it is evil. However, as stated above, a rational, universal ethic must be independent of purely personal or cultural views. Any rule of the universal ethic cannot be based on purely personal biases or predilections. Hence the universal cannot logically take a purely personal view that a particular practice is disagreeable and turn it into a universal judgement that such a practice is evil; instead, the personal view is neutralized. The universal ethic must assign to an offense the ethical value of 'neutral', neither good nor evil. This neutrality keeps the universal ethic independent of purely personal views.

By this derivation we arrive at the Lockean rule for evil: 'no one ought to harm another in his life, health, liberty, or possessions'. This rule can be rephrased to translate the baggage-laden 'ought' into an 'evil' and to reduce Locke's four categories of harm into harm in general: *all acts, and only those acts, which coercively harm others are evil.* The universal rule for good, which Locke omits, would then be: *all acts, and only those acts, which are welcomed benefits are good.* The third rule is that all other acts are assigned a moral value of 'neutral'. There are of course many refinements that can be made to these basic rules, and there are complications involving difficult borderline cases, but, for the purpose of this discussion, the above level of generality can suffice.[1] With these three rules (for good, evil, and neutral acts) formulating what Locke called the moral 'law of nature', or what can alternatively be called the 'universal ethic', the term 'voluntary' can now be given a non-arbitrary meaning. *An act is 'voluntary' if and only if the universal ethic does not assign to it a value of evil.* All neutral and all good acts are voluntary.

This definition likewise determines the synonymous meanings of 'market', 'consensual' and 'multilateral' governance, all of which consist of voluntary acts. The term 'association' will be used for a community with multilateral governance. The opposite of 'voluntary' are the synonymous terms 'involuntary', 'coercive', 'imposed' and 'unilateral'. Unless otherwise indicated, the term 'government' is used here for an imposed governance, that is, one imposed on at least one adult, conscious, sane member of a community. This usage is consistent with the literature that uses 'government' to mean typical sovereign country and local governments. A 'market' is therefore the totality of the voluntary economic acts of agents, including the non-coercive transactions of government agents (such as their use of donated funds). Non-market action consists of involuntary acts mandated by government agents, as well as any acts of coercion by governments or individuals.

Civic governance can be accomplished by a unilateral agency imposed on some participants, or by a multilateral, voluntary agreement among all the participants. In Chapter 1, the former type was identified as synonymous with the terms 'government', 'sovereign', 'political process' and 'public sector', and the latter was identified as synonymous with 'contractual', 'voluntary', 'market' and 'private sector'. Because the terms 'public' and 'private' refer both to goods and to governance, with quite different meanings, the distinction for governance will be indicated here also with the terms 'unilateral' and 'imposed' versus 'multilateral' and 'voluntary' governance.

Market competition, being an inherently rivalrous process, leaves some participants with losses, and laws preventing potential competitors from inflicting losses are sometimes defended by the claim that the losers are injured. However, financial injuries due to competition are non-invasive. Since the successful competitor does not directly invade the property of the loser, the loss is an incidental injury, not a harm, and therefore, under the Lockeian universal ethic, has a moral value of 'neutral'. Indeed, any restriction on competition would be an invasion into the activity of a market agent, an intervention that would infringe on rather than protect a market process.

Just as a restriction on the non-harmful acts of a market agent is a harmful intervention, any arbitrary cost imposed on an agent is also a harmful intrusion. Taxes on enterprise as such, whether on labor, profits or exchanges, are thus precluded from a pure market economy. Subsidies using tax funds also impose an intervention, since the agent receiving them obtains a competitive advantage which is imposed rather than incidental. Empirical findings in economics therefore cannot by themselves imply conclusions about failure in the provision of public goods in a pure market economy, since the effects may be caused by interventions as well. Likewise, empirical findings of success in the contractual provision of collective goods imply conclusions about market provision only if the provision is truly voluntary, as when not subsidized by government.

If the above derivation of Locke's moral law or universal ethic is accepted, then rights which are inherent in human beings, variously called moral, natural or human rights, can then be defined. A moral right is a function, or a correlative, of moral evil. A right to do X means, as a definition, that the negation of X (the coercive prevention of a person's ability to do X) is assigned a value of evil by the universal ethic. A right to own property, for example, means that the negation of that property by another person (by theft or destruction) is evil according to the universal ethic. The statement 'I have a right to speak', means 'it is evil for anyone to forcibly prevent me from speaking'. The expression of a right to do or to have something is therefore nothing more than a different way of expressing the wrongfulness of negating it.

The Lockeian premises of independence and equality and the universal ethic they imply are also foundational for constitutional agreements. The persons entering a contractual association do so as independent and equal persons and, for the agreement to be ethically valid, it must not be imposed on any of the participants. Since the rules of the universal ethic always apply, regardless of any human circumstances, the rights implied by it are inalienable. Therefore a slave contract, permanently impairing such rights, is not ethically valid. This implies that any agreement must allow for the ability of a participant to exit from the association, otherwise it becomes a lifetime slave contract. The agreed upon constitutional rules can otherwise contain anything that the participants desire. These constitutional principles were stated by Algernon Sidney (1990 [1698], p. 105): 'Those multitudes that enter into such contracts, and thereupon form civil societies, act according to their own will: Those that are engaged in none, take their authority from the law of nature; their rights cannot be limited or diminished by any man, or number of men.'

Hence contractual communities may be organized according to the voluntary will of the members, so long as inherent rights are respected, and relationships among those persons who are not in a contractual agreement are subject to the moral 'law of nature'.

Legal sovereignty

In addition to the moral distinction between unilateral and multilateral governance, there is a legal distinction between 'government' and 'market' having to do with sovereignty. The word 'sovereign' derives from the Latin word 'super', meaning 'above' or 'supreme'. A sovereign being is one which is not under the ultimate authority of others, but is self-governing, supreme in one's own domain. Sovereignty can be a moral, legal or *de facto* concept. Here 'sovereignty' will be used as a legal concept, the sovereign being the agent that is so authorized by the constitution of an organization.

A sovereign, such as a monarch, has authority over the persons in his dominion. The sovereign also has authority over the land within his jurisdiction, and hence has authority over all activity taking place in that space and over all wealth which is located in the space. Such control over wealth and activity gives the sovereign a legal (though not necessarily moral) property right over his dominion. Whereas each individual has a moral property right to his own personhood in the moral standard derived above, legal rights are determined by the laws of a sovereign agency. A legal property right permits a title holder to control property, subject to the constraints imposed by law; equivalently, legal property rights prohibit others from taking away property whose title is recognized by the government. But the sovereign also retains some property rights to the property of his subjects.

In a society whose basic law is congruent with the Lockeian 'law of nature', the premise of equality implies that each adult is individually sovereign and has a complete property right to his person and his production, so long as others are not coercively harmed. The equality premise logically implies that, where individual claims are not justified, as in the use of the oceans or the atmosphere, the opportunities or benefits are shared in common or equally. In such a pure libertarian world, legal and moral rights coincide. Persons may then enter into rules agreements which, for example, may specify that subsequent decisions be made by majority vote, so long as a member is free to remove himself from the agreement. This would constitute a democratic multilateral governance, which is typical in clubs and residential associations.

In a pure dictatorship, the dictator is the legal sovereign (though the subjects are still morally sovereign) and has ultimate control over his dominion; hence legal property rights are vested in the dictator. Any governance that is not purely libertarian is dictatorial in being imposed on some persons, even if a majority is doing the dictating. In an imposed or unilateral democracy, the voting citizens as a group constitute the legal sovereign and jointly (as tenants in common) have ultimate property rights to the wealth in the jurisdiction in accordance with the voting rules specified in the constitution. For any one particular issue, the sovereign agents are the number of members legally entitled to decide the issue. Ultimate legal sovereignty consists in the ability to alter the constitution.

In a pure unilateral democracy, because all the voters are potentially sovereign (part of a ruling coalition in any particular issue), rules may only be changed according to previously established rules, creating a 'rule of law'. The rules in effect at some particular moment endow the holders of property titles with some property rights, the ability to control their property within the constraints of the laws. Imposed governance thus has two levels of ownership: that of the sovereign and that of a subject, a person legally subject to the will of the sovereign, with ultimate control of all property held by the former, since the sovereign can change the law.

Legal property ownership by a sovereign can be termed 'sovereign ownership'. The property ownership rights held by a subject would then be 'residual ownership', since the rights of a subject are the residual of those not claimed at the moment by the sovereign. The case where the individual is legally sovereign can be termed 'complete ownership'. The earth today is, of course, divided into states which exercise legal sovereign ownership. Within states, firms and families govern themselves within their domains, exercising the level of individual sovereign ownership authorized to them by the constitution and the residual ownership the sovereign permits them over their assets.

The United States of America, like many countries, has a combination of democratic–collective and individual legal sovereignty. There is an imposed unilateral democracy, but individuals also have certain formal Constitutional rights, making them individually sovereign, although in practice these legal rights depend on their recognition by a substantial number of the members of the society (so that, for example, in a typical jury, a prosecution involving a violation of a Constitutional right would be unenforceable). Whether these Constitutional rights are recognized by the US Constitution itself as inherent, and thus citizens recognized as individually sovereign, depends, of course, on how one interprets the Constitution.[2]

In the USA, there are three legally sovereign levels of government: the federal government, the state governments and some aboriginal tribal governments. Since 1865, the federal government has assumed greater powers relative to the states, especially when making conditional grants to the states. However, as Dicey (1982 [1885], p. 81) pointed out, given their power to amend the US Constitution, ultimate sovereignty still rests with three-fourths of the state legislatures. Federal fiscal power may to some extent be regarded as a cartel among the states. Within the states, the local governmental agencies are subject to the sovereignty of the states, hence they in effect exercise sovereignty delegated to them by the states. Cities, for example, typically operate under charters issued by a state. They are essentially public corporations bound to enforce sovereign law.

Governance is concerned with the enactment and enforcement of rules.[3] A sovereign government has two basic defining elements: persons and space. Governments may, of course, also own other wealth, but such wealth is not a defining characteristic of governance. The two elements, persons and land, are distinct. There can be persons outside the territory who are citizens, and persons inside the territory who are not citizens or subjects. The two elements present a potential conflict, since the citizens outside the territory of one sovereign are, if not in non-sovereign territory such as the high seas, necessarily within the territory of another sovereign. Which sovereign then has the ultimate control over that person? By international practice, land has supremacy in determining power. The citizen of the USA who is located in Mexico, for example, is subject to Mexican law, and the USA may not normally enforce its laws on that citizen without the cooperation of Mexico.

Legally, the 'public sector' consists of sovereign governance, excluding individuals to the extent they are sovereign and including any agents working under the authority of a sovereign. Besides directly owning some property (such as highways), the public sector exercises sovereign ownership rights over the privately owned land, wealth and persons within a jurisdiction. The 'private sector' consists of all other persons and their property. The private sector can have governance as well; that is, agents who agree to form their own governance structure. A 'private community' is therefore a private-sector club with private, consensual governance.

In a contractual community, a member enters into a contract with the other free agents, and the contract provides for the ability of a member to withdraw. If he sues the governing agents, the two parties have an equal standing in the courts. Some theorists have characterized consent in a community as tacit – one implicitly agrees to the governance if one does not leave or protest in some significant way. But simply living in or even entering into a sovereign community does not imply any agreement with all its rules or its constitution. No contract is signed when one is born a citizen and, even if one immigrates, it can be from an unwanted imposed regime to one less bad but still imposed. In a genuinely contractual community, the agreement between community and member is explicit.

In a sovereign community, unless individuals are legally independently sovereign, the membership is not contractual, since the sovereign agency may impose laws upon the member without his explicit agreement. An individual is typically born into membership as a citizen. Even if people may emigrate, there is little option to create a new country, hence entry into the country business is barred.[4] The existing countries have created a monopolistic cartel over the available surface of the earth, and one only has a choice among the entities of the cartel. Even secession and independence movements have created new members of the cartel rather than permitted individuals to exercise individual sovereignty. Only when the right of individual, personal secession is constitutionally acknowledged is the membership contractual.

Subject to the law, consensual communities have absolute control over their own property, which enables them to enact rules which may not be possible under the sovereign governance. This control provides entrepreneurial opportunities for contractual communities that may not be feasible for sovereign governments. Since each household and firm constitutes its own private governance, a civic association is a government of governments. The ownership rights held by the members can be termed 'secondary residual', with the rights of the community government termed 'primary residual'. The rights of an owner/member are residual to those claimed by the community under its constitution.

A landed club has governing power greater than that of other types of clubs. The basis for its governing power is its spatial jurisdiction. A non-spatial club can sue a member for a violation of its contract with the member, but this is no different in kind from the ability of any person to sue another for a contract violation. In contrast, a spatial community has power over the behavior of any persons located within its jurisdiction, much as any owner has control over one's real estate property. Because persons live and work within the property jurisdiction of the community, its primary residual rights affect the permanent life of those involved, unlike other clubs which only have contractual rights with their members.

The proposition by Samuelson (1954) and others that provision of collective goods requires government overlooks not only the spatial aspect of typical civic goods, as discussed in Chapter 3, but the fact that governance can be accomplished by the contractual means as well as by an imposed political process. The industrial organization theory discussed in Chapter 4 forms the basis for private-sector governance by a contractual community. The following chapter presents a theory of the provision of collective goods by consensual communities.

Notes

1. The application of these rules is examined in detail in *The Soul of Liberty* (1980), by the present author.
2. See, for example, essays concerning the Ninth Amendment in Barnett (ed.), *The Rights Retained by the People* (1989).
3. Randall Holcombe (1989) defines a government as an organization that has the ability to finance its activities with compulsory payments from persons in some area on a continuing basis. This definition includes the two criteria of funds and geography in addition to rules enforcement. The Holcombe definition fits that of sovereign governments as well as private residential associations, such as condominiums, though not clubs in which members do not reside. But rules that do not impose explicit assessments nevertheless impose costs, which are in effect payments in kind. Moreover, countries extract payments from citizens even when they are not within the jurisdictional boundary. Also, the concept of an individual governing himself would be subsumed under the broader definition which encompasses all forms of governance.
4. See *How to Start Your Own Country* by Erwin Strauss (1984) for examples of attempts to start independent countries, and the difficulty and lack of success in doing so.

6 Competitive territorial clubs

Having analyzed the distinction between unilateral and multilateral governance, we turn now to an analysis of multilateral governance, or a theory of
clubs. In the first section, Buchanan's landmark model of a single club is
examined. In the second, the model is extended for the case of a territorial
club. Finally, we analyze the Tiebout model, in which communities or clubs
offer different types and levels of collective goods, and the member/
residents choose among them, as when choosing among severable goods.

A theory of clubs

The governance structure discussed in Chapter 4 concerned the organization
of the provision of collective goods. A club is an organization of persons
associated for some purpose. Clubs include firms, associations, governments
and families. Club theory concerns the size of the organization and the
selection of the amount of the collective goods to provide, as well as the
nature of the club revenues.

Buchanan's (1965) theory deals with a club providing collective goods
and seeks to determine the size of club which its members would consider
optimal in providing utility for the members. Such club theory usually
concerns a cooperative, a club in which each member (rather than share of
stock) has one vote and whose property is commonly owned by the membership. In Buchanan's model, the utility an individual obtains from using a
club good is a function of the good as well as of the number of members in
the club. Buchanan excludes camaraderie as a good, and so the collective
good is, in the terminology presented in Chapter 1, a 'clubhouse' good,
excludable and congestible. Since the cost of the good is divided among the
members as an equal per capita fee, the cost of the good to a member
decreases with club size.

Buchanan extends the Samuelson model to include the utility from the
number of members:

$$U^i = U^i[(X_1^i, N_1^i), (X_2^i, N_2^i), \dots , (X_{n+m}^i, N_{n+m}^i)], \qquad (6.1)$$

where U is utility, superscript i refers to an individual, X is an X good (a
physical good, using the terminology presented in Chapter 1), N the number
of persons in the club, n the number of purely severable (private) goods

(assuming in this model that physical goods are either collective or severable) and m the number of purely collective goods.

The production function also includes N, since additional members may affect the cost of the good per member:

$$F = F^i[(X_1^i, N_1^i), (X_2^i, N_2^i), \ldots, (X_{n+m}^i, N_{n+m}^i)].\tag{6.2}$$

For each individual, the optimal marginal rate of substitution between goods equals the marginal rate of transformation between the goods in production, and the (negative) marginal utility of club size equals the (negative number) cost of the good with an additional member.[1]

The equilibrium marginal conditions with respect to the consumption of goods X are met when

$$u_j^i / f_j^i = u_r^i / f_r^i = u_{Nj}^i / f_{Nj}^i,\tag{6.3}$$

where the lower-case u and f represent partial derivatives, j is a representative good, r signifies a numeraire good, and the subscripts Nj refer to the utility and cost of the number of members N of the club. An individual will have an optimal quantity of collective goods X and share this quantity optimally over a group of the determined size. If the optimum size is infinite, the second equal sign is replaced by 'greater than', for example if u_{Nj}^i equals zero, there is no cost per additional member. Then, of course, any finite size is smaller than optimal.

In a geometrical analysis, Buchanan adds the restriction that all club members are identical, noting that the results regarding optimal club size do not apply otherwise. Costs being subjective, without identical utilities, the problem of demand revelation and the charge per member once again has no solution in this model. A deeper problem concerns the nature of crowding, which itself is presumed but not analyzed. Under what situations would a public characteristic be in the congestible and excludable category? Once a characteristic is in fact congested, it is no longer public, as discussed in Chapter 1. But if it is not yet congested, what would make a characteristic capable of becoming congested?

The domain of the good, the field in which the good has a common availability, has a lower utility for some persons in the domain when additional persons enter the domain. If the domain is space, which seems to be the most common application regarding civic goods, then the impact of goods in space itself needs to be accounted for: that is, the induced rent, which the Buchanan model does not take into account. If the domain is not space, then, as it is an excludable good, some entry fee proportional to congestion may be charged offsetting the marginal cost. But the Buchanan model posits a fixed fee divided by the membership. A comprehensive theory of clubs which, as Buchanan states, is also a theory of optimal exclusion, needs to take into account the alternatives of user charges and rents.

Crowding may yield a vector of utilities rather than one value. Members may not like the quality rivalry itself, but may like some effects of crowding. Glazer and Niskanen (1991) model a club with members averse to congestion, yet who favor congestion in the club good because that induces some persons to choose alternatives to the club good. The club then produces a lower level of the good, reducing the expense for the members. If a majority do not suffer as much from the congestion as a minority (or a wealthy minority can afford to provide an alternative), then they will prefer crowded goods.

For many clubs, the domain is capacious, inherently incapable of becoming crowded, but there may still be a marginal cost of adding a member. A political association, for example, typically desires to have as many members as possible. A new member does not crowd the domain, but he does add some maintenance cost to the club. The members want entrants, but only if they at least pay their way. Such clubs are funded by an equal assessment of dues plus voluntary donations that the members may care to send. A discussion of such clubs is presented in Chapter 8. The point here is that such a club is neither infinite nor does it have a finite optimal size; the collective good is in the category of excludable and capacious, which does not fit the mold of the Buchanan model. Typically, clubs such as churches and political groups seek to convert others into their domain; their goods are not necessarily welcomed by those not in the club.

Ng (1973) presents a model of clubs which maximizes the utility of an individual subject to the constraint that the utility of others is held constant and the production possibilities are given. In the Buchanan model, the number of persons maximizes the benefit per person but, according to Ng, not necessarily the total net benefit. An increase in benefit for a new member may outweigh the aggregate decrease. Ng (1974) further notes that Buchanan's condition is that of a market equilibrium, where bargaining is ruled out by the assumption of equal cost sharing.

Ellickson (1973) states that, contrary to the Buchanan (1965) model, the determination of the optimal club size requires a global comparison among alternative clubs. A choice within a particular allocation is not sufficient to establish optimality. Equilibrium is relevant to the assignment of individuals to jurisdictions. This relates to Samuelson's (1958) statement that a determination of the *optimum optimorum* requires computing over all possible goods to determine the total optimum mix – an unattainable Pareto ideal raised to the second power! To argue against Ellickson, the Buchanan model does not seem to preclude competition among clubs, so the focus on the conditions within a club does not seem out of place. However, Ellickson has a point in saying that one may need to take the existence of other clubs into account; when Walt Disney grappled with the decision of the best size for Walt Disney World, he may well have included as a decision variable the existence of other theme parks around the world. The competition from other clubs, however, can be subsumed in the utility derived from the goods in one particular club.

Oakland (1972) analyzes the congestion of club goods, concluding that, if exclusion is costless, optimality conditions call for the rationing of such goods through user fees. Contrary to the Lindahl model, in which individuals pay different prices for a collective good, in the Oakland model rationing is achieved with a pricing system in which each participant pays the same price, equal to the marginal congestion cost. Berglass (1976) has a similar finding: that, with the free entry of clubs, congestion tolls equal to marginal social cost exactly suffice to finance the collective good. The models of Buchanan, Ng, Oakland and Berglass do not deal with the site rents generated by a club that owns land and provides territorial collective goods. If a good such as a bridge is provided by a club, it will generate a territorial rent which would be reduced but not necessarily eliminated by a congestion fee. For example, a bridge that is never crowded could generate rent.

A model of a territorial club

Buchanan's theory of clubs will be extended here by incorporating the rent R generated by a territorial collective good G, affecting some area A, with N number of units in the club. Such a club could be a residential association, with G consisting of goods such as swimming pools, parks, boats, trails and community meeting facilities. The members do not need to have identical utility functions, since payment by rent reveals demand, as discussed in Chapter 3. Besides the amount of the public good and the size of the club, the amount of rent an individual is willing to pay for the use of some collective good is a function of his income or wealth. Like the Buchanan (1965) model, this model abstracts from differences in wealth, just as it abstracts from individual tastes, cultural standards and the many other factors influencing the desire for goods.

The area A is divided up into residential lots. The utility of G for the users of the lots is independent of lot size (for example, the use of a common swimming pool is independent of the size of one's dwelling unit). Let the size of the lots be uniform and equal to some constant S; the number of units (lots) N is therefore A/S. Assume furthermore that there is some known average number of residents per residential unit, so that the total population in A is a multiple of the N lots. Suppose there is an entrepreneur who proposes to provide G within A. To maximize his profits, he needs to please the potential membership. His two choice variables are A and G, similar to the choice variables in Buchanan's model; that is, the public good and club membership number.

For the user of lot i, the utility derived from G is

$$U^i = u^i(G, N) = u^i(G, A/S) \qquad (6.4)$$

The first derivative of U with respect to G is positive; additional amounts of G yield greater utility. The first derivative of U with respect to N or A is negative, as in the Buchanan model, since camaraderie is excluded from the utility function, and crowding is assumed to have negative utility for all $N >$ 1. In this territorial case, there is a rationale for this negativity, since a larger N implies a larger A, which increases transportation costs within A and also increases the number of persons and thus the crowding of goods such as swimming pools. (The private characteristic of crowding in direct use still does not negate the public characteristics of G, such as its common availability, the times when it is not crowded and its physical qualities such as water temperature.)

A site is rented to the highest bidder during each time period (current residents either pay the rent or else are replaced). The rental revenue due to G is a function of the utility U derived from a lot by holder i:

$$R_i = r(U^i) = r(u^i[G, N]) \qquad (6.5)$$

There is a cost C in producing G,

$$C = c(G) \qquad (6.6)$$

which is a function of G and not directly dependent on A. For example, the cost of a swimming pool does not depend on the area of the resort. (Indirectly, since the optimal G is jointly determined with A, A will feed back on C.) Included in C is the increasing governance costs of managing a greater amount of G.

The entrepreneur's objective is to maximize the present value of a future profit stream. It is assumed that, once the club and G are created, the size of A and G will not change. With constant A and G in all time periods, profits are maximized by maximizing the profit P within each time period, where the profit consists of the total rental revenue from (6.5) minus the cost in (6.6). Assuming that the utility and thus the rent for each lot is identical,

$$P = NR_i - c(G) = Nr(u^i[G, N]) - c(G). \tag{6.7}$$

Profit is maximized where the first derivatives are zero:

$$\partial P/\partial G = N\partial R_i/\partial G - \partial C/\partial G = 0, \tag{6.8}$$

given some A, where $\partial R_i/\partial G = (\partial R_i/\partial u^i)(\partial u^i/\partial G)$ per the chain rule, and

$$\partial P/\partial N = N\partial R_i/\partial N + r(u^i[G, N]) = 0, \tag{6.9}$$

given some G. Hence, from (6.8),

$$N\partial R_i/\partial G = \partial C/\partial G, \tag{6.10}$$

and from (6.9),

$$r(u^i[G, N]) = -N\partial R_i/\partial N \tag{6.11}$$

Since $\partial R/\partial N$ is negative, the right-hand term in (6.11) is positive.

As area and the number of units increase, the marginal renter is willing to pay ever less rent. From (6.11), the optimal club membership N, and equivalently the optimal area A, is that at which the per-unit rent equals the negative of the number of units times the decrease in rent from the marginal unit. From (6.10), the optimal supply of G, for a given A or N, is that amount where the marginal cost of G equals N times the marginal unit rent induced by the marginal amount of G. Since the units are identical, this is simply the amount of G in which the marginal cost equals the total marginal rent.

Equations (6.10) and (6.11) provide two equations and two unknowns, G and N. Solving (6.11) for N, the optimal number of units equals the per-unit rent divided by the negative of $\partial R_i/\partial N$:

$$N = r(u^i[G, N])/(-\partial R_i/\partial N) \tag{6.12}$$

The optimal number varies directly with rent and inversely with the negative of $\partial R_i/\partial N$. This suggests that high-rent fancy hotels or residential associations, with luxurious public areas such as lobbies, would be correlated with a greater number of units than less fancy ones, a proposition one could test if one could control for $\partial R_i/\partial N$. Equation (6.12) also suggests that a greater decrease in marginal rent per extra unit would decrease the number of units, not surprisingly.

At the extreme, families who greatly value privacy or exclusivity have a very high negative $\partial R_i/\partial N$ and, if that value is about equal to R, then $N = 1$, a single family residence. If the decrease in rent per extra unit is zero for all values of N, the good is capacious, the optimal club size A is infinite, and G is not a territorial good.

Substituting for N in (6.10),

$$\partial C/\partial G = \partial R_i/\partial G(r(u^i[G, N])/[-\partial R_i/\partial N]) \tag{6.13}$$

At the optimal supply of G, the marginal cost of G equals the marginal per-unit rent times the unit rent divided by the negative of the decrease in rent from the marginal unit. A solution to G and N will exist if along some interval of G the marginal cost curve crosses the marginal rent curve from below and then remains above it with increasing G.

Solving (6.13) for $r(u^i[G, N])$,

$$r(u^i[G, N]) = \{\partial C/\partial G(-\partial R_i/\partial N)\}/(\partial R_i/\partial G) \tag{6.14}$$

The greater the marginal cost of the good and the marginal decrease in rent for additional units, the greater the optimal rent must be. The greater the marginal rent induced by the good, the less the rent has to be. If these marginal schedules are known, then $r(u^i[G, N])$ or $\check{R}$ is determined, and that value can be entered in (6.12) to determine N as $\check{N}$, and therefore A, if A has not been set exogenously. Since $\check{R}$ is a function of G and $\check{N}$, G can now be determined:

$$\check{R} = r(u^i[G, \check{N}]), \tag{6.15}$$

with $\check{R}$ and $\check{N}$ now known. If functions r and u (or their combination) are known, the inverse function g of the combined functions r and u can be derived. That is, if we know the amount of rent induced by an amount of G, then we can know the amount of G required to induce a given amount of rent. Given the optimal rent and unit numbers, the entrepreneur will produce that level of G which induces that much rent for those units:

$$G = g(\check{R}, \check{N}) \tag{6.16}$$

With G now determined as $\check{G}$, the total cost C is determined by (6.6). From (6.7), profit is now determined:

$$P = \check{N}\check{R} - c(\check{G}) \tag{6.17}$$

If the profit P is greater than zero and if the profit divided by the cost is greater than other opportunities offer, the club entrepreneur proceeds to develop the community. He acquires space of size $A = \check{N}/S$ and produces the quantity and quality of G equal to $\check{G}$. This completes the model.

As Buchanan (1965) stated, the theory of clubs is one of 'optimal exclusion' as well as inclusion. For territorial goods, exclusion is often possible by erecting physical and legal barriers to entry; laws fortified by fences prohibit trespass on private property. Even when entry is possible, the more frequent use of a public good by the permanent residents in the location creates a form of territorial inclusivity by proximity. Lower transportation and other transaction costs can make a good such as a park inclusive for the site residents relative to those outside.

Once the club is created and all lots are sold, the interests of the entrepreneur and the membership may diverge. If G is controlled by the entrepreneur, who by contract may charge any rent he wishes, the industrial-organization theory presented in Chapter 4 becomes relevant. The owners of lots now have site-specific investments, and the provider of G may behave opportunistically by increasing the rental payment above that which was charged when the lots were first sold. This increase in rental cost is capitalized into lower site values. Hence the lot owners will demand a governance structure which prevents such exploitation, and in practice this has been supplied by a democratic governance that prevents the rental payments from benefiting a party other than the co-owners, plus a constitution that limits assessments and provides other safeguards.

The assumption in the model of a land-owning club that area A is a choice variable has some empirical validity. The Walt Disney Company, discussed in Chapter 9, deliberately obtained a large area for Walt Disney World in order to capture the rents generated by the large G they were planning. Both Columbia and Reston were chosen for the large available areas for communities of 50 000 to 100 000 persons, capturing the site value generated by large economies of scale, but they also included smaller villages and clusters appropriate to local governance for the provision of congestible and lower-scale goods. Condominiums are an example of smaller-scale developments (compared to large towns), owing to the costs that a large membership and area would incur, with no offsetting economies of scale.

The cost C in the model is the monetary cost of providing G. Though costs are subjective, in a private investment, where an owner pays the cost and obtains the gain, the monetary cost is the appropriate cost, since the opportunity cost of one investment is the next best investment, and it is monetary profits that are under consideration. As stated by Buchanan (1981 [1973], p. 4), 'So long as the object for discussion, and for theorizing, is either the individual decision maker or the interactions of separate decision makers *in markets,* no harm is done and perhaps some good is added by conceptual objectification.' It is when the deciding agent does not personally bear the cost that the costs in the model are no longer relevant. The model does not take into account goods funded by user fees as well as the voluntary work typical in many residential associations. In practice, an entrepreneur must guess at many costs and, in the course of a development, may alter his plans, the creation of an enterprise being a discovery process.

The social engineering a developer necessarily attempts has significant differences from large-scale engineering by governments, since it must meet a market demand by customers and owners, and they are local in impact. The human choice is not planning or engineering versus not doing these, but at what scale and by whose choice. The industrial-organization theory presented in Chapter 4 implies that there will be some engineered governance in site-specific developments. When one builds a single-family house, the design necessarily engineers the life of the family dwelling in it, but it is their choice whether to build, purchase or rent it, and scale is small. Social engineering on a country-wide scale is imposed by force on unwilling citizens and on a scale so large that the problems of central planning arise. The design of a residential development (like Reston, described in Chapter 12) or shopping center involves some unavoidable social engineering, but on a small scale and offered in the market in competition with other similar projects, just as single houses are. Moreover, the plan for a development will generally be a flexible instrument that can adapt to discoveries and changing market conditions, as will be illustrated in the case study of Reston.

Despite the necessary simplifications of any model, the above model of a territorial club lays out the basic relationships between the public good, the area served and the rents that constitute the club's income.

Club monopoly and competition

The theory of territorial collective goods, discussed in Chapter 3, can now be integrated with the theory of clubs, discussed above, with regard to the question of competition among territorial clubs and the complementary question of the potential of monopoly within a territorial club. Since territorial goods are excludable, there can be several local providers within some region, which makes a civic good such as fire protection severable among the communities; the total amount of the collective good in a region equals the sum of the amounts provided in each community. Moreover, communities can offer different types of excludable goods, so that the demand for a goods package is revealed by persons choosing to live, work or play in the community.

The landmark model of competition among communities in the provision of collective goods is that of Tiebout (1956), which, as Hamilton (1991) [1987] puts it, offered an 'antidote to Samuelson's rather gloomy results'. The antidote actually consisted in the recognition that most civic goods are territorial. Tiebout concluded that the Samuelsonian conclusions need not hold for local expenditures, since consumer-voters can select the communities which best satisfy their preferences regarding collective goods. The choosing of a public-goods package implies that the goods are territorial, since otherwise there would be no need to move, and in the model the goods are also congestible. With perfect mobility, residents dissatisfied with their community's civic goods will leave, resulting in homogeneous communities with respect to the civic goods desired by the residents. Stiglitz (1983) points out, however, that homogeneity is not necessary if there are productive interactions among people, if there are transportation costs, and if people have different utility functions for land.

Samuelson (1958), criticizing the Tiebout model, compares it to the problem of finding the right marriage partners – no one might be exactly suitable, and it is difficult to find the right match among the many possibilities. But, unlike marriage partners, communities can be created anew and fashioned to suit the preferences of a group. Besides, people do find mates that approximately fit their preferences and circumstances, even if matches are not perfect. People often select one or two key goods, which often then come with other complementary goods. For example, some people buy their food at natural- or health-food stores; the stores do not perfectly fit their preferences, but the category as a whole is selected as a key alternative to the predominant type of food. Retirement communities are another instance of a key selection criterion; having selected 'retirement' as a key criterion, a prospective resident then examines the secondary characteristics of the community. Facilities are often divided into sections according to key selection criteria, such as non-smoking sections in restaurants. In a free market, product differentiation is carried out to the degree supported by demand, relative to costs. Contractual communities would provide more differentiation than imposed governance by offering several key goods or secondary characteristics, not impossibly perfect matches.

A premise of the Tiebout model is that there is an optimal community size in terms of the number of residents for which a bundle of collective goods can be provided at the lowest average cost. This is in accord with the model of a territorial club presented above, although Tiebout does not encompass land rent in his model. Consumers reveal their demands for collective goods through a choice of community, and competition among communities ensures that local collective goods are provided at minimum cost. Tiebout acknowledged that this is an 'extreme model' in which persons are fully mobile and there are a large number of community choices. The model nevertheless shows how a second-best solution could be achieved.

The choice of community is equivalent to the purchase of a good and reveals the consumer's demand for the local goods. A policy implication offered by Tiebout is that increased mobility and knowledge improve the allocation of collective goods. In answer to Samuelson's (1954) contention that no decentralized pricing system can determine the optimal levels of collective consumption, Tiebout contends that, for local collective goods, the problem does have a conceptual solution; the fact that the solution is not perfect does not invalidate it if it is the best that can be obtained. Like competition among producers of private goods, competition among providers of local collective goods is a spontaneous order produced by the action but not design of agents in a market process. Hayek's (1976) distinction between an economy and a catallaxy is analogous to the distinction between the theory of governance structure within a firm versus competition among governance units. An economy or community, like a household, is organized with a 'unitary plan' (Hayek, 1976, p. 107), like the model of a landed club above. Besides this deliberately designed organizational order, there is a market order, or catallaxy, 'brought about by the mutual adjustments of many individual economies in a market' (p. 109).

Also relevant to the concept of competition among communities is Hayek's (1985 [1978]) treatment of competition as a discovery procedure. How do we know in practice which items are actually scarce goods, and the value of the goods? As Hayek states, these are discovered by competition, by the bids and offers of goods in a rivalrous market. Two types of technical (as contrasted with Pareto) efficiency emerge for landed clubs: the provision of goods within a club where marginal costs equal the marginal rents induced, and the marginal choice of a bundle of goods among various competing clubs. One community may be providing goods in a technically efficient way, given the choice of good, but then a second community may come up with superior goods, revealed by the fact that members of the first community migrate to the second, thereby inducing the first community to improve its goods.

The theory of a catallaxy of private territorial communities is incomplete without including cooperation as well as competition. Being spatially distinct, neighboring communities share area-wide externalities, and it is in their interest to form associations of associations to provide goods with larger spatial economies of scale and scope. Mancur Olson (1971, p. 63) theorizes that, in large groups, the incentive is lacking to provide collective goods, but that there is one case in which the incentives could be present, namely a federal group. This makes the problem of providing the good to a large area a small-numbers matter. The federation would have an incentive to offer a package of goods to the constituent members, such that the refusal of one of the member associations to join the federation would involve the loss of cooperation and goods that its members desire, tied into those goods which are more subject to free-riders. At the same time, if the federation becomes wasteful, its members can secede and regroup to form an alternative, rather than try to reform the first one.

Though Tiebout in his model recognizes the importance of space, the model itself has no spatial dimensions, as though the various communities exist as points in space rather than themselves having space. As discussed in Chapter 3, the effect of a local collective good permeates the space around it like a magnetic field, giving a 'charge' or value to the space, which is manifested in the market as site rent. Hence an individual residing in that space must pay a rental price for the good.

Many analysts have incorporated capitalization into the Tiebout model. Wallace Oates (1969) recognizes that collective goods could be capitalized in real estate values. His empirical examination found evidence for the capitalization of the benefits of local collective goods and of property taxes. Hence property taxes are akin to user charges for local collective goods. Bruce Hamilton (1975) shows that under certain conditions a property tax is equivalent to a head tax if zoning is used to maintain equal house values, thereby achieving the Tiebout result. This conclusion is applicable to private communities, where covenants do indeed enforce homogeneity beyond that required by government zoning, and in which the units are somewhat homogeneous by design, as in condominiums. Joseph Stiglitz (1983) presents the case where communities differ and a community can increase its land values by providing collective goods that are valued by a marginal migrant rather than those in the community. Stiglitz states that the resulting equilibrium is not in general Pareto-optimal. But if the increase in rental income or land value is itself considered a collective good, then the provision of the goods is not necessarily irrational or technically sub-optimal. Moreover, given n identical lots and an active turnover of lots, if only a fraction m were bid on by migrants at a higher rate, the m lots would only increase a slight amount in value over the others.

If rent versus goods-value is the only factor, one only needs a minor increment to bid a lot away from a present owner. Hence only when almost all lots are taken over by the migrants desiring the new goods will the land rent go up to reflect the new good. In an open auction market of n identical lots, the $(n+1)$th bidder sets the price, the others needing only to bid slightly higher. If there are less than n bidders, and all lots are to be let go, then the price of the lots will be zero. Thus, if the relevant information is universally available, the rent induced by a new good will be zero until all (or mostly all) the lots are taken by those valuing the good. In practice, of course, information on all bids is not available; real estate markets are heterogeneous and localized, so a collective good may induce some rent even if only some of the residents value it, but the principle still applies that the mere existence of migrants does not necessarily induce rents from goods devoted to them.

Buchanan and Goetz (1972) present a model in which two features restrict the efficiency of the Tiebout process, the spatial dimensions and the lack of proprietary ownership. Regarding the spatial aspect, the per unit cost of collective goods falls as group size expands. Hence mobility does not ensure Pareto efficiency among the communities of different size. But this result depends on the per capita finance of a fixed amount of a collective good, and does not take into account the increased demand for space that a newcomer creates. When rent is incorporated into the model, a newcomer affects either the intensive or the extensive rental margins, increasing the population density or the area of residency. Even if the amount and cost of the good remains the same as newcomers arrive, an increased density increases the demand for space and the land rent in the community. If the goods are funded from the land rent, then there may not be a fall in the total cost of living in the community due to newcomers, but only a reduction in that amount of rent used for the collective good. For those who already own land in the community, the newcomers add to congestion costs but also add to land value, so the net gain in utility is inconclusive. If the newcomers increase the residential area at the edge of the community, then they will induce increased rents in the commercial center and may add to transportation costs as well as congestion. Although this model assumes that there can be immigration, some private communities (such as a condominium) have a fixed maximum size once fully developed, so the problem of immigration would not arise in the first place.

Even with their financing method, Buchanan and Goetz (1972) find that the internalization of the externalities could occur if the communities are proprietary and competition equalizes the value of the externality. 'Tax shares would have to be related to the size of the *locational rent* component in individual income receipts' (p. 35). 'If all valued "space" should be privately owned and if competition among proprietary ownership units were effective in all respects, allocational efficiency might emerge' (p. 40). The Buchanan and Goetz model was extended by Flatters, Henderson and Mieszkowski (1974) with results that, at the optimum, wage income is devoted to private goods and rent to collective goods and the private-good consumption of the landowners, a result similar to the Henry George theorem (HGT) discussed in Chapter 3.

Though the Tiebout model can attain efficiency with a head tax, such taxes give rise to inefficiencies if the regions are of different size (Mieszkowski and Zodrow, 1989, p. 1134). But when taxes are derived from land rent, a decentralized provision of collective goods can be efficient (p. 1135). However, when congestion is added to the model, as in Boadway and Flatters (1982), a head tax is efficient in accounting for the congestion effect. As mentioned above, the models by Berglass (1976) and Oakland (1972) also find that fees based on congestion costs suffice to finance collective goods when rent is absent. Thus, as Mieszkowski and Zodrow (1989, p. 1136) put it, 'the modified version of the HGT states that the sum of land rents plus congestion charges (head taxes) should equal public expenditures'.

Another such Tiebout model is that of Hochman (1981), who has a land and labor model with congestion. He concludes that, besides Pigouvian corrective taxes (including those that account for congestion), the only taxes necessary and sufficient to finance local collective goods are taxes on land rents, in which case local authorities can be fully autonomous. Stiglitz (1977) notes that the HGT does not hold when sites vary in quality, such as having different natural resource endowments. However, natural resource rents and the like are not generated by the local collective goods, hence the HGT as modified in Chapter 3 still holds for those rents generated by the goods. Even when rents not generated by the goods are included in the model, Flatters, Henderson and Mieszkowski (1974) show that, if the land is owned by a group separate from the general population, the optimum population is again that in which the marginal product of labor equals per capita private good consumption. Hence, as noted above, land rents would equal collective goods plus the private consumption of the landlords, achieving efficiency despite variations in the quality of land. Similarly, in the model by Berglass (1984), where the quality of land varies among communities, landlords control the government and finance collective goods with taxes on land rent, seeking to maximize after-tax rents. Efficient expenditures are smaller than rents, leaving a residual profit for the landlords. This literature, then, states that, not only within but among communities, the provision of collective goods by territorial clubs via a combination of land rent and user (congestion) fees, especially by proprietary communities, is efficient.

A complementary aspect of the Tiebout model is the question of political power. As Epple and Zelenitz (1981) ask, 'does Tiebout need politics?' They argue that competition among jurisdictions is not sufficient to guarantee efficiency, because land is immobile even if residents are not. 'Hence, governments can usurp some land rents for their own ends' (p. 1197), giving governments some monopoly power, the power to exploit the residents. 'Fixity of boundaries prevents the tax on land from being competed away. ... Jurisdictions do not compete for land.' This is because 'The tax reduces the unit price of housing received by suppliers, thereby reducing the supply of housing relative to the no-tax equilibrium.' The usurpation of land rents by the governing agency will be called here 'site exploitation'. The tax increases the gross price of housing.

However, while a tax on real estate as a whole may increase the gross-of-tax price of housing, a tax on land alone would not do so. In the 'classical' theory of the incidence of land-value taxes, Harry Gunnison Brown (1979 [1924], p. 216) states that 'A tax on the rental value of land, however used, can neither be shifted from one landowner to others nor from landowners as a class to any other class.' With this primary effect of a tax on land rent, there is no effect on the supply of housing other than possibly to increase it, since vacant or sub-optimally used land (which could be earning a larger rental) has a high carrying cost relative to the zero-tax case. There would be no effect on the gross-of-tax price of construction, and a tax on rent *per se* would lower the sale price of housing. Hence the effects indicated by the Epple and Zelenitz model hold for taxes on improvements but not for taxes on land rent.

Martin Feldstein (1977) challenges the classical theory, such as expressed by Brown, by introducing dynamic effects. A tax on rent induces an increase in the capital stock (fewer funds being invested in land), raising the marginal productivity of land and reducing the rate of interest. This increases the capitalized value of land. If land is less risky than other investments, the price of land will also fall less than strict capitalization would suggest. Hence part of the tax is shifted to lower returns on capital goods. But such results hold for a tax on the rent of a very large area, not on that of a small location. As Brown (1979 [1924], p. 246) argues, the incidence of a purely local land-value tax falls on the landowners of that community. Hence the Feldstein result does not affect the local monopoly question.

John Yinger (1982), like Oates (1969), notes the absence of capitalization from the Tiebout model. His model has a household bid for housing as a function of collective services and taxes. Yinger concludes that 'The capitalization of local fiscal variables into house values is a long-run equilibrium condition for households' (p. 935), but that capitalization does not support Tiebout's conclusion that the provision of local collective goods is efficient because 'the property tax distorts the housing market' (p. 937). However, such distortion does not take place if buildings and other improvements are exempt from real estate taxation, as argued by Brown (1979 [1924]) and the HGT literature discussed above. Hence, when collective goods are financed by land rent and congestion fees, the 'site exploitation' due to the fixity of boundaries, as analyzed by Epple and Zelenitz (1981), does not occur as a distortion of housing prices and supply. However, monopoly exploitation is still possible because of the site specificity of land and improvements in the community.

Owing to the lack of mobility of land and structures, the government (or landlord or association directors) can increase taxes (or assessments) or impose other costs, which decreases the price of the sites. Competition among communities by itself is not sufficient to prevent site exploitation. Democracy may help in providing a 'voice option' to the residents in addition to their exit option, but politics by itself does not eliminate site exploitation since, in a democracy, one faction may induce the government to grant it benefits at the expense of the others. What Tiebout needs is constitutions which provide legal protection against such exploitation. Constitutional methods of minimizing exploitation include limitations on assessments and expenditures, the requirement of super-majorities for major decisions, the guarantee of an investment (such as a put option on improvements, discussed in the case of the Shannon community in Chapter 10) and, for large communities, the ability to secede from the jurisdiction. Hence Tiebout needs governance constraints and guarantees of exit.

Just as sovereignty consist of persons and territory, exit consists either in a person's leaving the jurisdiction of a government or else the secession of some of the territory from a jurisdiction. Generally, the smaller the jurisdictions of the governments in a region, the less costly it is to move from one to another, since one gives up fewer of the attributes of the larger region, and the move itself is less costly. Hence local monopoly power is reduced when there are many small jurisdictions in a region. As noted by Hamilton (1991 [1987], p. 675), the evidence from several studies suggests that 'we have no particular reason to believe that scale economies are an impediment to wide community choice'.

Within the greater regional government, since leaving the area is costly for individuals, legalized secession from the jurisdiction, that is, flexible boundaries, offers one possible way to prevent monopoly exploitation due to what Epple and Zelenitz (1981, p. 1207) call the 'fixity of boundaries'. The possibility of such secession would serve to deter exploitation. Secession itself may be exploitative unless the seceding unit leaves with its share of the assets and liabilities of the parent country. The economics of secession is discussed further in Chapter 15.

Various studies support the principle that the ability to form new jurisdictions decreases the potential of monopoly power. Martin and Wagner (1978) show that barriers to the formation of new communities affect the competitiveness of local government services. In a model of local monopoly power, Gonzales and Mehay (1987) demonstrate that annexation increases municipal fiscal power.

While much of the above analysis and literature has been applied to public-sector governments, the same principles apply to private-sector or proprietary governments, especially as noted above with regard to regional Tiebout models. As Cowen (1988, p. 14) states, models such as that of Buchanan and Goetz (1972) 'offer the intriguing suggestion that Tiebout's model is better suited to analyses of collective goods provision through proprietary communities', a conclusion reinforced by the HGT models in which the landowners retain the residual rents after providing collective goods. Henderson (1985) argued that Tiebout needs entrepreneurs and flexible community boundaries. In the long run, 'population movements and land use adjustment will also eliminate the negative impact of bad politics' (p. 249). With active developers, in the long run, landowners 'refuse to allocate their land in any community to those attempting to usurp their incomes' (p. 267).

The theoretical basis for the contractual provision of collective goods has now been established. The chapters above set forth the elements of territorial civic goods, site rent, governance, the public/private distinction with respect to governance, and clubs. The next chapter rounds out the theoretical foundation of voluntary provision by examining non-excludable goods.

Note

1. In the Holtermann (1972) model of mixed or club goods, crowding is not taken into account. Instead, the model distinguishes between the direct utilization of a public good, which has a private characteristic, and the availability of a good, which has a public characteristic.

7 Non-territorial goods and Smithian sympathy

Chapters 3 to 6 have set forth a theory of the provision of territorial civic goods by competing clubs. This chapter rounds out the theory of public goods by examining the voluntary provision of non-territorial goods.

Excludable collective goods

An excludable good implies the existence of some *club gate* through which members must enter and exit. There may also be an *evictor,* some agency that can expel a member. An eviction may simply be the elimination of a person from a club roster, which acts as the club gate. A club gate may be classified according to the type of exclusion, such as by person, by event, by purchase of a good, by time or by space. An entrance fee is paid at the gate, either once (on entrance or exit) or periodically. A periodic fee implicitly sets a time limit to the membership; when it expires, one must again pass through the gate. A literal or figurative fence and gate enables a fee to be collected, making it possible to fund the club good.

If a club good is congestible, then the utility of the members may be best satisfied by including a fee proportional to the congestion, as analyzed in Chapter 6. An example of a congestion fee is the higher fare that transportation systems charge during rush hour. Fees may be reduced when congestion is absent, for example the reduced prices that restaurants charge during the late afternoon. Much congestion, such as the transportation and restaurant examples, or the usage of airline routes, is territorial, being the addition of persons to some limited space.

Many clubs, however, do not impose congestion fees. A swimming pool may be offered at a fixed rate; price discrimination may be based on age (such as for children or seniors) rather than by congestion. Hotels typically provide free elevator service, even during hours when they are crowded. Whether congestion fees are charged depends on social custom as well as transaction costs. Even when it is feasible to charge more for the swimming pool, later users may consider it unfair to pay more than earlier users, or the earlier users may not consider it fair to pay an extra charge when the area becomes crowded. The literature on crowding seldom distinguishes between a congestion fee charged to the additional users and a fee charged to users already in the domain of a good when it becomes more crowded. From a purely economic perspective, it would seem efficient to charge all those in a domain the same rate at any particular time interval, but, in practice, this is seldom done except when a user is in the domain only for a short time, such as in crossing a bridge.

Non-territorial congestion may be offset by benefits, such as the additional dues received. For example, a club may offer a library that most members use by mail. Additional members make it more likely that a particular book may be loaned out, thus making the library congestible, but the club members may still welcome additional members, since the added dues enable the club to provide more books and other services, and club size itself may be a desired good, adding to the prestige or effectiveness of the club.

Congestion is based on the sheer number of members in a club, as in the Buchanan model discussed in Chapter 6. But additional members may also decrease utility as a result of the qualities rather than the quantities of the entrants. Members may be biased for or against persons of a certain sex, age, race, religion, nationality, ethnicity, ideology, lifestyle or interest. All clubs are organized for some common purpose, so a bias in favor of the belief or interest in that purpose (such as religion in the case of a church) is necessary for the club to function well. Some clubs are subsets of other clubs, requiring members of the subset to be members of the superset – for example, clubs in universities may be limited to students.

A different type of discrimination occurs in *friendship clubs*, in which the members are acquaintances, who may only want to admit those who become friends or are endorsed by some members, rather than simply being additional minds and bodies. Club theory thus needs to take into account that social clubs may have entrance requirements such as acquaintanceship, character and identity, in addition to the fees.

Many clubs have non-congestible, or capacious, services that predominate, and their members therefore desire to have as many members as possible. These clubs are typically funded by periodic dues, the club gate being the membership roster. These clubs may not wish to exclude persons, but need to, owing to the cost of the services. The services of an excludable but capacious club can include severable goods such as a newsletter and collective goods such as a central facility, a research service or services intended for non-members as well. Goods for non-members may be given without cost or may be by nature non-excludable. Clubs advocating religious, political and social doctrines typically provide goods and propaganda to non-members. Such clubs are often funded by donations in addition to dues, which help pay for the non-excludable goods. Thus club theory as well as public-goods theory needs to take into account these non-excludable goods. Much of the theory of public goods implicitly deals with non-excludables and posits a market-failure argument. Yet the evidence is that many such goods are provided voluntarily, and a theory of its provision is required in order to have a comprehensive theory of public goods.

Non-excludable collective goods

Both congestible and non-congestible non-excludable goods can be treated as one category with regard to their funding. Without exclusion there is no club gate, and without a gate there can be no entrance fee for the good. Only if everyone on the planet can be charged a fee does the good becomes territorial and excludable; the gate becomes the use of space. Short of world-wide governance, a congestion fee or any entrance charge is not feasible.

Since all human action is performed by independently thinking individuals, any act presumes individual motivation. This implies that any voluntary provision of a non-excludable collective good requires some tie-in to a severable or excludable good, a good which is specific to the individual or requires an entrance fee. A tie-in can involve either catallactic production and exchange, in which an individual sells or purchases goods for purely pecuniary or mercenary reasons, or benevolent production, in which either an individual contributes to the production of a good without expecting to receive goods of similar market value in return, or else he expects to benefit from some common good regardless of his personal contribution, but contributes anyway.

Examples of catallactic, narrowly self-centered tie-ins include: (1) the approval of members of the community, which can further one's social or business goals; (2) social contacts and an entry in one's résumé; (3) the listing of one's name in a program, plaque or structure as a donor, which can promote one's interests or the satisfaction of preserving one's name for posterity;[1] (4) a key participant can influence the type of good provided towards one of his liking. But though non-benevolent tie-ins are important, such tie-ins do not account for all provision. The purely benevolent private tie-in requires an explanation.

Adam Smith, who related the 'invisible hand' provision of private goods by narrowly self-interested behavior in *The Wealth of Nations*, also provided a 'visible hand-out' theory of benevolent provision in *The Theory of Moral Sentiments* (1982 [1790]). He began this work with the following proposition:

> How selfish soever man may be supposed, there are evidently some principles in his nature, which interest him in the fortune of others, and render their happiness necessary to him, though he derives nothing from it except the pleasure in seeing it. (p. 9)

These principles are manifested in 'sympathy', by which Smith meant 'our fellow-feeling with any passion whatever' (p. 10). Smithian sympathy is a feeling of affinity, accord and empathy with a person, group, culture, organization or other entity: 'Nature, therefore, exhorts mankind to acts of beneficence, by the pleasing consciousness of deserved reward' (p. 86). This sympathy, said Smith, is not necessarily with those who benefit from a service, but can be with a 'noble and magnificent' objective, the achievement of a 'beautiful and orderly system' (p. 185). The sympathy can apply to an idea or project.

Sympathy is a different sentiment from altruism. A selfless altruistic utility function can be regarded as deriving no positive utility, otherwise the altruist would act to please himself as well as others. Therefore a pure altruist can only act to avoid disutility, such as the guilt or shame suffered when one does not do what one regards as one's moral duty. An altruist may feel pained when others suffer, but he never experiences joy.[2] Altruism can be formulated as $U(i)=f(V(j))$, where U is the utility of altruist i and V the utility of another person j. Altruist i seeks to minimize the disutility he obtains due to his failure to do some perceived duty to help j or from any negative utility suffered by j. In contrast, sympathy can be formulated as $U(i)=g\{V(j),x(i)\}$, where $x(i)$ is the provision of some set x of goods to i. A person i with sympathetic sentiments obtains positive utility when some other persons j obtain utility and also from goods x which satisfy him directly. The function g does not indiscriminately bring i joy from any utility that j may obtain, but can selectively obtain utility for i from only some of the utility experienced by j (unlike the case of the altruist who obtains negative utility from any source of disutility experienced by j).

A community of altruists presents us with a paradox, since all of the members are only interested in the utility of the others. A member would not know whether to sacrifice his own consumption in favor of that of others or else to consume, knowing that reducing his own consumption would give displeasure to the others. But no such paradox occurs in a community of sympathizers, since their utility functions include both their own consumption and, selectively, that of others, where each person seeks to balance the two.

The sentiment of sympathy can be divided into two types: benevolent and ethical. 'Benevolent sympathy' is the fellow-feeling manifested in the provision of goods (deemed good by the recipients) to persons, without the expectation of a catallactic exchange. 'Ethical sympathy' is the fellow-feeling manifested in the avoidance of committing harm to others. The utility of an ethically sympathetic person is, like that of an altruist, a negative function of the disutility of others, but only to the extent that they suffer harm. The complete absence of sympathy is apathy, literally 'without feeling'. An apathetic person will exploit an opportunity to steal goods from others if there is no risk, since the disutility of others does not enter into his utility function. Finally, negative sympathy or antipathy exists when one's utility is enhanced by the suffering of others. An angry mob has antipathy, whereas the ordinary criminal may have apathy towards his victims. A 'widely self-interested' person would then have both ethical and benevolent sympathy.

Ruling out pure altruism as empirically rare, when a person contributes to the provision of a non-excludable good, and narrowly self-interested motives are lacking, then the motivation for the contribution is benevolent sympathy with the good, its recipients or some other association with the good. (It is possible for antipathy to function in an analogous way; for example, one contributes to eliminate a hated target, so the discussion will be confined to positive sympathy.) The sympathy can be with a community obtaining the good rather than the good itself. In the absence of a narrowly self-interested tie-in, the act of contributing to the provision of a collective good reveals the existence of benevolent sympathy. The increase in utility (marginally superior to alternatives) due to a benevolent donation is a severable tie-in to the collective good.

Benevolent sympathy overcomes the prisoner's dilemma of free-riders unable to cooperate in the provision of a non-excludable public good. If a person has benevolent sympathy for a community and its goods, he will not wish to free-ride; the act of contributing itself provides satisfaction, or even joy. As the philosopher Benedict de Spinoza observed, a principle upon which cooperation rests, the 'imitation of affects', is a foundational desire to please others (Den Uyl, 1985). The principle of mutual aid is seen in animal life as well. As described by Petr Kropotkin (1974 [1914], p. 30), 'mutual aid is as much a law of nature as mutual struggle'.

Robert Wuthnow's (1991) survey and interviews of volunteers found that they wish to keep alive the notion of community, and to live in a society which shows compassion towards those afflicted with misfortune, consistent with the motivation of sympathy with a community. Douglas Young's (1989) model of voluntary public-good provision based on the proposition that people may feel a responsibility to pay what they perceive to be a 'fair share' of the costs is consistent with the sentiment of sympathy, since the feeling of responsibility may be due to sympathy with a community or project. Moral duty, of course, may also be a motivation not due to sympathy itself but to inculcated beliefs. David Schmidtz (1991) also notes the experiments on voluntary donations for public goods, including the use of assurance contracts (agreements to contribute) and money-back guarantees in case the minimum funds are not generated. In experiments, contributions have been positive even though narrow self-interest would generate a contribution of zero. Though tests results vary and some subjects free-ride, 'subjects contribute to public goods projects even when noncontribution is a dominant strategy' (p. 132).

However, sympathy might not overcome the prisoner's dilemma when action in a broad context is not truly voluntary, that is, when there are coercive restrictions, costs or threats on such action. When such acts are threatened with penalties, then it may require an extraordinarily high degree of sympathy because it must also overcome the cost of the threat. This is why, for example, it is difficult to organize the overthrow of a dictator when any co-conspirator can be a spy. But that situation is not a market failure in the usual sense.

Sympathy with a community fosters loyalty to it, which then affects both its governance and property value. As Hirschman (1970, p. 78) observes, 'loyalty holds exit at bay and activates voice'. Loyal members are less likely to leave when the community is in trouble, and they are more likely to vote and participate. Why, then, is benevolent sympathy not also a factor in the provision of severable goods? Why are most consumer goods produced via catallactic rather than benevolent means? The answer lies in the nature of sympathy itself. Sympathy is a scarce resource. Most persons are busy providing for their self-centered wants, and the well-being of the community is only one of many arguments in their utility functions. Since one will wish to maximize the utility derived from benevolent sympathy, one's production function of such utility will induce one to put funds allocated to public goods to their most productive use. Charity, for example, will be given to those organizations or persons that the giver subjectively feels are most deserving or for whom he has the greatest sympathy, those who 'need' the funds the most. A blind child in a wheelchair holding a cup will elicit more benevolent sympathy than a healthy, able-bodied man gruffly asking for money.

Non-excludable collective goods can be obtained through a benevolent provision which itself is tied in to excludable goods. Memberships in excludable but non-territorial clubs, such as a hobby society or a social movement, often have 'benefactor', 'patron', 'sustaining' and other above-minimum member rates. These levels provide some narrowly self-interested benefits, such as prestige, special publications, invitations to exclusive events and special access to the leadership, but they also induce benevolent donations. The *quid pro quo is* largely symbolic.

As discussed in Chapter 2, the concept of a Pareto-optimal amount of a good is problematic, if not meaningless. An 'optimal' ideal based on a hypothetical social welfare function or how much individuals would give if one had a 'truth meter' to measure their true utility is unattainable. For example, an 'ideal' amount of ideological propaganda as a collective good has no evident meaning, unless as a good subjectively deemed good by the propagandists and revealed as a good to the donors by their effective demand, their contributions. The theory of benevolent sympathy is an explanation of how non-excludable collective goods can be and are actually being funded. It is a theory of feasible provision, the amount depending on the circumstances that induce sympathy.

All categories of collective goods have now been discussed: territorial, excludable non-territorial and non-excludable goods, with or without congestion. Together these categories form a comprehensive theory of the contractual provision of collective goods. There is one case, however, in which sovereign provision is needed. It is impossible for all governance to be private, that is, non-sovereign. The highest-level, or sovereign, governance must provide at least the collective good of a constitutional rule of law governing its subordinate elements. Being sovereign, it belongs by definition to the public sector. But the sovereign government can still be a voluntary association and therefore its collective-goods provisions would be contractual, albeit by a sovereign agency.

Notes

1. In Alexandria, Virginia, the 'King Street Gardens Park' is being built, using 40 000 bricks. Some 12 000 of the bricks are being offered with the engraved name or message of donors at prices from $50 for a one-line name to $250 for a business name and logo ('King Street Gardens Park', n.d.).
2. Ayn Rand (1964, p. viii) wrote of altruism as a philosophy that regards action that benefits others as good, and in which the beneficiary of an act is the only criterion of moral value. In the altruistic ethic, selfish acts, done solely for one's own benefit, are evil. Here altruism is treated, not as an ethic, but as a utility function.

8 Proprietary communities and community associations

We now apply the territorial aspect of civic goods, examined in Chapter 3, with the theory of governance in industrial organization, examined in Chapter 4, to an analysis of contractual communities. Besides residential associations, consensual communities providing civic goods include hotels, shopping centers, condominiums and recreational areas. These types of communities are analyzed by Spencer Heath MacCallum in *The Art of Community* (1970). MacCallum credits his grandfather, Spencer Heath, with originating the concepts of proprietary community administration (p. ix), so we turn first to Heath's work.

Heath on proprietary communities

Heath's main work, *Citadel, Market and Altar* (1957), appeared, ironically, shortly after the Samuelson and Tiebout models, but evidently did not attract academic attention. Heath had developed his concepts over twenty years earlier in a manuscript, *Politics versus Proprietorship* (1936), subtitled 'A Fragmentary Study of Social and Economic Phenomena with Particular Reference to the Public Administrative Functions Belonging to Proprietorship in Land – Proprietorship as a Creative Social Agency'. It was a collection of his papers which Heath compiled and distributed 'as a record of the development and earliest expression' of this work (p. iii).

In one paper, 'Creative Association', Heath wrote that the value of public services is manifested as the rent 'which attaches to exclusive locations in proportion to benefits received by or at these locations' (p. 2). This central idea he obtained from Henry George, and the major essay in the 1936 collection is entitled 'Henry George: A Further Application of his General Principles'. Heath sees himself as extending the concepts of George, quoting from the preface to the fourth edition of *Progress* and *Poverty* (1975 [1879], p. xi): 'What I have most endeavored to do is to establish general principles, trusting to my readers to carry further their applications where this is needed.'

But though Heath's theory of rent was adopted from George, Heath turned George's political program on its head. Whereas George regarded the landowner *qua* landowner as a passive receiver of rent which he has no part in creating, to Heath the landowner as an entrepreneur has the potential of becoming 'a producer of and a restorer of land values' (1936, p. 14). Since

George himself (1975 [1879], p. 343) agreed that the value of improvements to land, such as clearing a forest or draining a swamp, belonged to the one doing the exertion, Heath did not directly contradict George, but he took George's concepts in a new direction, towards a society whose collective goods are provided by entrepreneurs who create location-specific capital goods which generate the rents that finance the goods. George (p. 452) recognized that, as persons, landowners are typically also laborers and owners of capital goods, but he did not envision the owner's role as a creator of land value. 'The great Henry George,' wrote Heath, did not discern 'this natural, at once private and public function, of landowners to invest their rents and also apply their services in the administration of public affairs and to receive in compensation for their services all the increase of rent above the cost of government' (1936, p. 15).

Heath appeals to the historical example of medieval Europe, where 'it was a frequent practice for lords of the land to organize free communities' (p. 16). The lords advertised for inhabitants, who received protection and services in exchange for the payment of rent. David Beito (1988), in his analysis of urban voluntary associations, also refers to historical studies by Thierry and Pirenne on the voluntary character of medieval cities. Each member of a 'sworn commune' took a public oath to obey the city charter, agreements which 'are the root of the restrictive covenants of modern times' (Beito, 1988, p. 2). Violators of the peace would be expelled from the city walls. Merchants dominated the leadership of the communes, and voluntary associations provided collective goods such as roads and defense.

H. Berman (1983, p. 362) in his studies of medieval towns also found that they 'did not simply emerge' but were founded, and their charters generally established liberties and self-government. These 'new municipal governments of Europe were the first purely secular political bodies, the first modern secular states' (p. 389). The 'commune' was based on a covenant; the city charter was a social contract; 'it must, indeed, have been one of the principal historical sources from which the modern contract theory of government emerged'. The community was a 'corporation (universitas)', a corporation being a 'body of people sharing common legal functions and acting as a legal entity' (p. 393), much like modern civic associations. As Heath noted, these free cities were later absorbed by the emerging national states. In the present time, 'what vitiates capitalism ... is not its growth but its immaturity; that the use of [private] capital ... has not been properly extended to community goods' (Heath, 1957, p. 20). The payment for such goods by rent would constitute a 'welding of the particular interest with the general interest' (p. 21). The concept of the proprietary provision of community goods can be developed 'with reference to the general sovereignty extending to the entire territory and the particular or residual sovereignty reposed in those who hold particular parcels of the territory by delegation of sovereign power' (p. 23), a concept similar to that presented in Chapter 5.

In another paper, 'Outline of the Economic, Political, and Proprietary Departments of Society', Heath viewed his concepts as a refinement of those of George (Heath, 1936, pp. 65–6):

> The proposal of Henry George to deprive the service department of society[,] that is, the political authority, of all its power of predatory taxation and thus restore the proprietary department to its function of disbursing the public revenue of rent to those public servants who collectively constitute the political department, carries with it the necessary implication that the proprietary department eventually will take on and exercise its full administrative functions over all the public services.

But in a non-Georgian twist, Heath adds, 'the balance of rent not required for these purposes will be the clear earnings of the proprietors who have administered and supervised the enterprise'. Heath lumped together the site rent generated by civic goods with that due to natural conditions or population. Only the former are 'clear earnings', and George's emphasis on site rents as a non-destructive source of community funds was based on the latter. What George did not envision was the possibility that governance itself could be proprietary or contractual.

Heath's concept was expanded in his *Citadel, Market and Altar* (1957). The historical appeal this time is to 'Saxon England', in which community services were paid from ground rent by free holders to the land lords: 'And it was only from the hand of a public authority acting as *owner* of the community, and not as ruler over the persons and properties of its inhabitants, that these community services could be obtained by voluntary contract and for market value received' (p. 77). Anglo-Saxon community organization, culminating in the 'Alfredian Renaissance', was proprietary government, and 'there was no public revenue but rent' (p. 80). Lysander Spooner (n.d. [1852], p. 145) also described the Anglo-Saxon system as that in which 'the state rested for support on the land, and not upon taxation levied upon the people personally'. Freeholders held their lands on the condition of paying rents, in part by rendering military and civil services (p. 146), jury duty being among the latter. Although there is no present-day example of nation-wide proprietary administration,

> In a modern hotel community, however, the pattern is plain. It is an organized community with such services in common as policing, water, drainage, heat, light and power, communications and transportation, even educational and recreational facilities such as libraries, musical and literary entertainment, swimming pools, gardens and golf courses, with courteous services by the community officers and employees. (Heath, 1957, p. 82)

As to its operation, 'The entire community is operated *for* and not by its inhabitants. Other than good behavior, they have no obligation beyond making the agreed on customary payments for the services they receive. And what they pay is voluntary, very different from taxation.' Moreover, the payment is limited 'by the competition of the market' (ibid.). Long-term residents in a hotel may have a contract obligating them to make payments, but one becomes a resident by making a voluntary contractual agreement. The agreement obligates the hotel proprietor to certain payment rates, unlike governments, which may arbitrarily change tax rates without being bound by any contractual agreements.

Heath stated that 'in all respects a public community is, in principle, the same as a hotel' (ibid., p. 146). When the proprietary concept is broadened to a larger community, the owners give 'not mere occupancy alone, but positive and protective public services as well, for sake of the new rents and higher values that will accrue'. He foresaw 'proprietary community-service authorities, organized as local community proprietors over extensive areas, comprising many communities and establishing associative relationships among themselves in order to provide wider services on a regional, a national and eventually on an international and world-wide scale' (p. 96).

Unlike sovereign governance, proprietary administration is subject to a market discipline. As Heath put it, 'the slightest neglect of the public interest or lapse in the form of corruption or oppression would itself penalize them by decline in rents and values'. This is so relative to public governments, where, as Heath recognized, ownership and management are separate. 'Political public officers, unlike the owners of land, have no ownership hence no business interest in the public values.'

A 'neglect' is still possible where a proprietary community has some degree of monopoly, as discussed in Chapter 6, and where neglect affects only a few parties and therefore has little effect on rent. If the proprietor owns the land and the tenants own their buildings, the proprietor can in the short run increase rents or reduce services relative to rents, which decreases the value of the buildings below the value of the construction, since new entrants would capitalize the increased cost into lower purchasing bids. Without upkeep, the community would eventually decay. This deterioration and site exploitation is, as discussed in Chapter 6, avoided through increased mobility and constitutional constraints. If the owner owns the buildings, then the tenants' investments in inventories and fixtures are not nearly as site-specific. Democratic governance reduces the likelihood of dictatorial exploitation, or leases can specify performance standards for the public services and guarantee the resale value of the buildings.

There are economies of scale in the provision of some public goods. Industry needs 'public rights of way for communications and exchange, and other common services that can be supplied only by or under a united public authority, either political or proprietary' (ibid., p. 160). To do so, 'it is only necessary that the site-owning interests, or substantial portions of it duly organized in corporate or similarly effective form, merge their separate titles and interests and take in exchange corresponding undivided interests in the whole' (p. 135). Some owners could hold out, 'but they and their unincluded properties will naturally receive second consideration in all matters of public benefit or preferment. Unfranchised as owners, their influence and advantages all will be of second rate' (p. 136), many of the benefits being excludable.

Heath noted that owners of enterprises 'cannot afford to have their capital tied up' in assets not relevant to their chief operations. Businesses and professionals seldom own the premises they occupy, which require specialized administrative services (p. 154). Hence specialized firms arise that own land and provide public-goods services. They not only provide for administration over the sites and various services, but also strive to 'keep up the public demand' for that space, including protecting the tenants from theft and injury and keeping them comfortable (ibid., p. 155). The rents generated by the sites depend on the prosperity of the enterprises on the sites. As examples of specialized firms serving sites, Heath includes apartment housing, professional buildings and shopping centers.

MacCallum on proprietary communities

Spencer Heath MacCallum, pursuing the concepts pioneered by his grandfather, wrote his thesis on 'Proprietary Community' in 1961, merging themes from anthropology, economics and real estate studies. In 'The Social Nature of Ownership' (1965), MacCallum considers the relationship between property and society. He notes that 'propriety' and 'property' were interchangeable terms in 16th- and 17th-century usage, the former having connotations of customary aspects. 'Property' comes from the Latin term 'proprius', meaning 'self' or 'one's own', but legal ownership also involves the recognition by others of jurisdiction and hence 'is a social phenomenon' (p. 53).

MacCallum's view of property also has an implication for severable goods. Consisting of socially determined legal rights, all private property has that public characteristic. There is therefore no purely private (severable) good in the economic sense. But ubiquitous collective characteristics do not imply a need for sovereign governance. 'It can be argued today,' states MacCallum, 'that there are no longer any political functions being performed at the municipal level and upward in our society that differ substantially from those that we can observe being performed on a smaller scale entirely within the context of normal property relations.' This is the central theme of the work of MacCallum and Heath.

More specifically, 'in the United States and Canada there has been a major development since World War II of a distinctive form of association based on the organized ownership and unified administration of land' (ibid., p. 57). Examples include 'shopping centers, industrial parks, professional and research centers, marinas, mobile home parks, medical centers, and scores of multifunctional building complexes, such as Prudential Center, Century City, Gateway Center and so forth of which Rockefeller Center was the prototype' (pp. 57–8). These have been evolving to include complementary land uses, such as occurs in shopping centers with many different enterprises (banks, theaters) besides retail stores. Such clusters have on a smaller scale 'all of the functional requirements of municipalities' (p. 58).

MacCallum notes that property is a 'far more versatile institution than is commonly imagined' (ibid., p. 58). In the public field, contemporary society 'suffers a schizophrenia', whereby 'the same agency that provides wanted public services also performs such public disservices' in 'cannibalizing the society'. Government becomes ambiguous, both benign in its services and yet also a threat to society. 'The modern dilemma is that we have a continually growing need for community service that we know no way of getting except through the technique of sovereignty, which in turn exists by ... the abrogation of ownership' (p. 58).

The public-goods literature analyzed in Chapters 1 and 2 posits the dominant view that only state agencies can override the free-rider problem inherent in collective goods, and the public-choice literature on rent or transfer seeking posits the problem of government failure. But MacCallum offers a way out of this dismal-science dilemma, that of proprietary governance. In *The Art of Community* (1970), based on his thesis, MacCallum examines the proprietary community as a vehicle that resolves the twin public-goods dilemma, free-riding and transfer seeking, combining governance with market. He observes that 'an empirical art of community has developed within Western society since mid-century ... in the real-estate field, outside the cognizance of the social sciences' (p. 1). Heath (1957, pp. 93–4) too had remarked that such 'endless examples today' were 'too long neglected in scholarly research'. The proprietary community fulfils Wicksell's proposition that government can be a positive-sum participant in the economic process if it adheres to the market rules of property and contract (Wagner, 1988a, p. 161). By 'proprietary' MacCallum means property under a 'single ownership' (1970, p. 55) as opposed to fractionated titles, such as occurs both in sovereign governance and with civic associations. A proprietary owner has a contractual relationship with his tenants or customers.

MacCallum first examines hotels as communities. He observes that there is, as noted earlier by Heath (1957), a homology between hotels and cities: 'The hotel has its public and private areas, corridors for streets, and a lobby for its town square. In the lobby is the municipal park with its sculpture, fountains, and plantings. ... Its public transit system, as it happens, operates vertically instead of horizontally' (MacCallum, 1970, p. 2). One can add that major hotels also often operate a horizontal public transit system as vans or shuttles to airports, parking lots and downtown locations. Like cities, hotels provide utilities such as electricity, water and sewerage. The administration provides for security and fire protection. Some hotels provide chapels, concerts, child care and 'community-wide credit arrangements' (p. 2).

Economic or contractual organization has been discussed by some scholars. Charles Noyes (1936, p. 422) posited the three types of organization as domestic (family), political and economic. Henry Sumner Maine (1986 [1861], p. 141) wrote that 'the movement of the progressive societies has hitherto been a movement *from status to contract*' (though Maine did not have a specific reference to communities). Nevertheless, the economic, contractual type of social organization has not been taken into account in the prevailing literature on public goods, as discussed in Chapter 2, or even with regard to local government, as discussed in Chapter 6. MacCallum (1970, p. 3) defines a community as 'an occupation by two or more persons of a place divided into private and public areas according to a system of relations which defines and allocates responsibility for the performance of all activities that might be required for its continuity'. Hence the basic ingredients are persons, space, goods and rules. Besides hotels, examples of communities given by MacCallum include office buildings, theaters during a performance, apartment houses, trailer camps, restaurants and private residences with more than one inhabitant. 'Airplanes, ships, and trains in transit meet the requirements of the definition' (p. 4).

The principle on which a hotel is organized is contract. MacCallum (1970, p. 5) states that 'The manner of the relationship of each toward others is specified in the terms of the individual contracts, the sum of which at any time is the social charter or constitution of the community.' This is so if 'constitution' refers to the makeup of the organization. In terms of governance or constitutional economics, however, a constitution constitutes a 'choice of constraints' rather than 'choice within constraints' (Buchanan, 1989 [1987a], p. 58). A constitution of a hotel would be its articles of incorporation, and its agreements with its staff and guests would constitute its law. Indeed, in the commercial law that developed in medieval Europe, contract law referred, not to law about contracts, but that 'law' which contracting parties bring into existence by their agreement (Benson, 1990, p. 32).

A hotel, then, is a proprietary community. Much of its contractual nature, such as the relations of the guests to one another, is tacit. 'A contract is nothing more than an agreement, a meeting of minds, and it is enough for such a purpose that much of it be unwritten' (MacCallum, 1970, p. 5). The modern hotel, with its services, is an American invention (p. 9). The word 'hotel' is a French import, meaning large house or town hall, and one of the first uses of the term in the USA was the City Hotel in New York, built in 1794, the first inn to be financed by a stock company. The Tremont House in Boston, completed in 1829, was the first to provide 'hotel service' (p. 10). It became a model copied in many American towns. On the frontier, the public hall of the inn was often the only place to entertain and became the center of community life. The hotel industry since World War II has been characterized by chain and franchise operation and professional management. The trend now is to combine hotel accommodation with office space and shopping facilities, 'aiming at a more balanced and complementary use of land' (p. 14).

MacCallum points out that proprietary communities are special-purpose organizations, although they have developed a 'generalizing trend' away from their original character as shopping centers, for example, to include office buildings (1970, p. 7). Shopping centers are a recent development, their number rising from little more than 100 before 1950 to many thousands today. Developers of shopping centers found that, since the developments increased site values in the vicinity, they could appropriate these value increments by buying more land than was strictly needed for the center. They then became involved in developing the surrounding area (Galantay, 1975, p. 72).

In the early 1900s, a few land developers realized that the value of a development could be increased if land uses could be clustered according to some plan 'instead of being strung out haphazardly' (MacCallum, 1970, p. 15). Edward Bouton of Baltimore is credited with the first shopping center, in 1907. The automobile made it feasible to have a community of shops offset from the street, with integrated parking. In an analysis of firm location decisions, Marc Dudey (1990) determines that firms may choose to cluster together to facilitate convenient price comparison. After World War II, regional shopping centers began to replace downtown facilities, offering major department stores and a careful selection of tenants, including competing stores to provide comparison shopping (MacCallum, 1970, p. 16). 'Planned competition' is no longer an oxymoron. Another evolutionary step was service-oriented center management, following the example of 'hotel service', serving the tenants as well as the customers. At the same time, merchants' associations evolved in a symbiotic relationship with the management, the owner of the center having a role in coordination and promotion (p. 17). Shopping center management is community governance, coordinating many interests (p. 19).

Industrial estates and parks began at the end of the 19th century and have a history of growth similar to that of shopping centers. An industrial park consists of a subdivision of land used by a community of industries, whereas an industrial estate – the preferred pattern in Great Britain – is a tract of land leased to industries according to some overall plan. Many developers began with the intention of selling sites but ended up leasing sites owing to the preferences of the occupants. Though industrial parks typically include restrictive covenants, they have often been inflexible and difficult to enforce. With the estate leasehold system, the owner has an interest in the future land value and has both the incentive and the power to enforce the covenants, as well as the ability to modify any covenants that prove to be burdensome as the needs of the enterprises change (MacCallum, 1970, pp. 23–4). Land economist Richard Ratcliff has noted that, once lots are sold into individual ownership, it becomes impractical to replan or resubdivide (p. 24). This difficulty, notes MacCallum, has not yet become a major problem owing to the newness of industrial parks; dealers in real estate have not drawn attention to it because it would be 'knocking the merchandise', their interest being sales.

Though MacCallum sees inflexible land usage as a problem, if the problem has not been recognized by the purchasers of the lots in an industrial park or residential association, it may lie so far in the future that it has been effectively discounted. Real estate improvements being normally long-lived, redevelopment has not been a significant issue in the recently developed residential community associations. As with shopping centers, the owner or association of an industrial park or estate offers services such as ground and building maintenance, financing, publicity, warehousing, trucking, banking, medical and club facilities, and police and fire protection. The services of a developer include planning for complementary land uses such as warehousing, computing services, hotels, restaurants, banking and recreation. There is potential for an expansion of services into areas such as waste disposal.

The mobile home park represents another type of proprietary community, 'the first substantial use of ground lease for single-family homes' (MacCallum, 1970, p. 28) and also the first successful use of factory-constructed homes. Mobile homes are larger than trailers and require special equipment to move. Trailer parks developed from automobile campgrounds. The mobile home park mutated from them after World War II, providing residential rather than recreational services. Mobile home parks have been restricted by a shortage of sites as a result of zoning ordinances. The zoning protects the existing operations from competition, to the general detriment of the industry, and reduces the mobility of the homes. Mobile home parks offer services such as landscaping, parking, utilities (including central television antennas), laundries, recreation and community meeting rooms. According to MacCallum, a major determinant of the quality of life in these communities is management, which includes fostering a community spirit, with good relations among the residents (p. 30). Mobile home parks again offer a contrast between associations of landowners and leaseholds under one owner. Some older parks, sold as subdivisions, 'their land pattern frozen by fragmentation of title', have became obsolete as the homes grew larger (p. 31). 'This is the problem in miniature of all cities, which are simply larger, agglomerate subdivisions.' Under unified ownership, obsolescence can be 'programmed out systematically' (p. 32).

Another type of proprietary community is a 'real estate complex', such as Rockefeller Center in New York City, combining many different land uses. Other types include medical clinics, campgrounds and marinas. MacCallum also forecast the growth of 'new towns', developed on the leasehold plan, combining residential and commercial areas. Though many private new towns did develop, they have been divided into lots sold to individual owners.

As noted by MacCallum (1970, p. 35), all of these forms of proprietary community are enterprises in which land is improved in exchange for compensation in the form of rent. The improvements are capital goods, and the return is actually the yield from these capital goods, but the returns take the form of rentals paid by users of particular sites and goods, induced by the value of the services – the collective goods[1] – offered to the sites. The rents are paid for rights of occupancy, the 'quiet possession' of some space serviced by these goods. The public goods are financed as tie-ins to the space used by the user. In the case of hotels, the value of the land beneath a building is not necessarily increased by the existence of the hotel but, in an analogous way, the rooms become sites whose value depends on the constructed environment.

As MacCallum puts it, 'Multi-story buildings are but so much increased land area stacked vertically in one place. The layers being sheltered by one another and screened and consequently "indoor" does not change its nature, for land use must be planned whether the land is dispersed or piled up – whether it lies in one plane or in successive planes' (p. 35). Actually, the land volume *per se* is not increased; the three-dimensional air space is made useful, just as the clearing and leveling of land makes surface sites useful. The increase in rent derives from the increased usefulness of the vertical space, just as making the surface more useful increases its site rent.

The trend toward larger size of projects and more varied land uses within them requires both more comprehensive planning and greater control and coordination in their operation. MacCallum (1970, p. 39) also notes the growing trend of the retention of land ownership by one agency for continuing administration. This could slow the overall process of subdivision, and in particular cases even reverse it as sites are assembled for effective management. The real estate industry is thereby being transformed from selling sites to a long-term ownership and management. Real estate developers have realized that the environment surrounding a site is a key to determining its land value. They have also realized that a neighborhood can deteriorate after the sites are sold off unless there is some provision for the continuing coordination of land uses (p. 42). The expected future status of a neighborhood is reflected in its present land value.

The 'new town' movement is part of the trend towards larger projects, variety and private governance. Developers of housing sought a product for customers desiring amenities as well as housing, thus creating 'new towns' (Galantay, 1975, p. 72). Among towns created entirely with private funding are Lake Havasu City, Arizona, and Irvine Ranch, California (Christensen, 1978, p. 281). Many unincorporated towns governed by residential associations, such as Reston, Virginia, described in Chapter 12, have been built with private funds as well.

Neither zoning nor covenants, MacCallum states, is sufficiently flexible for the coordination of land uses. John Mowbray, a past president of the Urban Land Institute, called zoning 'unwieldy', encompassing many nuisances. Zoning is difficult to change for a landowner yet subject to change at any time by the city (MacCallum, 1970, p. 43). Private covenants have been used widely with some success but, if there is no organization enforcing them, individual home owners often hesitate to call attention to infractions of their neighbors. Residential associations offer one form of governance, and leaseholds by one owner another. Leaseholds have been slow to develop in the United States owing to the historical role of landlords as little more than rent collectors. Another reason MacCallum offers is the prestige of land ownership, which he believes may be largely due to government interventions. However, says MacCallum, the 'tide has turned' for commercial real estate, and mobile home parks are an example for residential land (p. 44).

MacCallum (1970, p. 46) states that, so long as projects are subdivided and sold, they are being planned 'for the present and inadequately for the future. Obsolescence begins with their subdivision into parts.' Though in many of the large recent projects some parts, such as commercial areas, are kept under a single ownership, only in a few have entire communities remained under a single proprietor for on-going management on a leasehold basis. But real estate is developing into an industry whose product is the creation and maintenance of 'human environment' (p. 48). 'The objective is to optimize the total environment of each site within a system of sites in order to maximize the combined rents they will command' (p. 50).

Rent, therefore, provides a 'quantitative measure of the successful functioning of the community ... *Pathology is signaled by a declining income line*' (MacCallum, 1970, p. 50). Such social pathology can occur as the result of a lack of community organization when land titles in a neighborhood are 'fractionated'. In a typical town under a sovereign government, titles are 'scattered', and there is potential for conflicts of interest (p. 55). Various proposals affect land values unevenly. Divided interests and the lack of a leadership not identified with special interests show up clearly in the older downtown business districts, 'as compared with merchants in shopping centers' (p. 57) characterized by a single landlord. A proprietary ownership, with primary residual ownership (as discussed in Chapter 5), can provide for effective organization and realize the 'functional role of real estate' (p. 55). A merchant in a shopping center buys not only a site and associated public goods, but also leadership (p. 59), that is, effective governance. An entrepreneur creating a community needs to provide for land planning, selection of tenants or club members, and leadership (p. 63).

The theory of governance, discussed in Chapter 4, can be applied here, since the site-specific investments and on-going relationships with tenants, members and customers would induce complex contracts and flexible conflict resolution. The long-term nature of the real estate improvements and their fixed location induces the governance of the development. Opportunistic tenants can ruin the investment of the owner, and the tenant desires to be protected from opportunism by the owner. Although there can be competition among many communities, once a tenant becomes located in one, his investment becomes site specific, and the result is seen in the contracts and law that are especially complex for real-estate-based relationships.

Proprietary administration fulfils the needs of community life and therein provides an 'alternative to tax-supported institutions' (ibid., p. 63). This is most effective, says MacCallum, under a single land title (whether that title vests in a person or a corporation) rather than under fractionated ownership by a civic association of owners. The popularity of subdivisions in the USA is, he states, due to fiscal interventions such as Federal Housing Association subsidies and tax laws (p. 83). However, MacCallum may be overlooking the economic and cultural values of living in a democratically run community, that is, a residential association. Democratic governance can foster a sense of community and induce volunteer efforts, as shown by the case studies in Chapters 10 to 12. At any rate, in a world of private communities, there would be competition among both types of governance, and the relative merits of either would be demonstrated by the market process.

As Samuelson (1954, 1955) states, and as echoed in much of the public-goods literature (discussed in Chapter 2), the provision of many public goods requires governance, but it does not follow that such governance need preclude a decentralized pricing system or market process if, as MacCallum argues, proprietary governance can deliver the goods as well as or better than sovereign governance. MacCallum (1970) observes a trend at the local level towards 'social reintegration in the proprietary pattern, a trend that has not sprung from any conscious design' (p. 95). Here he echoes Hayek (1967), who writes of evolving institutions, in terminology originally used by Adam Ferguson, as 'the results of human action but not of human design'. Though each particular local proprietary community is individually designed and planned, a nexus of proprietary communities is evolving despite 'recurrent crises of civic affairs' (MacCallum, 1970, p. 95).

As noted by MacCallum, the revolutions of the 18th century purged land ownership of sovereignty, divorcing the landed nobility from government. Land could then be transferred like other types of property. The function of landowners was thereafter at first distributive, with civic improvements financed by governments via taxes rather than by the landlords. But in the 20th century, land owners and developers 'have begun to assume responsibility for some of the public improvements of land. … Such a development has become increasingly necessary as sovereignty has failed to meet the advancing demand' for such improvements as well as for localized governance. Indeed, many cities have shifted the responsibility for developing and paying for the local civic goods to developers (p. 101). The trend of increasing landowner responsibility is a function of developers retaining their interest intact in their properties after development; that is, developing income properties instead of subdividing land.

Some developments continue to grow after becoming established. Rockefeller Center, for example, has expanded by purchasing or administering adjacent sites. Architect Arthur Holden suggested in the 1930s that landowners could form an owning and managing corporation, pooling their titles in exchange for shares in the corporation with a higher total value. The corporation could then redevelop the area, and each owner would also obtain a more liquid investment (MacCallum, 1970, p. 102). MacCallum foresees, as Heath did, that, as islands of profitable proprietary administration grow in number and size, they will tend to federate their interests to gain regional advantages, collective goods over a greater area (p. 103). A proprietary 'art of community' could replace much of sovereign governance.

Residential associations

Contractual communities can be divided into three types: residential, industrial and retail (or a combination of these). Shopping centers or recreational areas sell services to non-resident consumers, and so are retail communities, as opposed to industrial parks which produce intermediate goods. Aside from apartment houses, contractual residential communities have tended to be associations of owners.

A 'residential community association' (RCA) is a club which provides collective goods for a membership of residents in some geographical neighborhood. As territorial clubs, they are governed by real estate contract law and by their internal private rules, such as the CC&Rs (conditions, covenants and restrictions). In many cities, RCAs exist as 'neighborhood associations' and cooperatives as well as planned developments. RCAs are providing local public services such as safety, cleanliness and community property improvements. They are of three legal types. In a *cooperative*, instead of owning a particular unit, a member has shares in a corporation that owns the real estate. In a *condominium*, a member has title to a particular unit and, tied to that unit, a fractional ownership of the common space and facilities in common interest with the other owners. While the condominium association manages the common property for the owners, the association itself does not own the property. In the third type, called a 'home owners' association', a member has title only to a unit, such as a lot, which is tied into the association membership. The home owners' association itself owns the common elements. The Reston Association, examined in Chapter 12, is an example. In practice, condominiums and home owners' associations operate similarly, except that the assessments and voting share of a condominium owner are typically proportional to his share of the common property, whereas, in home owners' associations, the assessments and voting can take any form, such as equal parts or based on property value.

Barton and Silverman (1989) note that RCAs have moved politics into a private setting of private governments which share many of the characteristics of public-sector politics. Politics in terms of coordinating common interests is inherent when people associate, as they do after joining an RCA. An example of such politics is a decision on the participation of renters in the governance. Other divergent interests include those with and without children, absentee owners versus resident owners and disputes over parking rules. Some associations have difficulty collecting special assessments for capital improvements or repairs (Oakerson, 1989).

The Tiebout model of consumers choosing a community presumes a level of knowledge of its public goods, whereas, aside from the physical goods, some purchasers of RCA units do not fully understand the association they are being tied into and are thus subject to the public-goods illusion discussed in Chapter 3. Barton and Silverman (1989, p. 35) deduce that, because of poor-quality information for many buyers, and the expense of moving, an RCA is as involuntary as a small town government. A typical problem in RCAs occurs when a member makes an improvement that is later disallowed by the association (for example Twomey, 1993). But these phenomena do not imply involuntariness; the purchase of an automobile is also subject to poor information and an expense in exit (resale), yet the choice is still voluntary. It is the contractual nature of the purchase and the tie-in of information to property rather than to sheer location or personhood that make these purchases voluntary.

Whereas Barton and Silverman advocate a greater role for local government in the affairs of RCAs and a reduction in the scope of RCAs, that policy subjects them to more remote politics whose interests may not be congruent with that of many of the RCA owners, and a governance which itself is not voluntary for all. Governments can play a constructive role, however, in specifying defaults when the association rules are unclear so that disputes, for example over property improvements, can be more easily resolved. As discussed below, greater autonomy would enable RCAs to become more diverse yet more internally homogeneous, as well as to increase in overall importance, creating a greater awareness of their characteristics for potential purchasers. In addition, better information by RCAs in cooperation with real estate agents would be in the mutual interests of RCAs and agents who are possibly subject to lawsuits for the failure to disclose some known public bads. Despite such political concerns, Miller (1989) reports that few RCAs have failed, even when they had severe management problems. Many of the troubles occur when the developer turns over the facilities to the RCA, which discovers deficiencies and unexpected costs.

The earliest known use of deed-related associations took place in the mid 1700s in London. Lord Leicester established a park in Leicester Square, and adjacent property owners agreed to an assessment to fund it, which benefited them by increasing their property values (Frazier, 1980, p. 96). Another private community in Great Britain was Victoria Park, near Manchester, which was laid out in 1837 and operated privately until 1954. The sale of its lots carried with it 'certain conditions, the "laws" of the Park, which would protect its amenities' (Spiers, 1976, p. 13). Besides annual 'rates', Victoria Park levied tolls on some of its roads.

Ebenezer Howard developed a theory of civic associations in *Tomorrow: A Peaceful Path To Real Reform* (1898), the second edition entitled *Garden Cities of To-morrow (1902)*. The basic idea was a 'voluntary plan of public finance' using leaseholds of land:

> One essential feature of the plan is that all ground rents, which are to be based upon the annual value of the land, shall be paid to the trustees, who, after providing for interest and sinking fund, will hand the balance to the Central Council of the new municipality, to be employed by such Council in the creation and maintenance of all necessary public works – roads, schools, parks, etc. (1902, p. 51)

Howard credits Thomas Spence with having thought of the concept in 1775 of assembling landed property and letting it out on leaseholds (pp. 119–23).

Howard envisioned combining the qualities of city and country environments: 'Human society and the beauty of nature are meant to be enjoyed
together ... Town and country *must be married*' (1902, p. 48). Howard
credited the idea of combining city and country to James Buckingham in
1849 (p. 125). The architecture of the garden city would be varied, but there
would be a 'general observance of street line or harmonious departure from
it', over which the municipal authority would have control (p. 54). The town
would have a unity of design, planned as a whole (p. 76). There would be a
cluster of towns around a central city. To the lease holders, the town would
issue a prospectus indicating the scope of operations. A Board of Management, elected by leaseholders, would govern the city. The extent of town
services would be limited by the willingness of leaseholders to pay the rents
(p. 91). Howard envisioned charitable institutions in the community sponsored by public-spirited residents. The case studies of Chapters 10 and 12 on
Arden village and the Reston Association show that these communities
implemented Howard's plan to a remarkable degree.

As pointed out by Christensen (1978, p. 116), communities, especially
cities, have been a focus of utopian thought, where 'utopian' has connotations of being impractical or unattainable. However, as Christensen notes,
the goal has often been not perfection but reform, to be brought about by
changing the institutions rather than human nature (p. 117). Howard's primary goal was the reform of economic arrangements rather than mere architectural innovation (Christensen, 1978, p. 122). The 'Garden City' was to be
a model for a large-scale reform of society. His emphasis was on the city
rather than the garden (p. 128), with a view towards decentralizing government (p. 147). Likewise, MacCallum has economy-wide reforms in mind,
with the proprietary community a building-block as well as prototype of
institutional innovations. Howard recognized two camps of reformers: those
who advocated increased production and greater efficiency, and those who
urged a more equitable distribution of wealth. The 'Garden City' approach
merged both goals, in Howard's view (Howard, 1965 [1902], p. 130). Howard
was responsible for the creation of two towns in England, Letchworth and
Welwyn, which were successful, but, as MacCallum (1972, p. 21) states,
they 'ironically provided the model for the present Satellite Towns program
in England under which they were themselves nationalized'. The two towns,
says MacCallum, 'fell far short of their potential' owing to the setting up of
a government 'without any equity interest in its administration', using a
democratic non-profit trust.

Early examples of developments with RCAs in the USA are Louisburg
Square in Boston and Gramercy Park in New York City, both established in
the early 1800s. Louisburg Square, established in 1828, was the first home
owners' association in the USA, made up of townhouses. In St. Louis,

neighborhoods with privately owned streets were developed within the city (described in Chapter 13). By the end of the 1800s, developers were incorporating RCAs into deeds to support common areas and maintain architectural standards. In 1891, for example, an RCA organized in conjunction with a 1230-acre development by Edward G. Boulton in Baltimore provided water, roads and sewers (Frazier, 1980, p. 97). The first housing cooperative in the USA was established in New York City in 1918, and the first condominium, The Greystoke, was constructed in Salt Lake City in 1962 (*Community Associations Factbook,* 1988). Large-scale development began to replace lot-by-lot subdivisions during the 1960s (Dean, 1989a, p. 4). During the 1970s, RCAs were mainly found in California, New York and Florida, but since then they have been spreading throughout the country.

Residential associations have themselves associated, like many industries. The Greater Boston Association of RCA presidents was formed to promote RCA political concerns (Dean, 1989a, p. 6), and RCAs have formed alliances in other cities. The Community Associations Institute (CAI), with headquarters in Alexandria, Virginia, was established in 1973 by the Urban Land Institute and the National Association of Homebuilders to serve condominium, cooperative and home owner associations. Members may be either individuals (for example, board members) or RCAs; there are now 10 000 members. The Institute offers over 200 publications and seminars on creating, managing and marketing RCAs, and sells videotapes such as one for 'Serving on the Board'. It also offers a training program for community association managers, a recognized distinct profession. One of its publications, *The Homeowners Association Manual* (1988), is a guide to running and participating in a RCA. The institute also publishes information jointly with the Urban Land Institute, such as *Condominium and Homeowner Associations That Work* (1978). One of its affiliates is the Community Associations Institute Research Foundation, formed in 1975, which gathers and distributes information about operating an RCA. It conducts surveys, publishes practical information and conducts other research. The foundation has a 'loaner file program' that for a modest fee (currently $12 per file for members) loans out packages of information for two weeks on legal issues, management, association newsletters, maintenance, municipal relations, development and so on. Housing cooperatives also have an association, the National Association of Housing Cooperatives, organized in 1950. In 1991, the Association created the Center for Cooperative Housing, which offers services to coops.

There are some 130 000 residential community associations in the USA. In 1960 there were fewer than 5000. These contractual communities affect some 25–30 million persons (Dean, 1989b, p. 4). Of these RCAs, 54 per cent are organized as condominiums, 5 per cent as housing cooperatives, and 41 per cent are under home owner associations (HOAs). Over half of the RCAs are in townhouse and low-rise developments. Community associations spent $12.5 billion in 1987 and maintained another $5 billion in reserves. Their growing impact is evidenced by their contributing to more than 50 per cent of the market share of new home sales in the 50 largest metropolitan areas (*Community Associations Factbook,* 1988, p. 1). The housing stock of RCAs has a value of about $100 billion (p. 2). In some rapidly developing areas such as California, nearly all new residential developments create RCAs (Dean, 1989a, p. 3). RCAs may currently constitute the most significant privatization of civic goods in terms of its substitution for government operations (p. 18).

RCAs were once largely limited to retirement, luxury and resort developments, but are now available to 'all income levels' (*Community Associations Factbook,* 1988, p. 2). The growth and success of community associations also turns the market-failure argument on its head, since much sub-optimal provision of collective goods by contractual processes can be traced to interventions by sovereign governments rather than a failure of voluntary efforts. Members of RCAs are required to pay taxes for municipal services whether or not they provide local private substitutes. In addition, the amortization funds and the common property of RCAs have been subject to property and income taxation (Frazier, 1980, p. 92). The Community Associations Institute recognizes that, although RCAs perform many of the functions of government, their members 'also pay local government property taxes for similar services received by other homeowners, but not by the community association resident ... Increasingly, community associations are voicing their concern' (*Community Associations Factbook*, 1988, p. 15).

The use of RCAs gives developers a competitive advantage, enabling them to offer cost savings relative to autonomous housing. By clustering and stacking units, developers reduce construction costs per unit and make more efficient use of land. Clusters save costs in building streets and utilities, leave more open space and facilitate the production of an environment and amenities beyond that which local government officials wish to provide and maintain. A planned community also enables a developer to use a more flexible type of zoning, while offering buyers a wider range of choices (Dean, 1989a, p. 4).

Local governments benefit as well, by receiving tax revenues without having to supply and maintain the infrastructure. As noted, RCAs do not usually obtain reduced tax liabilities for services that replace those provided by local government.[2] Moreover, RCA owners pay a property tax on any higher land values that are due to their own services. In some cases, the amenities themselves are taxed (Dean, 1989a, p. 5). The implicit stream of income flowing to local government from RCAs induces the government to

enact paternalistic legal measures, such as accounting requirements, to protect its 'investment' by keeping the RCAs well managed, since, if they were
to cease operation, responsibility for the local goods such as parks could be
shifted to the government. Since the association assessments are not currently deductible from income taxes, the federal government and some state
governments also benefit from the substitution of privately provided services
for those paid from tax-deductible sources.

Among the facilities operated by RCAs are (with the percentage of RCAs
having these indicated) swimming pools (69 per cent), a community meeting
place (46 per cent), tennis courts (41 per cent), playground (28 per cent),
park or nature area (20 per cent), exercise facility (17 per cent), lakes (16 per
cent), and golf courses (4 per cent). Services offered include landscaping (94
per cent), exterior building maintenance (82 per cent), parking (79 per cent),
garbage removal (74 per cent), water and sewerage (68 per cent), private
streets (62 per cent), sidewalk maintenance (59 per cent), exterior lighting
(56 per cent), passive security (39 per cent) and active security and protection (33 per cent) (*Community Associations Factbook,* 1988, p. 9). All RCAs
provide rules enforcement. Many RCAs, especially the larger ones, hire a
professional manager or management company. Hence RCAs offer a combination of community goods and lower-cost individual (housing) goods.

Contrary to the practice of many sovereign governments, which issue debt
to finance capital goods and projects or even operating expenses, it is typical
for many RCAs to have a reserve fund for future repairs and other capital
goods. The above-mentioned CAI association manual (Dunbar, 1988) rec-
ommends that RCAs have a separate capital budget (p. 90), backed by studies of the useful life of the capital goods. Some 82 per cent of non-converted
condominiums (99 per cent of converted ones) and 96 per cent of HOAs
have reserves, the average HOA having $119 set aside per unit and the
average non-converted condominium having $407 (*Community Associations
Factbook,* 1988, p. 12).

With many condominiums now aging, reserve funds are vital to the continuing financial viability of these associations. As Wagner (1986, p. 209)
notes, 'When property comprises the tax base, liability for debt amortization
rests on property owners in proportion to their ownership shares. ... Hence,
debt choices are capitalized into property values.' Wagner adds that this is
nevertheless not equivalent to a personal debt choice. In residential associations, however, when the voters are also the property owners, the evidence
of these reserves shows that debt tends to be avoided and replaced by
advance funding, although reserve funds may also reflect the difficulty and
higher costs of the associations of borrowing funds. Also, unlike sovereign
municipal bonds, RCA interest income is taxable. Since the capital stock is
being consumed, that is, it depreciates, it is economically appropriate for

that consumption to be funded concurrently. The annual placement of funds into a reserve account is not an arbitrary savings account for funds left over after expenses but a payment for an annual expense that accrues.

The growth of neighborhood associations in recent decades is due in some degree to the decline of other voluntary or quasi-governmental clubs. Political party machines had formerly established neighborhood clubs. Precinct captains organized a local provision of public goods and also facilitated the local provision of municipal goods in return for political support. Beginning with the New Deal, government programs and transfer payments reduced the power of these political clubs. Civic associations arose to replace the lost services, providing items such as street lamps, miniparks, tutoring and emergency medical and fire protection. In New York City there were 1000 block associations in 1980 (Frazier, 1980, p. 94).

The fact that RCAs provide services that supplement if not replace those of government is evidence of both the feasibility of and the preference for such services. One would expect members of RCAs to be content with the arrangement, since otherwise there would be more exit from them as information, however opaque, does spread. Surveys of RCAs confirm this theoretical expectation; one study of 233 associations, conducted by the Urban Land Institute, showed a 91 per cent favorable response to deed stipulations. The enforcement of deed stipulations has also been effective; researchers have found little physical deterioration in the RCA housing (Frazier, 1980, p. 98).

On the cost side, in a study by Robert Deacon of 23 associations and 41 comparable towns, associations are reported as paying 58 per cent of what governments would spend for similar police services, and 70 per cent of similar sovereign expenditures for street maintenance (Frazier, 1980, p. 100). One factor accounting for the less efficient government service is the independent civil service, which is less responsive to the residents (ibid.), as MacCallum also notes.

Contractual constitutions and law

A 'constitution' can be considered to be a subset of the set of rules in a club such that no rule in the subset is entirely dependent upon or authorized by another rule in the superset (including the subset). In other words, all the rules of the club are derived from the rules of the constitution, and the constitutional rules themselves are not derived from other rules. A constitution is therefore the supreme body of rules for governance. These rules can be formal, as in a written document, or tacit, following tradition or the desires of those in power. The actual constitution is then a combination of the tacit and formal rules. All governance has rules and therefore necessarily has some supreme set of rules, or a constitution.

James Buchanan (1990, p. 3) has written that 'Constitutional economics directs analytical attention to the *choice among constraints.*' Actual restraints may well differ from the merely formal ones, and government agents may interpret them to the degree that the formal rules become a mere formality. The formal constitution of a contractual community may be less subject to being overridden by tacit rules, since typically an association can be sued, whereas a sovereign government often claims immunity from suits. However, if the government intervenes in suits against contractual communities, or itself violates previous agreements it had with them, the formal rules of associations obviously become overridden as well. In a world of contractual communities, under non-interventionist sovereign governments, the ability to sue for significant violations of a constitution would seem to keep the actual and formal constitutions closely related.

The constitutions of sovereign governments are typically decided upon by a committee of representatives or by a previous government that presents it to a legislative body for approval. In associations or proprietary governance, a constitution is often drawn up by the proprietor or developer of the community. Boudreaux and Holcombe (1989) analyze this practice, which economizes on the production of constitutional rules, avoiding the transaction costs involved when a large number of persons attempt to create rules (p. 266). Approval of the constitution is then expressed by entry into the community. The authors state that purchasers generally prefer that rules be 'inflexible and difficult to change' (p. 274). Inflexibility is a benefit, however, only for the most fundamental rules of an association. In the Vandeventer private neighborhood of St. Louis, described in Chapter 13, the charter required unanimous consent for amendments, which proved to be too inflexible as the surrounding area developed into commercial use. However, many residential associations do have unanimity clauses for changes that affect the basic investment of the owners, such as the percentage of common interest of each unit in a condominium.

Boudreaux and Holcombe (1993, p. 1) note that 'homeowners' associations ... have many of the characteristics of local governments', namely in the public goods provided, in collecting revenues and in 'the way in which their constitutions provide for collective decisions to be made' (p. 4). As noted in Chapter 6, competition alone will not curb inefficient government in such associations, just as it does not for governments, because of the capitalization of the inefficiency in property values (p. 2). Whereas Epple and Zelenitz (1981) argue that, with sovereign governments, Tiebout competition needs politics, Boudreaux and Holcombe (1991) argue that civic associations need constitutional rules 'because relocation is costly' (p. 2). 'Constitutions and intergovernmental competition are substitutes for each other' (p. 3). In the pure Tiebout model, with no cost to mobility, 'no constitution is needed'.

What Boudreaux and Holcombe must mean is that no constitutional constraints are needed since, as argued above, every government necessarily has some supreme set of rules, that is, a constitution. For example, in the Tiebout model, the constitution of a community permits free (unrestricted) exit. Contractual governance offers collective goods 'at a level of aggregation not coinciding with an existing local government' and also 'an environment that is conducive to the development of optimal constitutional rules' (p. 3). The first advantage, a size different from established political governments, was also recognized by Sutter (1991), with the insight that there are profit opportunities for entrepreneurs in reducing the size and negotiating costs of the types of civic goods being produced by the public sector. Size reduction is accomplished, for example, with the private streets in small neighborhoods within St. Louis, as discussed in Chapter 13.

The second advantage obtains because 'the existence of the contractual government may enhance the value of the property' (Boudreaux and Holcombe, 1993, p. 4). The incentives with regard to the creation of rules differ between sovereign and contractual governance. In the former, as noted above, there is no residual claimant. In the latter, the entrepreneur is a residual claimant and, if the constitution is created by him, then obviously the question of interest groups in the creation of the constitution does not arise. There is 'a market mechanism which reveals which constitutional rules are most valuable', namely property values, and, with experience and competition, 'the quality of the constitutions of contractual governments should increase over time' (p. 6). Such evolution occurred with the St. Louis private neighborhoods, described in Chapter 13, in which clauses for changing the charter, for example, were made less restrictive as they were found to impede adaption to surrounding land-use changes.

Barzell and Sass (1990) analyze voting systems in condominiums. Their results show that developers of 'voting organizations' provide constitutions that maximize the expected value of the unit shares by minimizing the feasibility of wealth transfers and the costs of decision making (cf. Buchanan and Tullock, 1965 [1962]). Constitutional constraints prevent a faction from transferring wealth from the other members. Voting rules for condominiums run as investments are less restrictive and less inclusive than those of owner-residents. Wealth transfers are minimized by matching assessments with benefits, and by developers' providing the major structures before transferring title to the association, which subsequently manages them with generally little discretion for creating major new goods.

MacCallum (1971, p. 6) notes that 'the formal written law' of a proprietary community under one landlord 'is simply the totality of the leases in effect at a given time'. The lease thus becomes an 'instrument of social policy', including also obligations of lessees to their neighbors. A second level of proprietary law is that of its subgroups, contracts made by the landlord or the lessees with their employees, contractors and suppliers (p. 7). A third group of persons, the visitors to the community or 'business invitees' (such as customers) are also subject to both levels of this law (such as dress codes, pet restrictions and denial of access ('keep off the grass')). MacCallum observes that the typically desired decision-making process of the governance of such retail communities, for example by merchants' councils, is by consensus rather than majority voting. If a measure can only be obtained by a majority vote, then, as one participant stated, 'we don't want it' (p. 10).

The principle of constitutional constraints was implemented by MacCallum (1977) in writing a constitution for 'Orbis', put forward as a hypothetical community in space. The same economic principles apply to a space colony as to earthly proprietary communities, the colony being a type of artificial surface site, as are ships and airplanes. The owner would foster an environment, and the tenants would pay 'ground rent' exclusive of the tenants' improvements (1977, p. 43). A tenant would be able to transfer a leasehold. The problem of 'site exploitation', the potential for an owner of sites to extract rents above what a newcomer would willingly pay, is dealt with for 'Orbis' by governance constraints. First, if the owner decides to replace a tenant in order to change the site use, the tenant is reimbursed for the value of his fixed improvements and is compensated for other losses (MacCallum, 1977, p. 42). Secondly, when the rental charge is revised, it is set 'to an amount estimated to be equal to the then market rate of said site', less a 10 per cent reduction as a preferred tenant, as appraised by three disinterested parties (p. 44). This second protection acts against arbitrary rental charges, but not against an extravagant owner who spends the rental funds for his personal benefit, thereby reducing the market rent of the sites. Hence there is a third provision by which the owner pledges to conduct its business such that the total site value as income property is maximized (p. 43). This implies that only those expenditures are made that increase site value or at least do not decrease it, preventing site exploitation on the expenditure side.

This application to space colonies demonstrates the universality of the proprietary principles set forth by Heath and MacCallum. The same constitution could be used, for example, in creating a new proprietary colony on earth. The possibility of the private-sector provision of all civic goods in a space craft or on ships, which are effectively sea-going cities, demonstrates the general feasibility of a market-process public-goods finance.

Community and entrepreneurship

The typical case made for market failure in the production of collective goods is that individuals may have no incentive to contribute to the provision of the good. This case, besides homogenizing collective goods and ignoring private governance, makes an institutional assumption about the nature of the society. It posits that there is no existing community, that households exist in an atomistic relationship. If an entrepreneur wishes to build a dam, he must contract with each household separately. Such an assumption does lead to theoretical insights but, empirically, such atomistic communities do not exist. It would therefore make sense to also have a theory that presumes the existence of community. The evolution of human society is one of changing but continuously existing communities. New communities evolve from previously existing ones. A realistic theory of public goods must recognize that society is always, already, in community.[3]

If a community necessarily exists, then the question of the provision of civic goods is transformed from whether the market can fail to that of the nature of the community. If the community has a sovereign government providing the goods, the alternative of voluntary provision concerns, not the possibility of market failure, but that of the devolution of power and authority from imposed to contractual governance that can provide the same goods. An intentional community can be created anew, but within the framework of previously existing communities. A ship at sea sails under the flag of some sovereign country; the creation of a new ship includes many civic goods, yet it is not claimed that there will be a prisoner's dilemma about funding the goods. The owner need not worry about individual demand revelation, so long as the expected total demand covers his costs. He ties in the collective services to the rent paid for a cabin, and the existence of many different types of ships provides for competitive pricing.

The example of a dam serving a valley, as illustrated by the story in Chapter 1, poses less of a problem for contractual provision when it is realized that the residents in the valley must be *already in community*. If the valley consists of several communities, the coordination problem is still vastly reduced from the atomistic case. An entrepreneur wishing to build the dam need only contract with a few community associations, rather than with the individual households. Furthermore, the communities themselves may have formed a greater community with intercommunity agreements.

Whereas the above discussion is centered around territorial communities, Gordon Tullock (1985) proposes non-territorial contractual associations. He notes the example of the Millet system of the old Turkish empire, under which autonomous non-Muslim religious communities were formed. Tullock proposes 'associations with quasi governmental power', without a geographic domain. They would provide services which are not geographical in scope, somewhat like those churches provide today. Aspects of law which these 'sociological' associations could assume could include those concerned with family, probate and contract.

The provision of a civic good is typically theorized as an isolated good but, in reality, a community offers a package of goods, and potential members have the choice of accepting or rejecting the package. If one of the communities refuses to contribute towards a dam, the others can confront it with the withdrawal from the greater community and the loss of the package of goods which it offers. Some intercommunity agreements will be excludable; for example, law enforcement officers can enter another community in pursuit of criminals, and the refusing community can be cut off from trade, mutual law enforcement and other benefits. The refusal of one community to cooperate in the provision of a common good, when it is recognized that they in fact wish to benefit from the good, would involve the loss of good will, which itself is a public good. Hence the refusal of one community to participate in the provision of a public good would not be costless, as Heath pointed out.

A community is not a set of atomistic members who happen to be located within some boundary line, but also a web of relationships. Emotional attachments may create benevolent sympathy for persons in the community and for the community as a whole, and this sympathy can be tapped for the voluntary provision of civic goods. A community therefore has the feasibility of providing for goods by catallactic means and by sympathetic means as well as by tie-ins to club and severable goods. Feasibility does not make the provision of collective goods automatic or inevitable, but possible. What transforms possibility into actuality is entrepreneurship. Douglas Den Uyl (1985, p. 33) states that leaders reduce the number of prisoner dilemma games. The entrepreneur not only creates civic goods but also generates institutions – traditions, festivals – that elicit sympathy for the community. Sympathy itself is a public good generated by entrepreneurship.

Daniel Klein (1990, p. 799), describing the turnpikes constructed in 19th-century USA, notes that many of these efforts were not profitable and the 'investors' knew this in advance, which seems counter to a 'straight application of the simple public-goods model'. He notes that, in early 19th-century New England, there was no sharp distinction between private and public works. De Tocqueville (1946 [1835], p. 191) had observed the large number of societies in 19th-century America, 'formed and maintained by the agency of private individuals'. The free-rider problem was overcome by the culture of the early American towns. They were largely self-governing and there was a high degree of participation in the government by the residents. Church congregations provided schools, libraries and poor relief (Klein, 1990, p. 800). These social relationships constituted what Coleman (1988) calls 'social capital'. Cooperative societies flourished during this era, providing religious, scientific and civic services. Some turnpike companies explicitly called themselves a 'society' (Klein, 1990, p. 802).

The main incentive at work for the turnpikes, in Klein's theory, was negative: a failure to cooperate would be noticed. Social pressure was applied to obtain cooperation in these communities of up to a few thousand persons (p. 803). At town meetings to decide on the turnpikes, important residents were expected to participate. Stock pledges were made in public. Committees were formed to solicit subscriptions. The motive to contribute was not, however, entirely negative, since recognition and approval from others have positive utility. Moreover, the instigators of the project did not themselves act out of social pressure. As stated by Klein (1990, p. 809), 'The ability of voluntary association to provide infrastructure, education, security, and poor relief depends on the exercise and spontaneous development of certain institutions, activities, and sentiments.' But entrepreneurship was also required, which raises a question. Why did the entrepreneurs initiate the projects in the first place? Since the leaders did not always believe that their private gain would be greater than the costs, there must have been some element of benevolent sympathy in their acts.

To sum up, the theory of contractual community thus has these elements. The private ownership of space permits the collection of the rents generated by the civic services which induce the rents. Communities such as hotels, shopping centers, industrial parks and estates, and ships are examples of the proprietary provision of civic goods. Residential community associations are another form of contractual governance, many of which implement Ebenezer Howard's conception of city services financed by site leases. Their constitutions are typically provided for by the developers, enhancing the value of the property with constraints against future exploitation by the association governance. Civic entrepreneurs also foster community spirit, sympathy with the community, which enables non-excludable civic goods to be produced in addition to funding by rental assessments. Finally, a theory of public goods needs to recognize that society is always in community, and that the realistic choice in the provision of civic goods is not market versus governance, but whether the governance that provides the goods is imposed or voluntary.

The significance of the case studies

Having presented a theoretical analysis of the voluntary provision of collective goods, five case studies will be examined in depth to test the hypothesis of market failure as well as to illustrate how contractual communities operate. The argument of market failure states that, in general, civic goods cannot be provided by a market process; thus only one counter-example is required to reject that proposition. However, five cases are presented to show how the market-failure proposition is rejected in various community forms and contexts.

An argument could be made, erroneously, that, to test the proposition that the voluntary provision of collective goods is feasible, many cases must be examined – indeed that, to test it thoroughly, all such communities need to be measured, the test consisting of how large a percentage of them are successful. But the case studies are not data points to be added up. The test requires a logical 'or' function rather than an 'and' function. In an 'or' test, given cases A, B and C, the test has a positive outcome if any of the cases is positive – A, B or C – rather than all having to be positive, as in the 'and' case. The case is analogous to testing the false proposition in physics that falling bodies of different mass *must* accelerate at different speeds in a vacuum. Only one valid test is needed to reject the hypothesis. If another test did not reject it, after a valid previous one did, suspicion would fall on the latter test.

One does need a numerical verification for statistical propositions, such as the correlation, lower than 100 per cent, of two variables. However, the market-failure argument is not a statistical proposition. It is not stated that contractual provision will fail a certain percentage of the time. As usually stated, it is an unconditional proposition about market processes in general. The wording, as shown in the examples provided in Chapters 1 and 2, is usually that a decentralized market system 'cannot' provide for civic goods, analogous to the proposition that bodies of different weights *cannot* fall at the same rate. A similar example would be the proposition that human society cannot be vegetarian. If one group is found that is, then the proposition is rejected. It could be possible that the conditions that make it feasible are empirically unique, so further examples would demonstrate that it is not a freak case. The existence of several such groups would demonstrate its general feasibility, and then a close examination of one particular group would show how it is done in detail. This is the methodology used in these case studies, especially the residential communities.

The rejection of the market-failure argument does not imply that 'the market' will always work, or that there are not particular cases where voluntary efforts failed to provide some goods that were wanted. Even if, in many or most cases, there is failure, it does not invalidate the rejection of the market-failure argument. The rejection only implies that the voluntary provision of collective goods is feasible, just as the production of severable goods is feasible, although there will be many failures in producing these goods as well. Uncertainty and bounded cognition will make most human endeavor fail to reach perfection.

The proposition that a contractual provision of collective goods is feasible requires only one, or a few, case studies demonstrating success, plus some indication that these are typical rather than unique examples. Hence the case studies, especially of the residential communities, are representative cases. Similar examples are described briefly to indicate their non-uniqueness.

The cases

Walt Disney World was selected as an example of a proprietary community. Although typical of resorts and hotels, its autonomous legal status makes it a prime case study for the commercial provision of collective goods.

Arden Village was chosen as a prime example of a community financing its collective goods from site rents on privately owned land. It also demonstrates a high degree of voluntary activity.

Fort Ellsworth is an example of a condominium, a common type of contractual community which provides a limited range of goods, and implements the economic principle of funding them from rent.

The Reston Association is an example of a large civic association, resembling a sovereign town, demonstrating that such large-scale operations can be run as contractual communities.

Finally, the St. Louis 'private places' show how neighborhoods within a metropolitan area have associations which own the streets and utilities, providing protection and a sense of community.

Together the case studies demonstrate the feasibility of contractual governance and the provision of civic goods under different conditions, each being an example of a more general type of community.

Notes

1. As noted above, these collective goods are public characteristics of physical goods and services, which also have private characteristics in their direct use. The finance of the physical goods is generally not as direct prices for use, but as rent paid for being in the environment in which the goods are present; hence the public characteristic is significant for their funding. A hotel elevator is an example.
2. There are exceptions. Montgomery County, Maryland reimburses an RCA for street maintenance if the public is allowed access. Rebates are also offered in Houston and Kansas City (Dean, 1989a, p. 20).
3. The wording 'always, already' was used in the philosophy of interpretive understanding, whereby 'understanding is "always, already" interpretive' (Lavine, 1989, p. 99).

9 Utopia for rent: Walt Disney World

When we see a wild animal's beautiful appearance and watch it run hither and yon, we know that beneath the furry surface there is something awesome going on: a complex brain and muscle makes its life possible. When a visitor enters the world-famous Walt Disney World, there too lies a complex physiology beneath the surface of the animated displays and rides. It is not just the physical works that lie literally underneath, but a mind, a governance that makes it possible. Walt Disney World too is an organism living free in the world of competitive enterprise, having to struggle for its supper, like other creatures in the field. It cannot command subjects to feed it, so it must attract them as a beautiful scented flower attracts bees by offering an irresistible scent that signals a most delicious nectar inside.

Walt Disney World is a proprietary community, a corporation running a retail community and transient residential communities. It is also noteworthy in having influenced the design of other communities, and it offers an example of proprietary autonomy.

The hypothesis

This Walt Disney World (WDW) case study is framed in terms of a hypothesis: a real estate complex in a large territory owned and operated by a private corporation, with little significant public-sector funding or control, does not provide as abundant a level of civic goods, both in quantity and in quality, wanted by the users, as a similar public-sector government would.

General description

The WDW destination resort, located southeast of Orlando, Florida, has an area of 45 square miles (28 000 acres), about equal in size to San Francisco. When it opened in 1971, it was the largest and most expensive tourist attraction ever built (Zehnder, 1975, p. 2). The territory encompasses a contiguous though irregularly shaped tract of land in both Orange and Osceola counties. The developed part is mostly in Orange County; half the Disney land in Osceola County is leased for cattle and timber (Allen, 1989, p. 17). The site includes a permanent wildlife conservation area of 8200 acres. The three principal tourist attractions are the Magic Kingdom Park, with 107 acres; EPCOT Center, 260 acres, and the Disney–MGM Studios Theme

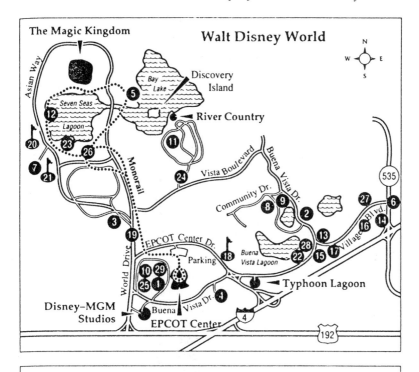

Legend

1. Beach Club Resort
2. Buena Vista Palace
3. Car Care Center
4. Caribbean Beach Resort
5. Contemporary Resort Hotel
6. The Crossroads at
   Lake Buena Vista
7. Disney Inn
8. Disney Village
9. Disney Village Conference
   Center
10. Dolphin Hotel
11. Fort Wilderness Campground
12. Grand Floridian Beach Resort
13. Grosvenor Resort
14. Guest Quarters Resort

15. The Hilton
16. Hotel Royal Plaza
17. Howard Johnson's
    Resort Hotel
18. Lake Buena Vista Golf Course
19. Magic Kingdom Toll Plaza
20. Magnolia Golf Course
21. Palm Golf Course
22. Pleasure Island
23. Polynesian Village Resort
24. Reception Outpost
25. Swan Resort
26. Transportation & Ticket Center
27. Travelodge Hotel
28. Village Marketplace
29. Yacht Club Resort

Map of Walt Disney World, reproduced with permission from Bob Sehlinger, *The Unofficial Guide to Walt Disney World and EPCOT*, 1991 edn, p. 45.

Park, 135 acres. Over 5000 acres of the resort have been developed. During the peak tourist season, total employment is about 35 000 (*Facts & Figures*, 1990, p. 1). There were 30 million visits in 1989, up to 150 000 visitors per day, three-quarters of them adults. WDW calls the visitors 'guests', as a hotel would. About 70 per cent of the guests are return customers.

Half of the revenues and two-thirds of the operating profits of The Walt Disney Company derive from its theme parks (Kerwin and Fins, 1990), which also include Disneyland, Tokyo Disneyland and Euro Disneyland, which opened in April 1992 near Paris. The operating margin (operating income divided by revenues) from the theme parks and resorts for 1990 was 29 per cent (*Walt Disney Company Annual Report*, 1990, p. 38).

The Disney products

To understand the variety and extent of the proprietary activity in WDW, a brief description of some of its parks, resorts, and other goods is outlined here. The Magic Kingdom Park, the heart of WDW, opened in 1971 and contains Main Street and 43 attractions within six other theme 'lands': Adventureland, Frontierland, Liberty Square, Fantasyland, Tomorrowland and Mickey's Starland. The park is designed so that, at any of the lands, one has the feeling of being in one specific environment – each is visually closed off from the others (Sehlinger, 1991, p. 166). The park has 35 food outlets and 56 stores selling merchandise. All 300 retail outlets in the three Disney resorts have some kind of theme, reflected in props, store design and music ('Disney World: putting money where the mouse is', 1991). The Disney services extend to labor as well, with its friendly employees and the cartoon-character figures that walk around.

The EPCOT (Experimental Prototype Community of Tomorrow) Center, dating from 1982, is an international showplace with 23 attractions, 13 exhibits, 36 food outlets and 66 stores. Prior to opening, Disney landscapers planted 12 500 trees and 100 000 shrubs. The two theme areas are Future World, featuring science and the prototype community envisioned by Walt Disney, and World Showcase, featuring country exhibits similar to those in world fairs. The Disney–MGM Studios Theme Park opened in 1989 and has eight attractions related to motion pictures and television, two exhibits, 11 food outlets and 20 stores. It includes working motion picture and television studios, which offer tours. There are two water theme parks. Typhoon Lagoon has streams, a lagoon, a wave pool and saltwater snorkeling. River Country offers a swimming hole, white-water rapids, a nature trail, heated swimming pool and white-sand beaches. Besides its theme parks, WDW has an employee recreational area at Little Lake Bryan. The company also rents townhouses as retreats at Lake Buena Vista, a town by Interstate Highway 4.

In 1990, the 634-room Disney Yacht Club Resort and 580-room Beach Club Resort opened, both located by a 25-acre lake. These add to the 6200 rooms in seven resorts previously available, including 785 camp sites and 407 rental trailers. Disney's Village Resort has 585 family units, including villas and club suites. The Disney Village Hotel Plaza has an additional 5820 rooms, making a total of over 12 000 rooms. There is also a conference center that accommodates 350.

Pleasure Island, opened in 1989, offers evening entertainment for one cover charge (continuing the price policy practiced in the theme parks), with six themed night clubs, shows, films and restaurants (Sehlinger, 1991, p. 14). Discovery Island has a zoological park of 11 acres of flora and fauna, in a tropical setting, with trails, marked plants and an aviary. Disney's Boardwalk, an amusement park like Coney Island, but Disney-clean, opened in 1991 (ibid., p. 15). The resort facilities also include three golf courses, pools and lakes, boating, a night-time entertainment complex, a shopping village, a conference center and campgrounds. The Walt Disney World Village Office Plaza, at Interstate 4, contains 100 000 square feet of office space (*Facts and Figures*, 1990).

The Disney Company sells its own products in WDW, but it extracts revenue from the products of other firms as well. Most products sold at WDW have a name-brand co-sponsor that pays Disney Company for the exclusive right to sell the type of product (Allen, 1989, p. 8). In effect, WDW charges them a rent for the privilege of selling within the grounds.

The development of WDW

To avoid hold-outs as well as to keep the land prices in the area from escalating, Walt Disney had by 1964 acquired the land in small parcels using various holding companies, subsidiary corporations such as the Buena Vista Land Company. 'Using middlemen, stealth and more than 100 dummy corporations, he went on a secret land-buying spree near Orlando, paying about $400 an acre' (Allen, 1989, p. 13).[1] Disney's father had tried unsuccessfully to raise cattle and grow oranges in that same central Florida area before moving to the midwest (ibid.).

One reason for including so much land, much more than is currently developed or held for conservation, is to create a buffer zone and avoid the motels, fast-food stores and unsightly neon cacophony that developed around Disneyland in California (Clark, 1973). These developments are in part substitutes for goods sold in Disneyland, and the haphazard ugliness contrasts with the carefully planned image that WDW seeks to invoke. Hence Disney is able to control the immediate environment around its theme parks. Disney officials also learned from Disneyland that they would profit from owning the land surrounding the theme parks, which would rise in value as a result of the business the parks would attract (Zehnder, 1975, p. 5.)

If state or local governments had funded or mandated some of the civic goods, the test of the hypothesis would be weak, since the provision could be ascribed to these government provisions and requirements. However, Disney was able to obtain perhaps the greatest autonomy of any major proprietary community in the USA, providing a clear case of the private provision of collective goods. Government did play a role in making the external area attractive to WDW: the network of roads in central Florida and the prospect of highway improvements influenced Disney's decision to locate there (Zehnder, 1975, p. 52). But the internal civic goods were created privately with little help or interference from state or local governments.

WDW has obviously had an impact on the development of central Florida. The population in the greater Orlando area grew from 30 000 in 1965 to 450 000 in 1970 and 1.1 million in 1990. The labor force grew from 186 000 in 1970 to 620 000 in 1990 (*Facts and Figures*, 1990). With this growth, WDW has induced an increased land value in the area, but the surrounding developments in turn increase the value of its land, hence it is an open question how large the value received from external developments is, relative to the value exported to the region.

The legal foundation

Having obtained the land, Disney now needed self-government to fulfil his vision for WDW as a proprietary community. On 15 November 1965, Disney representatives met government officials at Orlando to discuss zoning and other laws, Disney's commitment being contingent on reaching an agreement (Zehnder, 1975, p. 43). The governor of Florida assured Disney of his cooperation (p. 63). The circuit court approved the request for a separate drainage district that included the WDW land and a few other small lots (p. 71). Roy Disney, Walt's brother, stated, 'We must have a solid legal foundation before we can proceed with Disney World. This foundation can be assured by the legislative proposals we are presenting to the next session of the Florida legislature' (p. 87).

The Reedy Creek Drainage District (RCDD) was formed in May 1966 under Chapter 298 of the Florida code, 'Drainage and Water Control'. The Disney Company proposed an improvement district that would assume the functions of the drainage district, enabling WDW as landowner to control the environment and construction (p. 89). In 1967, Florida enacted Chapter 67-764 (House Bill No. 486) for the benefit of the Walt Disney Corporation, radically transforming the governance of the Reedy Creek Drainage District. The new law, changing it from a 'Drainage District' to an 'Improvement

District', 'abrogated nearly all state laws' concerning building and development (Berliner, 1978, p. 4).[2] The RCID law combined features of different Florida district acts into one 'powerful entity' (Zehnder, 1975, p. 105). Included within the Reedy Creek Improvement District are two towns, Lake Buena Vista at the edge of the District, and Bay Lake, which contains the theme parks. The governor signed the bill on 12 May 1967 (p. 107).

The District's 180 workers are civil servants. Its $20 million annual operating budget is funded mainly from taxes which Disney pays to the District (De George, 1988, p. 49). The District has control over water, waste disposal, airport facilities, transportation, public utilities and roads – the civic goods normally provided by cities and counties. The District is governed by five supervisors who serve four-year terms. The law specifies that all board members be owners of land within the district, thereby providing for proprietary governance of a sovereign-authorized district. The board members are elected at annual meetings of the landowners. Each landowner is entitled to one vote, which may be by written proxy, for every acre or major fraction of an acre owned. In fact, the Walt Disney Corporation (WDC) owns nearly all the land (98 per cent according to De George, 1988) in the District, thereby controlling the Board. The District boundaries match the land owned by WDW, so that governing the District is tantamount to governing WDW (Berliner, 1978, p. 9).

The text of Chapter 67-764 recognizes the existence of 'year-round resorts and recreation-oriented communities in other states and parts of the world that vie with Florida for the tourist trade'; hence 'appropriate measures' can be taken to promote 'the creation of vacation, sports, and recreation facilities and residential communities of high quality and the utilization of the many technological advances achieved by American industry in developing new concepts in community living and recreation'.[3] This is an implicit recognition that lowering the regulatory and tax costs of an enterprise will promote its growth.

The text posits external benefits from the district: 'the conservation of natural resources and attractions, the creation of favorable conditions' and 'utilization of new concepts, ideas, designs and technological advances in the establishment of such facilities and communities are valid public purposes and the legitimate concern of special taxing districts created for that purpose'.[4] Since these are taxes paid mainly by WDW to the District, these benefits in this case are actually those of the proprietary provision of the goods, the specialness consisting of the independence of the District from government controls.

An objective of the District is 'to provide streets, roads, bridges and street lighting facilities, to adopt zoning and building codes and regulations'.[5] Moreover, the 'purposes of this Act cannot be realized except through a special taxing district having the powers hereinafter provided', the powers being necessary for the 'welfare of the District and all its inhabitants and landowners'.[6] Here again, what is politically a 'special taxing district' is, economically, an autonomous proprietary governance. These clauses are quoted at length to show how they describe the features that did develop in Walt Disney World, such as the conservation of wildlife, the promotion of tourism, the creation of civic goods and the use of innovative technology. They also reveal the recognition that the use of new technology and new ideas for communities may require a high degree of exemption from local and state laws, such as building codes and zoning.

Section 9 of the Act provides for the 'Powers of the District'. These include the ownership of the infrastructure, utilities, transportation and recreation facilities. The powers are explicitly open-ended. Section 10 endows the District with the power of special road districts.[7] This power is exclusive of and supersedes the jurisdiction of the State Road Department of Florida and any political subdivision of the State, except for two designated state roads and Interstate Highway 4, which cut through WDW. The roads within WDW are not considered to be part of the State or county public road systems.[8] Connections between the private and public roads are jointly determined by the District and the State.[9] Under Section 22, the budget and finances of the District are not subject to the requirements of Florida laws or State subdivisions.[10] Section 23 declares that the jurisdiction of the Board of Supervisors with respect to traffic and safety 'shall be exclusive of any and all codes, ordinances, requirements, plans, or other regulations of the respective Boards of County Commissioners of Orange and Osceola Counties ... with respect to zoning, building and construction, planning with respect to the subdividing of land, regulation of building safety, regulation of escalators, elevators and other lifting or transportation devices, regulation of amusement and recreation parks and facilities, regulation of plumbing and electrical installations and other safety or sanitary codes', although electrical and other contractors are still subject to licensing laws.[11]

A question that arises is whether, once developed, WDW would be vulnerable to a change in the District authorization by the State of Florida. Section 56 of the Chapter addresses this concern. It is entitled, 'Pledge by the State of Florida to the Bond Holders of the District and to the Federal Government', and states: 'The State of Florida pledges to the holders of any bonds issued under this Act that it will not limit or alter the rights of the District to own, acquire, construct, reconstruct, improve, maintain, operate or furnish the projects or to levy and collect the taxes, assessments, rentals, rates, fees, tolls, fares and other charges provided for herein ... until all such bonds together with interest thereon, and all costs and expenses in connection with any action or proceeding by or on behalf of such holders, are fully met and discharged.[12]

In 1972, the District issued $20 million of bonds, free of State taxation, for drainage and sewerage (Berliner, 1978, p. 8), and it has issued bonds subsequently. So long as bonds exist, the State evidently pledges to keep the Act intact. Whether terms of the statute can be altered is an open question, which, if it was attempted, would most likely be brought to the courts.

Section 60, recognizing its 'essential public functions', provides for some tax exemption within the District. It states that 'all assets and properties of the District', and the revenues derived by the District under the Act, 'shall be exempt from all taxes by the State' or any of its subdivisions.[13] As a government agency, the District is able to finance improvements with tax-free bonds and it is exempt from the impact fees which private developers have to pay. However, the Act does not exempt business activity which would be subject to taxation in Florida if such were owned by a municipal corporation, and enterprises which are not undertaken as a 'public function' are also not exempt.

The District does pay county and state taxes on the land, but the tax assessments are not kept at the market value (Clark, 1973, p. 37). The land value stated in the Walt Disney Company consolidated balance sheet for 1990 is only $67 million, compared to a total improvements (buildings and so on) value, less depreciation, of $3250 million (*Walt Disney Company Annual Report*, 1990, p. 43), which would put land at only 2 per cent of the real estate value, even excluding the value of construction in progress.

Since the Walt Disney Company does pay some property taxes, it is not evident that it is being subsidized by the state and local governments for the use of their public works. The exemption from regulations and some taxation (for example, on District bonds) amounts to the elimination of barriers and imposed costs, rather than necessarily constituting a subsidy. Clearly WDW benefits relative to the other enterprises in Florida, but this does not constitute a subsidy *per se*, but the imposition of costs by the state on these other businesses, which in a world of proprietary communities would not be the case. The importance of being free from such costs and restrictions was brought out in the case of the Walt Disney Company's plans for a $2 billion theme park in Long Beach, California, which was cancelled because of regulatory hurdles and the opposition of environmental groups ('Digest', 1991, p. D2). It should be noted that this Chapter of Florida law does not create a sovereign entity, but only grants the District autonomy from much of sovereign law, effectively granting WDW a substantial amount of residual ownership over its land.

Levy's analysis

WDW's local autonomy provides the basis for Walt Disney World as a significant test case for proprietary governance and the provision of public goods. One brief analysis of WDW's performance as a private community was done by David Levy (1975). He notes that the typical vision of contractually provided goods such as streets and transit posit explicit prices for each good, and often explicit contracts, which appears to make private provision cumbersome, if not unworkable, in practice. As Levy states, WDW offers an example of a 'contractual city' or proprietary community that in fact does not operate in this way. Indeed, this case study reveals a corporate community operating essentially along the lines theorized by Heath and MacCallum, as described in Chapter 8.

Levy (p. 29) notes that WDW provides a mass transit system, garbage disposal, a wildlife preserve and 'no pollution to speak of'. He sees one key difference between WDW and sovereign cities in the ownership of the land: in WDW, one entity owns the entire site, whereas in 'normal cities' the ownership of land is decentralized, a key point made by MacCallum. Levy contrasts garbage collection in the two types of communities. In sovereign cities, garbage is stuffed into cans by the residents, placed outside and then taken to dumps or incinerators by trucks. WDW faces the same problem of garbage disposal but, as a for-profit organization, it 'bears the burden' of its customers' displeasure at the sights and smells of the garbage. These are not externalities at WDW; being internalized, the displeasure reduces the revenue. Besides fewer fees from the theme parks, the unpleasantness induces less shopping, and 'the rent which Disney Corporation can charge will be reduced' (p. 29). The WDW garbage disposal system uses pneumatic tubes that take the refuse to a disposal plant. Its monetary cost is probably higher than conventional disposal would be, but WDW has evidently also taken into account the social costs of the alternative, making the pneumatic system the preferred approach. As Levy (p. 30) notes, it is in the interest of WDW to provide the pneumatic system if the increase in rent relative to the ugly alternative is sufficient to cover the monetary costs of avoiding ugliness. It is made feasible by a unitary owner which retains the residual profits. As he also notes (p. 31), whereas some services of a city might not be economically privatized separately, they can be provided privately as elements of an entire community.

Another example discussed by Levy (1975) is fire protection. Under a sovereign government, residents provide some private preventive protection, such as extinguishers and fire-resistant materials, but they rely mainly on the public service to deal with fires. 'In typical cities buildings often do not have sprinklers' (p. 30), whereas WDW has installed sprinklers in all its buildings, which provide more immediate protection. As Levy notes, the Disney Corporation has a stake in a reputation for safety.

Levy states that a contractual community such as WDW might not be 'libertarian' in the sense of permitting everything that does not coerce others (p. 31). Acts or materials are banned if they are offensive to many of the customers. But a proprietary community is 'libertarian' in the wider context of property rights, of property being controlled by its owners, who have a contractual relationship with the persons within its space. As Levy notes, in a world of proprietary communities, there would be a diverse assortment of interests and laws, offering competition among communities offering different types of civic goods.

WDW's physical goods

Walt Disney World is well known for its clean environment: 'Maintenance is performed so promptly that nothing is dirty or in disrepair' (Berliner, 1978, p. 11). However, the preservation of wildlife and avoidance of outside-area pollution are external benefits which theory would suggest would not be provided as readily, there not being direct payoffs to the owners.

The mission to conserve part of the area in its natural state may provide indirect benefits for the corporate image and utility to the owners, and it may reduce outside environmental regulation. The original planning team for the nature preserve included a Conservation Advisory Board, and it consulted major US conservation organizations. WDW established a Walt Disney World Environmental Protection Department. The conservation area includes wetlands and a stand of virgin cypress. One stated goal is to demonstrate that development can be achieved without disturbing the ecology of the adjacent areas (Zehnder, 1975, pp. 155–6). This includes a program of building new wetlands for wildlife disturbed by construction (Bloch, 1991, p. 32). However, environmental preservation has an opportunity cost, limiting its extent. Aside from the designated conservation area, the undeveloped land has been stripped of its native vegetation and bulldozed into a 'giant empty greenbelt' (Allen, 1989, p. 14), making the monuments of the park visible from afar.

As the District law indicates, WDW was to use innovative technology, and it takes pride in its high-tech civic goods. The resort has the first commercial all-fiber-optics telephone system in the USA and the world's first completely electronic telephone company, Vista-United Telecommunications, a Disney partnership (*Prototype*, 1987). The Digital Animation Control System (DACS) coordinates the hundreds of Audio-Animatronics puppets in the Magic Kingdom. DACS sends signals to the puppets, controlling their voices and gestures as well as stage lifts, doors, lighting and curtains. WDW has a computerized central monitoring system, the Automatic Monitoring and Control System (AMCS), for its utilities, which are operated in a 9.5 acre basement under the park, into which trucks can drive.

As Levy described, pneumatic tubes collect solid waste. The tubes, a Swedish system named the Automatic Vacuum Collecting System (AVAC), speed the garbage at 60 miles per hour to a central collecting area, where the trash is compacted and taken away by truck to be burned. The incinerator plant uses wet scrubbers to avoid pollution. Waste water is recycled for irrigation; it is fed into ponds where water hyacinths absorb the nutrients left after initial treatment. The energy plan includes a waste heat recovery system. The sprinkler system is tied into the AMCS, and use of sprinklers in all buildings reduces the extent and cost of the fire-fighting department. The Dynamic Economic Energy Dispatch System (DEEDS) compares several energy-generating options at the Reedy Creek Utilities Company Central Energy Plant and selects the most cost-effective methods. High-voltage electric power is monitored by computer for WDW, a system 'more sophisticated than those in most current municipal uses' (*Prototype*, 1987). The photovoltaic power system on top of the pyramid-shaped 'Universe of Energy' building at EPCOT is the largest privately funded solar power system in the world.

The exemption from building codes has enabled WDW to use innovative methods and building materials, as proposed in the Charter. WDW built what was at the time the tallest reinforced masonry building in the United States, the TraveLodge motel, 16 stories high. No code in the USA would have allowed such a building over 12 stories (De Michael, 1973, p. 61). As a result of its freedom to innovate, the Disney Company has become a premier patron of architecture, commissioning works by major architects. Recent constructions include hotels at WDW and an administrative building at Lake Buena Vista. (Prior to the administration of Chairman Michael Eisner in 1984, Disney buildings had been designed in-house.) As one example of innovation, the core of the Team Disney office building at Lake Buena Vista is an open cylinder fastened by a 74-foot beam at the rim, forming one of the world's largest sundials (Andersen, 1991, p. 66).

WDW has made extensive use of its power to provide for innovative transportation. Services, many provided with admission to the parks and hotels, include four monorail trains (13.7 miles of beamway), ferryboats, motor launches, trams, 123 buses and water taxis. The resort contains 125 miles of paved roads. WDW has what it calls the 'fifth largest Navy in the world', with over 750 watercraft. The Mark IV Monorail system links several parks and resorts using 250-passenger trains, moving 80 000 passengers per day. To service air transport, there is a STOLport for short take-offs and landings. As Levy notes, much of the ground transportation is not specifically charged for, being included in the general fees; the marginal price paid by a user is zero. Foot traffic has also been attended to. On Main Street, the sidewalks are paved with a resilient asphalt, which keeps legs from aching, and there are places to sit (Zehnder, 1975, p. 259).

The hypothesis that a privately owned real estate complex in a large territory, with little significant government funding or control, cannot provide as abundant a level of desired civic goods, both in quantity and in quality, as a government would is thus rejected. There is no evidence that the WDC has not provided the civic goods that would have an effective demand. The civic goods are territorial, and there is a way to induce individual users to pay for their share of the public goods, since an admission fee is charged for the use of the site.

WDW's psychic goods

The physical goods provided by WDW, however impressive, constitute only the surface of its public-goods provision. Families do not typically travel 3000 miles merely to experience a fancier carnival ride. The more psychic and emotional characteristics of WDW's public goods – the value of being in the WDW space itself, apart from 'consuming' rides and exhibits – need to be analyzed as well in order to provide a comprehensive understanding of the success of WDW.

As Sharon Zukin (1991, p. 221) explains, Walt Disney sought to transform the amusement park from mere physical entertainment: 'he wanted to project the vernacular of the American small town as an image of social harmony'; it would provide not just enjoyment, but a message. Disney was the 'son of a disappointed utopian' (p. 222). Both Disneyland, California, (established in 1955) and Walt Disney World, Florida, are images of utopia. One of Disneyland's planners stated that its Main Street is 'what the real Main Street should have been like' (ibid.). Main Street is actually an image of what one would wish it were like rather than a realistic reconstruction. The buildings are built from five-eighths to seven-eighths of full size, a movie-set technique that renders them friendly to children while creating the illusion to adults that everything is smaller than they remembered (Stern, 1986, p. 211). The street recreates Disney's home town, Marceline, Missouri. Main Street is the heart of WDW, the 'key to the secret of the Disney vision', a time when America was simpler and more coherent (ibid.).

Walt Disney was an example of an entrepreneur whose vision superseded narrow conventional profit calculations but ultimately provided greater profits than conventional wisdom would have likely gained. Amusement park owners in 1953 criticized the small number of rides in the Disneyland plans, as well as the large amount of open space and the expensive maintenance (Zukin, 1991, p. 223). However, Disney was selling not merely animal figures that went in circles, but a whole make-believe landscape. Making up for the reduced conventional vehicles of profit were the psychic elements of the park, a combination of myth and fantasy. The high-cost maintenance was necessary to prevent garbage and litter from spoiling the carefully imaged environment.

Disney pioneered the concept of charging an admission fee to an amusement park rather than by individual ride (Allen, 1989, p. 11). The Disney environment has a rental value, collected as entrance fees for a number of days. Indeed, the reproduction of the environment is an excludable good, and Disney has a copyright on many of its identifiable buildings; published images require Disney's permission (Sehlinger, 1991, p. 306). At WDW, one-day tickets are available for the individual parks, as well as 4-day and 5-day passes for all three parks, valid for a lifetime until used up, and also a one-year pass. As of June 1993, for adults a one-day, one park admission is $35, a four-day, three park Super Pass is $125, and a five-day, three park Super Duper Pass is $170. Disney hotel packages also include admission to the parks.

Bob Garfield (1991), a journalist and disgruntled visitor, reports the total cost, not including airfare, for his family of four at $1700. Calculating 6 hours and 47 minutes of actual 'fun', that is, excluding the time waiting in line, riding in buses, eating and so on, his $1700 amounted to a $261 'cost per hour of fun' for the family, by his reckoning. The fact that he paid it nevertheless demonstrates his revealed preference for the experience. According to Garfield, the Disney Company does not furnish elapsed-time figures for its attractions. One spokesman on the grounds is quoted as saying that 'It's not our policy to reduce a visit to Disney World to mundane statistics.' Garfield does do so, calculating his family cost per hour of fun in the Magic Kingdom at $579. However, he does not take into account that just being there is supposed to be part of the fun; he is paying rent during his entire stay. Hence, if the $1700 is divided into their total stay of 120 hours (five days), that would be $14.17 per hour for the family, or $3.54 per person per hour for the use of space and facilities in Walt Disney World. For pure admission, a 4-day pass of $186 would be $3.87 per hour for 12-hour days.

Charging at the gate is more appropriate for the Disney idea of selling an environment as well as the rides. As noted by Allen (1989, p. 12), charging at the gate also keeps out opportunists – the pickpockets and trouble makers that infect some carnivals. A fixed charge also provides for a more predictable expense than a per-attraction fee. Fixed fees also avoid the costs of charging at each attraction, which would also decrease the fee that the guests are willing to pay at the gate.

The mere existence of congestion does not necessarily make it more profitable to charge a user fee. Hotel elevators are crowded in the morning, but hotels still do not charge for their use. A fee that eliminated waiting could produce disgruntled guests who grudgingly use the stairwells. Culture and custom also play a part in what is charged for. There is also the desire of hotel owners to make the features of the premises available, which implies making transaction costs as low as possible, for example not charging for elevator service. These factors would apply to transportation at Walt Disney World as well as its attractions. The queues evidently do not grossly detract from the enjoyment of the park, since WDW surveys the guests as they leave the park and, on a scale of 1 to 10, satisfaction ratings were about 8 to 9 (Grover, 1991, p. 64). The Walt Disney Company is conscious of the queuing problem and has substantially reduced waiting time with new attractions, operating efficiencies and longer park hours (Walt Disney Company Annual Report, 1990, p. 7).

Visitors to WDW can gear their plans to avoid much of the congestion cost, if they wish to, since attendance has annual, weekly and daily cycles. The least crowding occurs early in the morning, on Fridays and Sundays, and between Thanksgiving Day and December 18 (Sehlinger, 1991, p. 19). The weeks between Easter and June are also less crowded (p. 25). In early December, the daily attendance of 20 000 is about a third that of the peak summer season or during holidays (p. 30). Main Street often opens half an hour before the announced time, and WDW maintains a flexible opening schedule to accommodate variations in attendance. A guest who seeks to avoid waiting can save a significant amount of time by careful planning, or by following suggestions such as are published by Sehlinger (1991), who provides detailed plans for time-efficient touring of WDW. Tests conducted by Sehlinger found that, with attendance at 48 000, a guest could save an average of 3.5 hours with his plan over those wandering about on their own, and thus experience more attractions (p. 59). Visitors can also save time by avoiding lines for food by buying from vendors rather than restaurants (p. 90). Hence, if time has a high opportunity cost for a visitor, there are ways to economize on it.

Disney's vision for Walt Disney World had two additional features. One was the model of a world fair, with the theme of world cultures. The other was the creation of EPCOT as an actual utopian city with a population of 20 000. Walt Disney said that EPCOT

will be a city that caters to the people as a service function. It will be a planned, controlled community, a showcase for American industry and research, schools, cultural and educational opportunities. In EPCOT there will be no landowners and therefore no voting control. No slum areas because we will not let them develop. People will rent houses instead of buying them, and at modest rentals. There will be no retirees. Everyone must be employed. (Zukin, 1991, p. 224)

The town was to have a 50 acre central hub enclosed by a dome, the tall buildings rising up through it. Transportation spokes would carry people to the outlying residential and industrial areas. The civic goods planned included a monorail, garbage disposal through tubes, underground utilities and a central computer system. It would be open to paying visitors (Taylor, 1987, p. 33).

Disney died on 15 December 1966, and the company decided that such a residential community would involve too much legal responsibility; instead it turned EPCOT into a 'temporary haven' (Zukin, 1991, p. 224). WDW is a residential community to some degree already, having, apart from the hotels, some townhouses and single-family homes at Lake Buena Vista. Some dwelling units are leased, and some are purchased under condominium ownership, with the Disney Corporation retaining title to the land.

Michael Eisner, chairman of Walt Disney Company, wants to redeem Disney's dream 'City of Tomorrow' by creating a high-tech town in the southern part of WDW (Andersen, 1991, p. 68). In 1990, the company obtained 2045 acres in Osceola County southwest of WDW for the new 'Dream City', to be built over a 25-year period. It will be a 4000 acre complex with houses, apartments, a shopping mall, schools, recreation, museums, office buildings and a 6000 acre greenbelt. There are also plans for time-sharing condominiums (Grover, 1991, p. 276; *Walt Disney Company Annual Report*, 1990, p. 13). Now called 'Celebration', the town will be a laboratory where humanity coexists with nature, like Ebenezer Howard's garden city, and will have a Disney Institute with classes that take advantage of WDW resources such as the conservation area (Bloch, 1991, p. 8). One of Walt Disney's aims for WDW was a city in which employees could live, and a showcase for new technology in fields such as transportation and sanitation (Greene and Greene, 1991, p. 10).

The idea of a utopian community was derived in part from Disney's own boyhood experiences (his father's problems during the depression) and also from previous world fairs. The 1893 exposition in Chicago featured a 'White City' of 200 buildings. The 1939 Fair in New York City had a utopian 'Town of Tomorrow' in a 'World of Tomorrow' featuring technical progress. Its exhibits were interactive, with viewers able to touch the exhibits and speak with the demonstrators (Zukin, 1991, p. 226). Zukin sees consumerism as a prime thematic intention of Walt Disney World: 'information blends into an implicit call to consume: Feel! Marvel! Buy!' (p. 228). But the 1939 Fair was a 'commercial disaster' (p. 227). Something more than fancy rides, technological utopia and consumerist propaganda is needed to draw the crowds.

An anthropological insight into the Disney parks' success is provided by Alexander Moore (1990). The form of WDW, he says, is borrowed unconsciously from the pilgrimage center, such as Mecca. It symbolically replicates the baroque capital, playful pilgrimage being appropriate to the secular 'technologized' society of today. A pilgrimage involves a rite of passage in which the pilgrims undergo some change. Moore calls attention to the myth-evoking name, 'Magic Kingdom'. To enter the Magic Kingdom, the visitor goes through symbolic entrances such as the ticket gate, trams, turnstiles and monorails. Main Street is lined with Victorian shops, an evocation of 'Main Street America'. Frontierland reflects the 'heroic mytho-historical American past' (p. 212). The themes are journeys in mythical time, past and future. To heighten the image, Disney characters wander around at random, encountering the guests. 'The reigning ikon' is Mickey Mouse (p. 215).

'Spectators behold five North American utopias: that of Main Street towns; that of the fantasy of childhood; that of the fantasy of adolescence; that of the epic history of the founding fathers, frontier and Lincoln; and finally that of the space travel of the North American future.' WDW 'evokes the supernatural in a context within which the supernatural has been banished' (Moore, 1990, p. 214).

The idea of a pilgrimage is echoed even by the disgruntled visitor, Garfield (1991), who describes it as 'an overwrought Mecca of mass-market escapism'. Only half facetiously, he states that Disneyland and Walt Disney World have become, for parents, childhood institutions, 'somewhere between an entitlement and a sacred duty ... the middle-class American hajj'. This was his second family trip, lest his older child be denied the expected rite. In fact, two out of every three Americans visit a Disney Park at some time (Kobliner, 1990, p. 152), lending evidence to the view that there is more to the Disney experience than mere amusement.

In Walt Disney World, the environmental atmosphere is maintained throughout the resort. The hotels have an 'entertainment architecture' and are 'theme parks in themselves' (Zukin, 1991, p. 228). The new Dolphin and Swan hotels, transient communities for 10 000 persons, have the animal motifs invoked by their names. Giant dolphin and swan figures sit on top of the roofs, symbols of Florida fauna, water, the tropics and Disney cartoon figures. The exterior walls are covered with waves and banana leaves, 'an imaginary landscape for visual consumption' (p. 229).

The psychic elements of Walt Disney World, so complementary to the rest of the Disney empire, create a unique site that the Disney Company has nurtured to extract its rents. Those rents, in turn, depend on maintaining complementary aspects of the other Disney business. For example, films that departed from the value system that Disney markets could erode attendance at the theme parks (Taylor, 1987). The importance of the psychic elements and the environment are illustrated by one visitor's description: 'Most of us live all year long in a world that is ugly and dirty, filled with worry and hard work. My annual visit to the Magic Kingdom, Epcot Center and MGM–Disney Studios [*sic*] gives me a chance to become part of a world where everything is clean, everyone is friendly, nothing is broken, and no matter how tired or grumpy I am, people are still glad to see me' (Ross, 1991). Utopia for rent, per diem.

The influence of WDW on communities

The various elements of WDW have been influential on other communities. First of all, the Disney rivals in Florida have copied some of the Disney characteristics, such as 'theming' with a decorative scheme (Allen, 1989, p. 12). Some of the competition, especially the older resorts too far from Orlando for the typical WDW tourist to travel to, went out of business or are barely surviving (Sehlinger, 1991, p. 6). In the 'Orlando Wall', satellite attractions have formed (p. 7). EPCOT created a second shock to the Orlando tourist industry, taking up one or two days more of the tourist's vacation week. Disney created multi-day admission prices, which were effective in keeping the guests in WDW territory for several days (p. 8), another reason for charging admission rather than relying more on per-ride fees. When Disney–MGM opened, the three-day pass was discontinued and the guests could either buy a one-day pass for one park or multi-day passes for four or five days, which takes up most of a family's vacation week (p. 9).

External to Orlando, WDW has stimulated the development of tourism combined with real estate development, as well as residential communities (Zukin, 1991, p. 230). Housing developments have borrowed Disney's 'abstraction of the Main Street vernacular' (p. 231). Andres Duany, a Miami architect, said that 'The newest idea in planning is the nineteenth-century town' (ibid.). The Disney Company itself has moved deeper into the residential field; The Disney Development Company, begun during the mid-1980s, plans to build residential communities near WDW (pp. 231–2). Zukin describes the creation of city landscapes as a 'creative frontier' of highly-industrialized society. This new landscaping 'requires neither centrality nor monumentality' and, instead, 'it visually reconciles the tension between public and private consumption, global and local capital, market and place' (p. 241). The theme of proprietary developments as reconciling public and private, market and place, echoes the thought of MacCallum, discussed in Chapter 8. Walt Disney World is thus much more than a resort or even a secular Mecca. It is, for Zukin, a model for residential communities of the future, the model being a 'multi-use exurban complex'. WDW has already served as a model for communities such as Seaside, Florida and Mashpee Commons, Massachusetts, both designed by 'historicist post-modern architects' (p. 265).

As Zukin (p. 268) states, space is not just a place to hold objects but also 'structures people's perceptions, interactions, and sense of well-being or despair, belonging or alienation' and, as he notes, these characteristics determine land values. Walt Disney World's financial success is a result of its shaping of the spatial environment, complementary to its other goods.

WDW as a firm

WDW's own promotional literature stresses its technological and physical innovations, but Walt Disney's utopia had a conscious financial aspect as well. According to Richard Nunis, president of Walt Disney Attractions and creator of Tokyo Disneyland, 'The aim of Disney World was to show that through free enterprise you could take virgin land and develop it without any government subsidy' (Allen, 1989, p. 13). The recent history of the Walt Disney Company points out a contrast between the market and government sectors in their provision of goods. Private enterprises do not automatically maximize profits, nor do they necessarily operate efficiently, that is, to generate maximal returns on investments. But when they do not, in contrast to the government sector, their stock values fall relative to their asset value, and they become candidates for takeovers, as discussed in Chapter 4.

The heirs of Walt Disney during the 1970s attempted to keep his vision intact, but business in a changing world requires constantly new visions. The new owners tried to do as Walt would do, but did not innovate and take chances as he had done (Grover, 1991, p. 12). As costs escalated (EPCOT was originally estimated to cost $600 million and ended up costing twice that), company earnings were declining (p. 13). Moreover, Disney's ticket prices were not even keeping up with inflation, the corporate officers being worried about negative reaction to price increases and an attendance decline (p. 64). One-day tickets cost only $17, a small fraction of the $1000 cost of a typical family trip to WDW (p. 41). Hotel business at Orlando was being taken by other firms (p. 14).

Faced with a takeover attempt, the directors brought in Michael Eisner, formerly president of Paramount (p. 16). From 1984 to 1990, ticket prices at WDW were raised 82 per cent under the new management, to about what the market can bear (Kerwin, 1990, p. 53). Price increases were combined with television advertising to increase demand, having learned from a trial run that it could cost $6.50 in advertising to bring in a guest who would pay $18 admission plus other spending (Grover, 1991, p. 67). 'Pleasure Island', with night clubs patterned after Orlando's Church Street Station, was an attempt to attract young adults (Grover, 1991, p. 179; Sehlinger, 1991, p. 9). In addition, the company upgraded WDW with attractions such as the 'Captain EO Show', a 3-D rock and roll space fantasy film with special effects, and

'Star Tours' (Grover, 1991, pp. 78–9). Attendance increased even with the increase in ticket prices, and theme park profits tripled from 1983 to 1987 (p. 79).

The management team also decided to add a third theme park, the Disney–MGM studio, which would induce guests to spend an extra day of their holiday week in WDW rather than some other park (p. 172), especially the new MCA Universal Studios. The Disney Company had a comparative advantage over MCA owing to its independent Reedy Creek Improvement District. A Disney project did not require the numerous regulatory reviews and licenses that other firms needed (p. 180). MCA competed by making its attractions more violent and thrilling than rides and attractions at WDW that teenagers consider tame (p. 183).

WDW as a community

The WDW facilities are not just a tourist-servicing business, but a community with the infrastructure and civic goods provision equivalent to a city. The 16 000 overnight guests constitute a sizeable, if transient, residential population, in addition to the daytime visitors. All these services are financed by the guests using a combination of user fees and rental charges. The entrance fee is, in effect, a rental charge paid to WDW for the use of all the grounds and facilities during a period of time. The utilities are paid for from these rental payments. The collective goods are thus financed from rent, just as a hotel guest pays rent for the short use of facilities.

WDW provides evidence of a sizeable private community that not only provides for civic goods, but does so abundantly and in an advanced way, made feasible by the legal autonomy granted to WDW by Florida law. The collective goods are excludable and territorial, funded by rent, paid as admission to the site. Admission to a site such as WDW is a contract between a guest and the owner, typically specifying certain conditions on the ticket itself. WDW also generates non-excludable public goods such as its influence on culture and on other communities. The evidence rejects the hypothesis that the contractual provision of community-wide civic goods is necessarily inferior to that of government. The Disney theme parks in California, Florida, Japan, and now France, also indicate the possibility of a corporate provision or franchising of a chain of communities of a certain style, which is achieved with hotels, campgrounds, resorts, student dormitories and YMCAs, and could conceivably be done with more permanent residencies as well.

WDW is primarily a retail community, and it could be argued that the feasibility of providing the civic goods to external customers does not apply to goods for mainly permanent resident users. The payment of admission is different in its details from residential communities, but not in kind, since residents in a contractual community also need to pay to have admission rights to the site. Residents make periodic payments suitable to their long-term stay. Nevertheless, an examination of residential communities will provide further tests of the market-failure argument for communities of various sizes and types. Four different types of residential communities will be examined as case studies in the following chapters.

Notes

1. Some $5 million was paid for the original 28 000 acres (Grover, 1991, p. 9), which averages out at $179 per acre.
2. The text of the law is included in the Berliner (1978) publication.
3. Berliner (1978, p. 15); Laws of Florida (1967), Chapter 67–764, part 3, paragraph 4.
4. Berliner (1978, p. 15); Laws of Florida (1967), Chapter 67–764, part 3, paragraph 5.
5. Berliner (1978, p. 16); Laws of Florida (1967), Chapter 67–764, part 3, paragraph 8.
6. Berliner (1978, p. 16); Laws of Florida (1967), Chapter 67–764, part 3, paragraph 10.
7. Berliner (1978, p. 17); Laws of Florida (1967), Chapter 67–764, part 5, section 10, clause 1.
8. Berliner (1978, p. 18); Laws of Florida (1967), Chapter 67–764, part 5, section 10, clause 2.
9. Berliner (1978, p. 18); Laws of Florida (1967), Chapter 67–764, part 5, section 10, clause 5.
10. Berliner (1978, p. 20); Laws of Florida (1967), Chapter 67–764, part 7, section 22, clause 2.
11. Berliner (1978, p. 20–21); Laws of Florida (1967), Chapter 67–764, part 8, section 23, clause 2.
12. Berliner (1978, p. 23–4); Laws of Florida (1967), Chapter 67–764, part 17, section 56.
13. Berliner (1978, p. 24); Laws of Florida (1967), Chapter 67–764, part 17, section 60.

10 As they like it: Arden and land trusts

Suppose we were to conduct an experiment on the voluntary provision of civic goods. To test it on a small scale, we could create a contractual municipality of about 500 persons. The land would be owned by a private firm, which would lease it out to the residents. The rents would be used for the expenses of the firm as well as to provide civic goods to the community. If the experiment were successful, we would have a prime laboratory example of a contractual community that provides for its civic goods in accord with the theory presented in the previous chapters.

Such an experiment actually exists. It is the Village of Arden, Delaware, north of Wilmington. While there are many contractual communities in the USA, most are limited in their scope of civic goods, since they are usually part of some municipality. Arden, in contrast, is an independent municipality. It is the only village in the USA on the National Register of Historic Places in its entirety, placed there in 1973 as a successful experimental community, an example of a garden city, a direct democracy, a center of the arts, and for the preservation of a 'true village feeling with a deep sense of community' (Liberman, 1974, p. 25).

The hypotheses

The Village of Arden tests the following hypothesis: a residential community with contractual governance and little significant public-sector funding or control does not provide as abundant a level of the civic goods desired by the community, both in quantity and in quality, as a similar imposed government would.

A second hypothesis to be tested is that the decentralized provision of civic goods is not feasible. The provision of streets, parks, community centers and so on by Arden-sized communities would constitute a decentralized production of such goods within the context of the United States and its states.

Other aspects of contractual provision that can be examined in the case of Arden include: (1) whether the civic goods produced by Arden are excludable; (2) whether the public goods increase the site values and rents; (3) whether there is a problem with demand revelation; (4) whether free-riders present a problem; (5) whether the provision of the goods requires the support of higher-level governments; and (6) whether it is impractical to separate the site and improvement values in the calculation of rent.

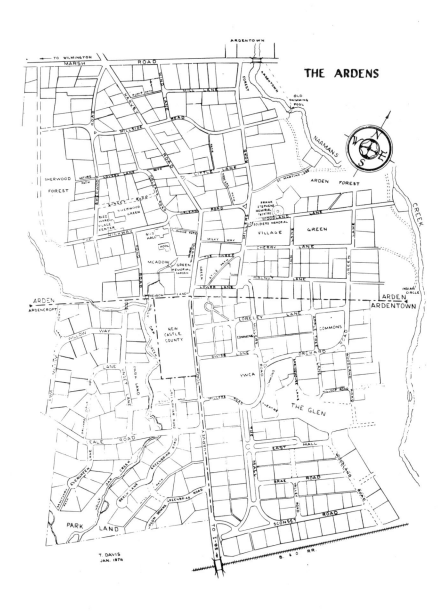

Map of the three Ardens, from *The Arden Book*, authorized by the Town
Assembly of Arden; map designed by Ted Davis.

If the two hypotheses are rejected, there remains the issue of whether Arden is a unique case or else can be replicated. Some other communities that have been founded on similar principles, that is, using land leases to fund civic goods, will be examined briefly as a comparison to Arden to test whether the Arden case is path-dependent or whether it is based on general principles.

General description

The residential land of Arden is owned by a non-profit trust which collects the site rent from the leaseholds, the buildings being owned separately by individuals. The rent, set by assessors elected by the residents, is then used by the community, governed by majority vote, to finance its civic goods. The trust also pays the county property taxes, including taxes on the buildings, so that the owners pay a charge independent of the value of their improvements. The site rent is also used to pay the expenses of the trust. Since only some of the economic land rent is collected by the trust, the rest is retained by the leaseholders, giving the sites positive site values much as occurs with fee simple land titles.

Since each leaseholder contracts with the trust for a leasehold, Arden is a contractual community, its civic goods provided by a market process.

Historical background of Arden

The following history is instructive for the market-failure proposition, because it reveals that not only was government of the sovereign type not needed for the provision of the Arden civic goods, but that in fact it impaired the contractual nature of the community and stifled its local provision of civic goods. Unlike the case of other intentional communities, the history of Arden also shows that this model works for a population not necessarily ideologically committed to that model.

Arden was founded in 1900 by followers of Henry George who wanted to build a model community which would test George's theory of public finance. George (1890, p. 1) had proposed implementing his theory of funding public goods from land rent by reforming the tax system: 'We propose to abolish all taxes save one single tax levied on the value of land, irrespective of the value of the improvements in or on it.' During 1895-6, some of George's followers from nearby Philadelphia had campaigned in the Delaware election to elect officials favorable to the single-tax concept. Delaware had only 40 000 voters. George's followers sought to have the state adopt the system, hoping that others would follow a successful model. But the officials of Delaware resisted this 'invasion', arresting over 20 of the speakers. The project backfired. Not only did the campaigners obtain only 3 per cent of the vote in 1896, but, in 1897, Delaware reacted to the campaign with a constitutional amendment preventing the legislature from enacting such a tax system (Wynn, 1965, p. 16; Wiencek, 1992, p. 128).

Two of the campaigners, Frank Stephens, a sculptor, and Will Price, an architect, then set out to found a settlement to demonstrate that a town could be operated with this system. The community trustees would implement the 'single tax' by collecting the community's land rent to provide for the community's goods. Price and Stephens bought an abandoned farm containing 162 acres for $9000, of which $6500 was financed by a mortgage from Joseph Fels, a Philadelphia soap manufacturer and supporter of George's ideas (Wynn, 1965, pp. 21–2). The rolling hill country looked to them like the beautiful woodlands of Warwickshire, England, site of the Arden Forest in Shakespeare's *As You Like It*. Stephens and other George adherents had used Shakespeare's plays as practice for their oratory for campaigns. They founded the town and named it 'Arden' in 1900, and the community has kept alive the memory of its origins ever since. 'Founders Day' in May is still celebrated as an 'Arden Day' holiday, and the Shakespeare legacy has been retained. Stephens built an open-air theater to present Shakespearean plays, performed by the Arden residents. The tradition is carried on by the Players Gild, and the theater, now called the Frank Stephens Memorial Theater, is still in use for weddings and memorial services. Also, in 1930 a barn in Ardentown was refashioned into a 'Robin Hood Theatre' and is still used.

The original Deed of Trust of 1901 gave the three trustees (Price, Stephens and Frank Martin, another Philadelphian) a high level of control over the community's operation and the assessment of the leaseholds. It was, though non-profit, a proprietary community. But then, to attract more residents, the Trustees altered the community's Deed of Trust in 1908,[1] providing for assessors elected by the residents and limiting the powers of the trustees, and new leases were drawn up. This was the beginning of a shift towards ever more democratic control over the governance, and it demonstrates the proclivity towards democratic governance common in contractual residential communities where the residents have site-specific investments, for the same reasons that citizens prefer a democracy over a dictatorship. Even though a single member has little control over the governance, the ability of a majority to overturn the leadership is regarded as a check against arbitrary power, not present under a non-elected governance. Perhaps stronger constitutional constraints against site exploitation might have reduced the desire for democracy. At any rate, the case of Arden as well as other contractual communities is consistent with this proposition: *Contractual communities tend to have a democratic governance unless the assets owned by the residents are mobile, or the site-specific investment is fungible or guaranteed by the management.* Entry and exit are key elements of a market process and, where the exit of one's assets is too uncertain, the exit (replacement) of the governors is a substitute, however imperfect.

Article I, Section 10, of the US Constitution states that 'No State shall ... pass any ... Law impairing the Obligation of Contracts.' The Trustees had entered into a contract with each leaseholder and by the terms of that contract the Trustees had the authority to set the rent, as with any landlord. But in 1935, despite the Constitutional provision, the government of Delaware impaired the contracts between the trustees and the leaseholders. In 1934, the Assessors had enacted a second 10 per cent reduction in rentals, and the Trustees rejected this recommendation. The dispute was brought before the Delaware Chancery Court, which determined that the Trustees must delegate their authority to the Town Meeting and elected Board of Assessors. The reasoning of the Court was that 'This is a charitable trust. Courts are disposed to greater liberality in dealing with trusts of that character than with trusts of a purely private nature.' Furthermore, the leases left the holders in a 'state of uncertainty and insecurity and the potential victims of the arbitrary will of the trustees in the matter of future rental obligations' (Court of Chancery, 1935, pp. 18–20).

The 14th Amendment requires 'the equal protection of the laws' and the language of the US Constitution does not specify any different treatment for charitable trusts. Moreover, any tenant is subject to the 'arbitrary will' of a landlord when a lease is renewed or if it allows the landlord to set the rent. He should know this when he commits the constitutional act of signing a lease agreement. The will of a landlord may be arbitrary, but his ability to set rent is not, since too high a rent will leave him without tenants. However, the site specificity of the leaseholders' investments in buildings at Arden reduced their exit option and led to the lawsuit. The founders failed to recognize this principle and enact safeguards (as MacCallum, 1977, does in his rules for Orbis) for the leaseholders' investments. This was a constitutional failure.

The State of Delaware by this court ruling effectively transformed Arden from a proprietary community owned by an outside corporation, like Walt Disney World, into a democratic civic association such as a condominium, although the Trust remained as the legal holder of the land title and the collector of the rent. In Walt Disney World, legal autonomy gave a private corporation the chance to demonstrate that the private provision of civic goods is feasible and successful. The proposition that the provision of residential civic goods requires a public sector was turned on its head with this court decision; rather than public goods requiring government, government prevented the proprietary provision of the goods. Aside from providing safeguards for the lessee's investments, the legal right of the trustees to set the rent might have been preserved by establishing instead a for-profit corporation which would keep the rental income left after paying for the village and trust expenditures, income which could have been used to purchase more land. The establishment of a charitable trust implies having some beneficial purpose, which can be subject to different interpretations, such as benefiting the residents themselves. Still, the concept of raising revenues through land rent remained in the Arden Deed of Trust, and this basic element of the Arden constitution has endured, a testimony to its sound principles. Arden thus remains a test case of the financing of community public goods explicitly from private land rent.

Stephens attracted not only George sympathizers from Philadelphia and Wilmington, but also others interested in an experimental colony, as well as those with conventional ideologies. The founders, also influenced by the ideas of the 19th-century artist William Morris (founder of the arts and crafts movement in England), envisioned a village of craftsmen and a community life filled with art, music and theater. A craft shop was built and artists, craftsmen and musicians were attracted to the rural enclave within easy commuting distance by railroad from Philadelphia. Stephens and Price did not wish to select the people who would live in Arden on ideological or artistic criteria, since the community model was meant to apply universally. One of the entrance gates was inscribed with the motto of Arden, 'You are Welcome Hither'. The land would be rented to anyone willing to apply for it, at equal terms for all (Wynn, 1965, p. 21). Today, few of the Arden residents are adherents of or even understand Henry George's ideas. The Arden case thus rejects the hypothesis that the model can only work if its members are ideologically committed to it.

Many of the settlers, not having to pay up-front costs for the leased land, built their own houses. Unlike many recent civic associations, such as Reston, Virginia, there were no restrictions imposed on the architecture. The houses were and remain different from one another: 'houses were placed randomly on their lots to give them privacy and room for gardens' (Liberman, 1974, p. 4). The predominant style is English Tudor, 'but aside from that, the place is the very definition of the term "radical diversity"' (Sayles, 1988, p. 27). This freedom of individual house style and placement on lots provides evidence that a residential association need not include restrictive covenants on the architecture. Reinke (1975, p. 53) goes so far as to say that 'Arden is known for its unkemptness; the fact that many residents cite as one of Arden's attractions the lack of pressure to keep up the lawn ... makes for a great deal of variety in appearance.'

Ebenezer Howard's idea of a 'garden city' (cf. Chapter 8) influenced the residents of Arden as well. Some 43 per cent of Arden (70 acres) was set aside as greens, forest and roads. A woodland perimeter separates Arden from the now-adjoining suburbia. The streets of Arden followed the contours of the land rather than being laid out in a straight-line grid. The Arden forests make the village land more desirable, adding to site rents, and the rental increment provides the funding for the maintenance of the forests.

In 1965, the trustees sought the incorporation of Arden as a village. In Delaware, incorporated municipalities obtain 'municipal street aid' from the state. The county government was also about to change the property tax system which levied lower tax rates on incorporated municipalities that provided their own services. Hence government again intervened, inducing the trustees to give up some of their property and authority. As a municipal corporation, the officially named 'Village of Arden' was also included in the General Revenue Sharing program of the federal government, now discontinued. Arden, however, has demonstrated the ability of a town to finance its own goods and services without any tax-paid aid.

In 1973, the common land was transferred to the incorporated village (except for a burying ground). Municipal lands being tax-exempt, the transfer reduced the amount of taxable property without reducing rental revenues, raising the value of the leaseholds by reducing the expenses of the Trust. This different tax treatment of government and private real estate is yet another example of intervention imposed on contractual governance. Arden at first had a separate school district, which became racially integrated in 1952. In 1969, state law compelled Arden to give up its educational control, and the village joined the Mt. Pleasant School District (Liberman, 1974, p. 16). The 'closing of the Arden School marked a significant loss for community life' (Reinke, 1975, p. 59). Here again, the state intervened.

The governance of Arden

The Arden Deed of Trust as amended in 1908 has continued as the legal document for the charitable trust. The three trustees fill their own vacancies subject to the approval of a majority of the residents, and they make decisions by majority vote. The Deed of Trust specifies that the trust shall collect the rental value of the leaseholds and, after paying taxes and the expenses of the trust, apply the funds to uses which 'are properly public in that they cannot be left to individuals without giving them advantages over the others'. The taxes externally imposed include New Castle County property taxes and school taxes. The budget is approved by a majority of the residents in annual referenda (Liberman, 1974, p. 6). The Town Assembly and its elected officials work closely with the trustees in the village's finance.

The private law of Arden also includes the Arden Lease, a 99-year contract (the longest allowable by law, but renewable) for a lot (Liberman,

1974, p. 6). The lease document provides for the enforcement of the community rules by cancellation of the lease. The trustees could terminate a lease if the lessee cut timber without permission or kept the land 'in such disorder as shall in the opinion of the Majority of the Town Meeting be injurious to the Rights of others' (Huntington, 1929, p. 137). Arden has held town meetings since its founding, but the early meetings did not have any legal powers. Since incorporation, the town meeting, the only one in Delaware, is the legally constituted legislature of the Village, and its committees constitute the executive branch of government. Residents at least 18 years of age who have resided at Arden for the six months preceding the Assembly may vote; leaseholders who are not also residents may not vote at the Town Assembly. About 75 dwellings are rented by leaseholders' tenants (Curtis, 1991). The Town Assembly has adopted only 13 ordinances, regarding subjects such as speed limits, the use of the commons, noise, firearms, dogs and roads.

Regular town meetings are held quarterly, and special meetings may also be called. A quorum consists of 35 residents. At the January meeting, candidates are nominated for the committees. There is also an Advisory Committee made up of the chairs of the standing committees, the town officers, senior trustee and the chair of the Board of Assessors. Elections for the committees are held at the March meeting, and residents may nominate themselves.

The Archives Committee, formed in 1988, preserves the history of the village and is working to create a museum. The Auditing Committee examines the accounts of the Trustees and of the Arden funds. The Budget Committee proposes an annual budget, presented to the September Town Assembly and then submitted to a village referendum. The budget cannot be adopted unless it receives the approval of a majority of all residents.

The Civic Committee is the equivalent of a department of public works and is responsible for the services normally associated with municipalities. It supervises the streets, drainage facilities, snow removal, mowing the greens, the upkeep of the woods and other supervision of the common land.

The Community Planning Committee is concerned with landscaping and trees, and administers the Memorial Garden, Arden's private cemetery. Arden residents are eligible for burial in the garden, with no required maintenance charges. The committee also produced *The Arden Book,* with Liberman (1974, 1992) as principal author.

The Legislative Reference Committee is responsible for codifying the governing documents of the village. Its members also act as parliamentarians at the town meetings.

The Playground Committee oversees the equipment on the Arden Green and Sherwood Green. They also spread mulch and contract for painting and repairs, as well as recommend the purchase of new playground equipment.

The Registration Committee includes the chairman of the trustees and the Town Assembly Secretary. It conducts the elections and annual budget referendum, and counts the ballots for the assessors.

The election for the Board of Assessors, of seven persons, uses the Hare system of proportional representation, a complex method that places the votes in piles according to the successive choices on each ballot (Liberman, 1974, p. 12). Arden is evidently the first US community to elect officials by proportional representation.

The Safety Committee was formerly delegated by the Town Assembly with responsibility to act as a police force; it now maintains contact with the County police force and sponsors a community watch program for the three Ardens.

When the Trustees of Arden deeded the Village Center building to the Village of Arden, the Town Assembly made the Buzz Ware Village Center Committee responsible for the supervision of the building. It is expected to encourage and initiate cultural, recreational and civic activities at the center.

The officers of the Town Assembly include the Advisory Committee chair, a Town chairperson (who acts as a mayor), a secretary and a treasurer, the latter three elected at the March meeting. The secretary and treasurer, part-time positions, are the only paid officers of the village. The volunteer nature of committee members evidently involves a high degree of benevolent sympathy as social glue.

Territorial asset specificity involves time in addition to space. Time specificity, the intent to reside in a community for many years, induces the volunteer effort seen in Arden, since an investment in relationships (person-specific) will pay off over many years. The traditions of Arden, going back almost a century, are also a capital good which requires maintenance. As in other real-estate-based organizations, asset specificity of various sorts induces the contractual trustee–lessee, democratic town governance and volunteer committee structure that exists.

Community assessments and rental value

The 1908 Deed of Trust requires that the leaseholders pay the 'full rental value' of the site, a stipulation repeated in the lease agreements. In practice, the full economic rent of the leaseholds has not been collected. 'The Assessors forecast the anticipated town expenses for the year and set the tax at the minimum rate that will meet expenses' (Wynn, 1965, pp. 51–2). The intention of the founders to charge the full rental value or economic rent was most likely futile, even without the Court's intervention. If the majority of the residents obtained greater utility from buying personal rather than communal goods from the rent funds beyond a certain amount, then it would be optimal (from their point of view) to distribute these excess funds as dividends to the population. This stream of private income would become capitalized as leasehold values. The most likely outcome of a democratic decision-making process would be the avoidance of dividends and the collection only of that amount of rent which at the margin provides the desired amount of public goods, as theorized in Chapter 3. This outcome is the actual practice at Arden.

Henry George himself recognized that the full economic rent of sites cannot be fairly collected and spent on a small scale (Stewart, 1970, p. 11, citing Young, 1916). George also wrote that a person who only wishes to collect whatever percentage of land rent suffices for the 'necessary' expenses of government is as good a single-tax man as one who wished to take it all, since the former would still favor one single charge on land values. 'If that does not constitute a single tax, what does?' (Alyea and Alyea, 1956, p. 109, citing *The Standard,* 17 August 1889). George called this view, which had been advocated by Thomas Shearman, 'the single tax limited' (ibid., p. 108).

The 1991 report of the Board of Assessors notes that a former trustee had stated that one yardstick for determining rental value is the 'community standard of living' (this and some other statements of principles have been repeated year after year in the Assessors' reports). The report states an agreement by the Board that 'our land value is a creation of the community' (Board of Assessors, 1991, p. 1). In the 1989 report, the Boards emphasize that 'the community of Arden must be free to determine its standard of living and that the Assessors must neither limit nor inflate expenditures. The community must determine its own standard of living in the annual budget referendum.'

In stating that the 'full rental value' is that amount required to pay for the desired collective goods, the Assessors are defining the value as that which is created by the community public goods, plus the outside taxes. They are putting into practice the idea expressed by Heath and MacCallum, that land values could be created by the territorial goods, generating the land rent used to pay for them. Arden residents are practicing the theory expressed in Chapter 3, by which an individual's rental payment is the price he is willing to pay for the collective goods. The goods/rent mix is not simply a function of what the majority feel is best for them, but of the effect on the market value of their leaseholds, as potential entrants take the mix into account in bidding the price of the leaseholds up or down.

The rent is calculated at a base rate per 1000 square feet of land, with proportional increases (called 'factors separately appraised') for lots facing the greens or bordering on woodlands or commons. There is also a 'lot size adjustment rate', since it is recognized that the larger lots have a lower value per square foot than the smaller ones. A 'multiple dwelling rate' is added to account for the value added to leaseholds permitted (with or without a zoning variance) the 'privilege' of more than one dwelling unit (with a kitchen). A commercial rate is applied to leaseholds with a 'commercial' use, which applies to only one lot (Board of Assessors, 1989, p. 2). The assessment system is attributed to W.A. Somers, who believed that the factors add value to all the lots in a uniform way (Wynn, 1965, p. 30). As a typical example, the rent on a 20 000 square foot lot with fronting on the village green and adjacent to Arden forest was $1202, which is the sum of a base rent of $1090, a forest factor of $75 and a greens factor of $37. The base rent on a 40 000 square foot lot was $1839 (Board of Assessors, 1989, p. 5; the amounts have been rounded here to the dollar).

Assessors study the sale prices of real estate in and near Arden and take into account rates of return on capital. Two assessment techniques used are the comparative and the residual methods (Wynn, 1965, p. 41). The comparative method compares properties with benchmark lots of similar characteristics, using past sales to obtain the data. The residual or abstractive method is useful if benchmark sales of land are not available; the value of the improvements is estimated from its replacement value less depreciation. The Assessors have relied on local real-estate dealers and appraisers, who, according to Wynn (p. 45) are interested in the Arden experiment and provide their services at no cost to Arden.

The separation of the site and improvement values is sometimes put forth as a problem of collecting site rents, making it impossible or impractical. The practice at Arden refutes this proposition. Of course, it is impossible to calculate the exact economic rent, but it suffices in practice to get a reasonably close approximation, tests of success being the number of complaints generated or the longevity of the practice. Facts do not create theory, but they do imply possibility. The fact that the system has been in effect in Arden for nearly a century rejects the argument that the method is theoretically not feasible.

One effect of the Arden leasehold system is that the carrying cost of unimproved land is significantly higher in Arden than in surrounding areas. In 1965, for example, an acre of land in Arden would cost $328 in annual rent, whereas a similar acre outside Arden would only have been taxed $10, excluding sewer charges (Wynn, 1965, p. 32). There are few unimproved sites left at Arden. One test of the efficacy of the public-goods provision at Arden is its land values relative to neighboring areas. The real estate in Arden has a higher market value than similar surrounding properties (Hamburger, 1991). This implies that the economic rent generated by the public goods exceeds the cost, as theorized in Chapter 3, with the premium retained by the leaseholders. It has been recognized in the minutes of the Board of

Assessors that some of the value is due to a 'community value factor', that is the community's artistic and social activities (Wynn, 1965, p. 49), which implies that the volunteer efforts generate land value in addition to the goods funded by the rent.

Clubs at Arden

The civic goods provided through the village budget form only part of the services enjoyed by Arden residents. Many of the cultural and recreational services are provided by volunteers. In 1974, the Village Center committee was created by the Town Assembly to oversee its use as a community center. It is used by the Arden Community Recreation Association (ACRA) and other groups. ACRA, founded in 1948, is a voluntary group sponsoring free recreational and educational programs, financed by residents' contributions solicited at an annual fund-raising drive. Among the ACRA activities are holiday celebrations for the community and a summer day-camp program for children.

The Arden Club is an important private corporation in the village. It owns the Gild Hall, built in 1900. Members, including non-residents, pay annual dues. Club members may use the swimming pool upon purchase of a bond. Branches of the club, called gilds, serve various interests, including the operation of a private library in Gild Hall staffed by volunteers. The Arden Club also sponsors an annual Arden Fair, which raises funds for the club. Ardenites no longer residing in the village come to the fair for an annual reunion. Another organization at Arden is the Merry-Go-Rounders, which began as a sewing circle and then became a service group, visiting patients in hospitals, awarding a scholarship and planting flowers in the commons. Also serving to create community spirit and Smithian sympathy are traditions such as the Saturday-night Gild Hall dinner, where volunteers cook food for some 80 persons who pay $4.50 each for the communal meal ($6 for non-members). As one participant states, 'this creates community' (Sayles, 1988, p. 29).

Among the gilds that operated in the early days was 'The Scholar's Gild, Frank Stephens, Gildmaster, which has study groups, classes in economics and Esperanto, and arranges meetings for speakers on live social questions from time to time' (Huntington, 1929, p. 111). The Arden Building and Loan Association has also served as an important enterprise, formed to finance construction at Arden. In the early days, the banking law classified Arden buildings as personal rather than real property, and banks would not provide mortgage loans on leased land. The Arden B&L was formed in 1917 to provide construction loans and still it operates.

Another financial institution, organized in 1911, was the Raiffeisen Gild, a credit union, so named because it followed the plan originated in the mid-

1800s by Burgomeister Raiffeisen of the village of Hedesdorf, Germany. Security for loans was not collateral, but the character of the borrower. Such a practice requires a membership that knows one another; the members were fellow 'Ardenfolk' known to 'keep their promises and pay their debts' (Huntington, 1922, p. 60). Further security was obtained by requiring the signatures of two neighbors as sureties. Loans were mainly for construction of buildings and starting small enterprises, hence for investment rather than consumption. Despite not paying dividends, the credit union had $15 708 in shares in 1922 and had extended $40 000 in loans during its first decade (pp. 61, 77). As of 1929, it had no defaults or losses.[2] When Ardentown was founded in 1922 next to Arden, a Raiffeisen Gild Two was started there (Huntington, 1929, p. 275). Both these institutions demonstrate the feasibility of mutual credit for the development of a community, when the conditions are suitable. As with many other civic services, the issue is not whether market or volunteer effort can provide them, but under what circumstances.

These gilds and institutions are listed in detail to demonstrate the sense of community and Smithian sympathy for the community that has existed in Arden, where the fraternal tradition has overcome free riding. This social and benevolent provision of public goods such as mutual financial, social and cultural services provides evidence for the theory of the provision of non-excludable goods, as analyzed in Chapter 7. Urban and suburban life is often noted for the detachment of households from one another, whereas Arden demonstrates how a small community can maintain relationships in a shared space and governance that has a high degree of local autonomy.

Contractual, decentralized collective goods

The vitality of the community activities and the abundance of public goods at Arden, and its independent source of financing, reject the hypothesis that a contractual community necessarily provides civic goods inferior to what government provides in similar communities. Moreover, as Wynn (1965, p. 62) states, Arden demonstrates that such a community 'can exist side by side with communities whose tax is levied primarily against improvements'. In the context of the United States or even Delaware, Arden constitutes a decentralized provision of public goods. Residents of Arden still consider the village to be an intentional community, and it is so recognized by the 1990/91 directory, *Intentional Communities* (p. 170), which states that its 'core ideals have remained in effect over the years'.

Arden is also a test case showing that, in contrast to the notion of public goods requiring sovereign provision, the privateness of the civic goods provision has been restricted by government policies. Without the taxation and subsidies provided by Delaware and the USA, there would have been no need to incorporate the village or to rely on the county and state for some services, such as schooling. Regarding the other aspects of contractual provision, the evidence of this case study demonstrates that (1) the civic goods produced by Arden are territorial, their benefit being confined mostly to the village residents; (2) the civic goods do increase the site values and rents (relative to the lack of provision with the same rent); (3) the fact that the leaseholders are willing to move in and pay the rents reveals the demand of at least a majority of the residents for the civic goods; (4) free-riders are discouraged by the need to pay rent for a site and, although free riding on volunteer effort of others is possible, much volunteer work takes place nevertheless; (5) the provision of the goods at Arden does not require the support of higher-level governments; indeed, more local goods, such as education, were provided when the interventions did not prevent it; and (6) since Arden has assessed a site rent apart from the value of the structures for one century, using Somers' system of evaluation, and there has been no agitation to change it, it can be done with no greater apparent difficulty than the usual property tax assessments. Finally, the provision of civic goods at Arden is clearly abundant.

Other land-rent enclaves

There remains the issue of whether Arden is a unique case, not reproducible. In fact, Arden has been reproduced, twice, in neighboring communities. In 1922, a committee headed by Frank Stephens founded a new Arden-type community, Ardentown, using funds lent by Fiske Warren, a friend of Stephens. It contains 110 acres, with a layout similar to Arden, including a woodland owned by the trustees. In 1975, Ardentown became incorporated, with a town-meeting governance like Arden.

A third community based on the Arden model, Ardencroft, was begun in 1950, bordering on Arden and Ardentown. It was founded by Donald Stephens, son of Frank Stephens, and attorney Phillip Cohen. With 63 acres, Ardencroft is intentionally racially integrated, and efforts to attract African-Americans have succeeded. Ardencroft is organized as a corporation rather than as a charitable trust; its three directors serve for life, and vacancies are filled by the remaining directors. One of the original directors was Henry George III, grandson of the namesake. Ardencroft also became incorporated during the 1970s (Liberman, 1974, p. 29; Liberman and Liberman, 1992, p. 11).

Followers of Henry George also founded several other communities. Free Acres in New Jersey (Berkeley Heights township) was begun in 1910, and others in the USA continued to be founded during the 1920s and 1930s (Geiger, 1933). The largest experiment has been Fairhope in Baldwin County, Alabama, begun in 1895. The Fairhope Single Tax Corporation (FSTC), a non-profit organization, owns 20 per cent of the land in the town of Fairhope, which was incorporated in 1908, and it also owns land outside the town. (Because of this mixed nature, Arden provides a clearer case study for an entire community.) Besides paying the property taxes on its own land, the Corporation allows a credit against rental payments for taxes paid by the leaseholders on their improvements (as well as crediting the poll tax), thus simulating the land-rent-only funding of public goods. Like Arden, the FSTC used the Somers method of assessment (Huntington, 1922, p. 12).

The community built parks, streets, waterfront facilities, bath houses, a sewage disposal system, schools, a library and other public goods, all financed by the rents. The original constitution of the organization also authorized the issuance of script, receivable in payment of rent, and the script (in effect non-interest-bearing credit) helped finance the settlement in the early years (Alyea and Alyea, 1956, p. 71). During the 1930s, after Alabama increased its assessments, the FSTC gave several parks to the town to avoid paying taxes on them (ibid., p. 212). The FSTC, as a private governing agent, invites a comparison with city governance with respect to 'rent keeping' as a type of rent seeking; that is, the keeping of some of the land rent by the corporate officers and staff. Alyea and Alyea (1956, p. 239) reports that 'Throughout its history the single tax corporation has leaned backward with respect to salaries in order to avoid any charge of self-interest being levied against its leaders.'

Aside from its longevity and the ample public goods provided, Fairhope offers a further test of the land rent financing of public goods: the growth of the town relative to nearby areas. From 1920 to 1960, Fairhope had an annual population growth rate of 4.8 per cent, exceeding the Alabama rate of 0.8 per cent, the Baldwin County rate of 2.2 per cent, and the town of Daphne (3.1 per cent), which is located on Mobile Bay a few miles north. The city of Mobile grew at a 3.1 per cent rate and the county seat, Bay Minette, at a 4.0 per cent rate. This growth occurred despite the errors made by the founders; according to Alyea and Alyea (1956, p. 37), the founders purchased too little bay frontage and the contiguous land holdings were too small, reducing the enclave's potential success. Hence a hypothesis that land rent funding by a corporate land ownership hampers the growth of a community is rejected by this evidence. Moreover, the 20 per cent of the city land owned by the FSTC constitutes about 50 per cent of the city land value (Stewart, 1970, p. 13), consistent with the theoretical expectation that the absence of a tax on the improvements encourages a more intensive use of the land relative to the sites so taxed.

Fairhope thus provides a parallel test case, rejecting also a hypothesis that Arden's development was due to unique historical circumstances not repeatable elsewhere. Alyea and Alyea (1956, pp. 288–9) reports that 'The urban community of Fairhope has outdistanced many small American cities both in material achievements and in those intangible, imponderable qualities which make a community worthwhile.'

Community land trusts

The viability of land-owning organizations has been further demonstrated by the recent development of land trusts created for the purpose of leasing sites or preserving a particular type of land use. Land trusts date back at least to 1891, when the Trustees of Reservations were established in Boston by nature preservationists (Poole, 1992, p. 54). A residential type of community land trust was developed by Ralph Borsodi in the 1960s, based on the Arden/ Fairhope models. Whereas Arden is controlled by its residents, land trusts are not incorporated towns, and the members and trustees include non-residents.

Borsodi founded the School of Living in 1934, which in 1936 established a residential cooperative at Bayard Lane near Suffern, close to New York City, and several others. During the 1960s, Robert Swann and others modified the organizational form to the Community Land Trust (CLT) to prevent sell-outs of the trusts and broaden the boards' expertise in interests by including a majority of non-residents (Stucki and Yeatman, 1990, p. 105). There are about 50 operating urban CLTs in the USA, and over 800 land trusts of various types (Naureckas, 1990, p. 115). Over 800 000 trust members are preserving some 2.7 million acres of land in the USA (Poole, 1992, p. 55).

One motivation for setting up land trusts is the perception that home ownership in the United States is becoming less affordable relative to wage earnings, and that land trusts as charitable organizations can help to reduce the acquisition and carrying costs. The leaseholders usually own the buildings and improvements in the leaseholds, and the CLT often facilitates the financing, either holding the mortgage or selling via a land contract, that is, by installment (The Institute for Community Economics, 1982, p. 18). Typically, a CLT retains a first option to buy the improvements at the real cost less depreciation, so that the seller does not capture the gains due to the community services or to general land value appreciation, yet retains the equity in his own investments. The leaseholds are passed on to heirs, so that the invested equity is retained as a family legacy. These complex contractual provisions again demonstrate a governance response to asset-specific real estate investments and uncertainty by both the trustees and the lessees.

Some CLTs have begun to federate; in 1976, the School of Living expanded its function to include an alliance of land trusts and acts as a landholding company for them. Since 1985, some intentional communities in Virginia have held conferences sponsored by InterCommunities, an informal association of private communities (Ringrose and Brown, 1990, p. 132). Several organizations have been established to aid CLTs, including the School of Living, the E.F. Schumacher Society, the Institute for Community Economics and the Land Trust Alliance, which serves as an umbrella organization for conservation land trusts.

The Shannon model: providing for mobility

Land-owning organizations have taken other forms as well. The Shannon Farm in the Virginia Blue Ridge mountains has a population of 75. Its 500 acres, held by a non-profit corporation, is not subdivided into leaseholds. Housing is built in clusters which share wells and springs, with large forested areas left uncleared. Decisions are made by consensus, with voting (requiring a 60 per cent super-majority) an option only after two successive attempts at meetings, thus coming quite close to a Wicksellian unanimity. The community services, including roads and utilities, are financed from dues consisting of 7 per cent of after-tax income, which drops to 5 per cent (with a minimum of $42.50 per month) after 12 years of membership.

Though Shannon holds title to the structures, the value of the houses belongs to the leaseholders, who can transfer the structures to others. Shannon obtained a line of credit with a local bank, using its land as collateral, from which members can draw loans after raising their own matching funds. Property taxes on the improvements are divided according to an internal valuation rather than using the county assessments. Owing to its rural location, where the real estate market may be thin, a problem arose as to the ability to obtain the improvement value when one moved away. Shannon members developed a plan in the lease to facilitate exit. A new member can choose to have the corporation guarantee a portion of his house value, from 30 per cent initially up to a maximum of 75 per cent after 15 years of membership. The exiting member also pays a transfer fee proportional to the guarantee percentage (Robinson, 1990, p. 88). This equity guarantee also offers a way to assure mobility for non-democratic land-owning companies. As mentioned above, MacCallum (1977) drafted a model constitution under which the owner of sites pledges to reimburse tenants for the value of their fixed improvements, which follows the same principle. The lease agreement of the Community Land Trust in the Southern Berkshires, which is offered by the E.F. Schumacher Society as a model form, gives the lessor a first option to purchase the improvements at the replacement cost less depreciation, as estimated by appraisers (E.F. Schumacher Society, 1990).

An interesting exception to democratic governance is provided by mobile home parks. The mobility of the houses makes them less site-specific and prevents the landlord from raising the rents to an exploitative level. The Shannon, E.F. Schumacher Society and MacCallum guarantee plans offer a way for land-owning companies to assure some mobility when the structures are immobile. Just as some CLTs have call options on the improvements, a landlord can offer its leaseholders a put option, an option to sell the improvements to the landlord at a previously set price, such as the replacement value (less depreciation) or the value estimated by an impartial appraiser. Shannon may some day be recognized as a pioneer of the sale option, making possible the type of proprietary community envisioned by Heath and MacCallum, but which has not yet developed widely, a company which profits from the land rent it creates by producing public goods and leasing the land.

Land trusts provide more evidence that Arden is not historically unique, and that the method of financing civic goods from the rents they generate can be implemented by various forms of governance and community sizes.

Notes

1. The text of the 1908 'Constitution and By-laws' and 'Deed of Trust' is reproduced in Huntington (1922, pp. 64–71). One section is reproduced in Liberman (1974, p. 17). An Arden lease agreement is reproduced in Huntington (1922, p. 72).
2. No information is at hand since Huntington (1929) as to the fate of this credit union.

11 Life at the fort: the Fort Ellsworth Condominium

Few condominium residents realize that their communities put into practice the principle of financing the goods and services of contractual communities from the rents they generate, as well as the theories regarding governance and landed clubs. As a test for the contractual provision of collective goods, this case study is redundant, since the Arden case is sufficient to demonstrate its feasibility. However, as a test for unique factors, this case is needed. Arden as well as the land trusts discussed in the previous chapter are intentional communities, deliberately founded on the principle of financing their services from the ground rents. It is conceivable that such contractual communities have in their production functions for collective goods a variable 'intent'; that is, the intent of the founders. Condominiums typically do not have this conscious intent, being more commercial in origin, hence the 'intent' variable would be null.

Another difference of this test case is that a condominium has a more limited scope of goods than a more self-contained village such as Arden. It therefore demonstrates the operation of a contractual community within a greater urban community. The contractual structure is also different from the leaseholds at Arden. A condominium is a common-interest community made up of co-owners. 'Condominium' means 'joint rule'. A member has full title to his unit and an undivided shared ownership of the common property. In the USA, condominiums are the most common type of private residential governance above the level of families, and for that reason too their provision of collective goods warrants a case study. The principal case examined here is the Fort Ellsworth Condominium Apartments in Alexandria, Virginia, within the metropolitan area of Washington, DC. A condominium in California is also investigated briefly to compare the generality of the features of Fort Ellsworth.

The hypothesis

The issue to be addressed is, as posed in Chapter 1, the feasibility of the contractual provision of collective goods, framed as the following hypothesis: *Incentives for personal gain do not induce private agents to provide the public goods that the people in a service domain effectively demand, be-*

*cause there is no way to induce individual users to each pay for a portion of
a good so that its total amount is paid for.*

As with Arden, the other hypotheses which will be tested are: (1) the
public goods produced by Forth Ellsworth are non-excludable; (2) the public
goods do not increase the site values and rents; (3) the funding for the public
goods has little relation to the site rents; (4) the demand for the public goods
cannot be truthfully revealed; (5) free-riders prevent the provision of the
goods; (6) the provision of the goods requires public-sector support, and (7)
the separation of the site and improvement values is impractical.

Fort Ellsworth's history

During the Civil War, Fort Ellsworth, built on a hill near what is now the
George Washington Masonic National Memorial, was one of many Union
forts circling Washington, DC, to protect the capital from Confederate invasion. This fort was named after Col. Elmer Ephraim Ellsworth, the first
Union officer to be killed in the conflict (Fort Ward Museum, 1990). During
the 1980s the association bought a large rock and plaque, placed near the
community room, noting the history. This expense was justified as enhancing the historical interest of the community and thereby adding to its site
value (Rader, 1991b). The newsletter of the condominium association also
recalls the history, its name being *The Cannonball.*

In 1972, the property, covering 7.4 acres, was deeded to the Savage-
Fogarty Companies, Inc., which constructed the condominium structures.
Fort Ellsworth was part of a condominium building boom which reached a
peak in 1973 (Wolfe, 1978, p. 7). Fort Ellsworth was one of the first condominiums built in Alexandria, and the very first condominium to obtain Veter-
ans Administration approval for its loan program. According to Dean
Morehouse (1992), project manager, one design innovation was 12-foot high
ceilings in some of the living rooms. In designing the amenities, the company relied on its previous experience in building apartment buildings. The
size of the development was basically a function of the land available for
purchase, although too-large projects do not generally obtain approval from
the city (Morehouse, 1992). Hence a large project that could provide local
civic goods in addition to those typically provided by condominiums does
not get built because of this intervention as well as the lack of tax rebates for
services replacing those of the local government.

The reason given by Morehouse (1992) for choosing to construct a condominium complex rather than something else was that at the time, traffic
congestion was increasing and there appeared to be a market for the ownership of housing closer to the urban center (Washington, DC), as well as for
the lower price and lack of external maintenance offered by a condominium.

Selling condominium units would also free capital and return the investment sooner than renting out apartments.

The condominium goods

The Fort Ellsworth condominium consists of 169 residential apartments in five buildings, each four stories high. The buildings are divided into sections, each with a stairwell, bulletin board and mailboxes. The common structures include a boiler room; a swimming pool, along with lounges; a small children's wading pool (which is inoperative and never worked well from the beginning); a tennis court; a picnic area with trees, tables, grills and rubbish containers; landscaping, including trees, lawns and shrubs; several 'dog walk' areas; a master television antenna (which does not include cable); storage rooms; a community meeting room; and parking spaces. These facilities are available to tenants but not to non-resident landlords. Snow removal and rubbish collection are also handled by the association.

The landscaping, swimming pool, picnic grounds and proximity to the George Washington Masonic Memorial Park give Fort Ellsworth a modest resemblance to Ebenezer Howard's garden city in miniature. There are 228 444 square feet of residential buildings, an average of 1352 per unit. Dividing by four stories, there are 57 111 square feet of residential surface, making up 17.7 per cent of the condominium area. The 82.3 per cent of the site surface held as undivided shared ownership comes to about 0.5 per cent per unit. The City of Alexandria only assesses and taxes the individual apartments since, in condominium ownership, the association itself owns nothing. The value of the common facilities is imputed in the value of the individual units, which is congruent with the theory presented in Chapter 3, that the rent of residential sites includes the value of the territorial collective goods in the neighborhood. As an example, in 1991 a typical one-bedroom unit was assessed by the city at $16 900 for the land and $98 000 for the building, totalling $114 900. This unit was sold in December 1989 for $119 000 but assessed in 1990 at $111 700, so the assessments do not match the current market values (Alexandria, 1991).

The services supplied by the condominium include a property management company, Condominium Management, Inc. (CMI). One of its employees is the manager of Fort Ellsworth. The condominium also hires a grounds supervisor. Many condominium residents live there in order to avoid working in a yard or shovelling snow. Labor-saving services provided by the condominium are collective goods as significant for many of the residents as the physical amenities (Kass, 1991b). Besides the individual parking space assigned to a unit, there are some unassigned parking spaces. The Association contracts with a towing company to remove unauthorized cars.

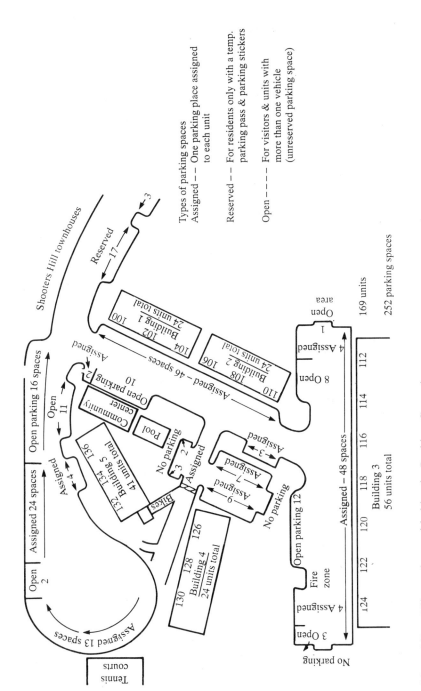

Types of parking spaces
Assigned – – One parking place assigned
to each unit

Reserved – – For residents only with a temp.
parking pass & parking stickers

Open – – – – For visitors & units with
more than one vehicle
(unreserved parking space)

Map of Fort Ellsworth, provided by the Parking Committee.

155

The social and community life offered by the condominium is another civic good. The association holds several community parties each year in the Community Room and, during summers, at the pool, to which all residents are invited. Donations are solicited, including 50–50 raffles where half the funds contribute to the party, the remaining expenses being borne by the Association. The condominium also provides utilities, including hot and cold water, air conditioning and heating. As discussed below, these utilities have significant private characteristics, but they are generated from a common physical plant and use some common piping, hence they have collective characteristics as well. In some condominiums, safety is an important feature. The Briarcrest condominium in Los Angeles, discussed below, has security gates with keys at the entrance to the buildings and the parking lot. Fort Ellsworth does not have such gates, but has some security services, such as 'no trespassing' signs, a gate around the swimming pool, a committee concerned with security and a liaison police officer assigned by the Alexandria police.

With respect to the secondary hypotheses, these facilities and services are clearly territorial, with little external spillover. They make the site more desirable: the better the maintenance of the exteriors and the gardens (in appearance as well as structural soundness), the more attractive the site is to the marginal purchaser, and the higher the unit rent and price. The swimming pool, tennis court and picnic tables also induce those who value these goods to bid more for units than otherwise. The demand for these goods is revealed by the entry of persons willing to pay the price of a unit plus the association expenses. Free riding is prevented by exclusion, since the use of a unit requires one to own or rent it. Geographic proximity rather than a fence makes these facilities exclusive for the most part to the residents. Finally, there is no significant government support for the internal goods and services of the condominium.

Condominium governance

The unit owners have site-specific investments vulnerable to possible opportunism by the governors of the condominium. They also face uncertainty as to future expenses and capital projects. They therefore have a complex contractual arrangement with one another as a 'Council of Co-Owners', the contract inscribed in the condominium's Master Deed and the bylaws. Schedule B of the Master Deed (cf. Savage/Fogarty, 1973) lists all the units, their square footage, initial value and the *percentage of interest in the common property*. This percentage of interest is of great importance, since it determines the percentage of the condominium expenses allotted to each unit as well as the percentage of the vote each unit owner is entitled to. This percentage interest, which remains fixed, is tantamount to a percentage of the land value of the condominium.

The boundaries of the units are specified in detail in the Master Deed; they establish the property rights and division of expenses between the units and the association. The collective facilities are divided into two categories: 'limited common elements' consist of patios, balconies and a few other facilities; 'general common elements' are all parts other than units and limited common elements. They include the land, foundations and exterior walls. The Master Deed specifies that the acceptance of a deed constitutes an agreement that the provisions of the governing documents are accepted. This statement is the constitutional agreement between a co-owner and the Council of Co-owners, making the governance unanimous at the constitutional level when one joins the community. In contrast to sovereign governments which have automatic jurisdiction over all persons within their areas, the condominium jurisdiction is established by an explicit contract.

The Master Deed also specifies several levels of agreement for subsequent constitutional changes. Amendments require a two-thirds vote. However, the percentage interest that each unit has in the common elements cannot be changed except by unanimous consent. Hence no owner may be deprived of his specified representation or ownership without his consent. The Master Deed provides an exit option for the entire association, allowing the co-owners to terminate the regime by three-quarters vote if the property is destroyed by some disaster, or unanimously otherwise. A co-owner is thus assured of the continuance of the condominium so long as he wishes it.

The by-laws of the condominium (Fort Ellsworth Condominium Apartments, 1973) are the second element of the association governance. They require that the administration be performed by a Board of Directors. This representative government is in contrast to the direct democracy of Arden. There is a sound economic reason for this. The physical connection of the apartment units to one another and the use of common utilities such as water, heating and air conditioning require a more continuous monitoring and decision making than the facilities at Arden, which is made up of detached houses. The parking spaces and grounds also require continuous monitoring by committees. However, as is typical with condominiums, the association holds annual meetings (in April) during which members elect the Board and transact other business. The Board or a petition of at least 25 per cent of the percentage interests may call a special meeting. The percentage of the vote to which a unit owner is entitled is the percentage interest assigned to that unit. Unless otherwise required, the voting is by majority rule of the percentage interests. An owner may not vote or serve on the Board if there is a lien against his unit. Proxies for a particular meeting may be executed in writing,

which is similar to voting in corporations and unlike voting in city governments. A quorum requires 40 per cent of the owners in person or by proxy.

The Board of Directors has five unit members, each Director serving for
three years. The Directors do not receive any compensation for their service
(except reimbursement for expenses) unless it is authorized by the owners at
an association meeting. They are volunteers serving for social reasons, to
influence policy, or out of sympathy for the community. The Board is endowed with 'all of the powers and duties necessary for the administration of
the affairs of the Condominium'. The duties of the Board include preparing
an annual budget and establishing the assessments, which are paid in equal
monthly installments. These broad powers are consistent with Williamson's
theory regarding successive adaption, described in Chapter 4, in which contingencies cannot be predicted in an uncertain world, inducing a flexible
governance structure that can keep transaction costs low.

The Board is specifically required to keep books in appropriate detail, to
be available for examination – reducing the chance of opportunistic behavior.
The records are to be audited annually by an outside auditor. Article III
mandates that the Board of Directors employ a professional managing agent
for the Condominium, constitutionally authorizing a council/manager type
of civic government. The Board is authorized to delegate powers to the
agent, except for setting assessments, enacting and enforcing the rules and
regulations, and some other specified powers. The section explicitly states
that 'the Condominium shall not undertake "self management" or otherwise
fail to employ a professional management agent without the prior approval
of all of the holders of such first mortgages'. The Condominium officers are
a president, vice president, secretary and treasurer, all elected and removable
by the Board. The president, a board member, has the powers of such an
office 'of a stock corporation organized under the business corporation laws
of the State of Virginia', including the power to appoint committees to the
extent the Board decides is appropriate.

The Board must adopt a budget by 25 November and send each Unit
owner a copy by 1 December, as well as an accounting of the actual revenues and expenses after the end of each year. These budget requirements
again safeguard against opportunism. The by-laws mandate that the budget
include reserves for contingencies and replacements. If the reserves are
inadequate, the Board is authorized to levy a further assessment, which the
Board may designate to be paid in a lump sum or by installments. A reserve
account ideally provides enough funds for periodic maintenance, such as
painting every few years; for repairs and replacements after the expected life
of depreciating assets; and for accidents and natural disasters. The fund
reduces uncertainty over future assessments, avoiding the unpleasant sur-
prise of a special assessment. An inadequate reserve fund is not evident to

the typical purchaser of a condominium unit and may constitute a public goods illusion, a liability that would lower property values if recognized. Hence the requirement for adequate reserves is a safeguard against both uncertainty and the opportunism of a board postponing such expenses to some future date in order to spend on present consumption.

The assessment paid by each unit owner is in proportion to his respective percentage interest and is a lien against the unit. An addition or change to the Common Elements in excess of 5 per cent of the annual budget must be approved by a majority of the unit owners, otherwise the Board may proceed with the measure. If 80 per cent or more of the Board members believe that such expenses substantially benefit the unit owners, the owners are assessed for them. Insurance must be purchased by the Board as trustees for the unit owners. The Board must attempt to obtain a single master policy for the property, each unit owner receiving a sub-policy. The Board must also attempt to secure a policy which is not affected by the conduct of any unit owner. Besides insuring the property, the insurance shall insure unit owners against liability incident to their ownership of the Common Elements. A default, failure to comply with contractual duties, entitles the Association, acting through the Board or its managing agent, to specified reliefs. These include legal action, including the 'foreclosure of the lien for payment of all assessments'. Relief may also be sought 'by any aggrieved Unit Owner'. A default by a unit owner of an assessment after 45 days obligates him to pay a late charge or interest, as determined by the Board.

Fort Ellsworth's law includes the parking regulations, enforced by towing (Fort Ellsworth Condominium Association, 1989a). Some 220 cars are registered, averaging 1.3 cars per unit. All parked cars require either stickers or visitor passes. The Alexandria police may also enter the parking areas to check on licenses and inspection stickers. One parking area has been designated for two-wheeled vehicles. Normally a car is not towed from a numbered space unless the owner so requests. A resident or visitor may appeal a towing to the Parking Committee, which in turn may submit reimbursement requests to the Board for final action. The Board thus has a judicial as well as a legislative role.

The detailed listing of mutual responsibilities is induced by the asset-specific investments of the owners. As the Williamson (1985) model indicates, high asset specificity and recurrent use of the goods induce the use of unified governance and provisions such as reserves and insurance, reducing uncertainty. A real estate-based firm with long-term residence is horizontally integrated within the territory, the common elements being under the control of one governing agency.

Fort Ellsworth's operations

The Board normally meets on the fourth Wednesday of the month in the Community Room. The first half hour is 'residents' time', during which residents are able to ask questions. Residents may also sit in on the rest of the Board meetings, except for executive sessions when personal issues such as defaults are discussed. Residents may also submit proposals to a Board member for consideration at the Board meetings. The property manager attends the Board meetings, where he reports on the management operations and answers questions.

Committees authorized by the Board include Architectural and Engineering, Grounds, Newsletter, Parking, Swimming Pool, Social Activities, Tennis, Safety and Security, and task forces for bylaw revision and Residence Guide. Renters may join and chair the committees; a Board member serves as a liaison. The committees are required to report on their activities to the Board. The committee chairs may join the Board at its meetings and participate in the discussions. Much of the work of the association, including the monitoring of contractors and the facilities, the recommendation of a contractor and the types of goods to provide (such as which trees to plant or the swimming pool hours), takes place in committees. The board often approves a committee recommendation with little disagreement. In addition to the governing committees, there is also a Pet Care Exchange in which residents care for each other's pets during vacations.

Each building sector (and street address) has a Stairwell Captain and assistants who coordinate local affairs with the Board. The captain reports problems which may occur, keeps a key to the storage area, distributes the newsletter, participates in an emergency telephone tree and hosts meetings of the stairwell residents, some more frequently than others. The volunteers, including committee members and stairwell captains, total about 50. Although the majority of the residents benefit as free-riders, nevertheless some do volunteer. The ability to influence outcomes plays a role in the volunteering, as well as other narrowly self-interested motives, but (going by personal observation as a resident) some benevolent sympathy with the community is likely to be present as well. I can infer this in part because some of the volunteers have said they would willingly let others take on the tasks if there were takers.

The swimming pool is normally open from Memorial Day to Labor Day, though the season may be extended. The City of Alexandria considers condominium pools to be 'public/private' areas and imposes its law on these pools, including the provision that there must be at least two and no more than nine people in the swimming *area* (not just the pool, but also the lounging area around it!) when there is no lifeguard.[1] The association has hired one of its members as a lifeguard for weekends, but this rule reduces the usability of the swimming pool during work-days. A single person is unable to do any swimming, and is not even allowed to sit in the pool area to signal his or her presence. The Briarcrest condominium in Los Angeles is not subject to such a rule.

In Alexandria, condominiums may pay the city a fee to service their rubbish or contract with a private firm. In 1992, the city offered its service for $11.67 monthly per unit. Fort Ellsworth instead contracts with a private firm, which picks up the rubbish twice as often as the city for only $4.74 per unit (Cheney, 1992).

The Fort Ellsworth budget

About one-fifth of the operating income is allocated to funding the reserves. As discussed in Chapter 8, condominiums typically pay for maintenance and capital-goods expenses from a reserve fund rather than by borrowing. A cooperative is able to borrow funds more easily than a condominium, since banks are less knowledgeable about residential associations. Although the common areas cannot be sold separately, associations do have collateral in their future assessments, just as government collateral is its future tax revenues. As associations increase in number, specialized banks may develop to finance association borrowing. For the present, investor pools in the secondary mortgage market require assurances that a reserve program is in place, hence mortgage officers require such reserves to approve loans to condominium units. As discussed in Chapter 8, it is more prudent to maintain reserves, since the capital goods are being consumed annually. The reserve funds are not a savings account made up of residuals after operating costs, but an accruing expense for this consumption. The American Institute of Certified Public Accountants has been creating guidelines requiring the inclusion of a capital reserve program in association audits.

In 1981, the management of Fort Ellsworth had prepared worksheets of various structures such as roofs and the heating plant, with estimates of replacement costs, lifetimes and the desirable annual reserve (Condominium Management, 1981), an analysis which is updated periodically. The Briarcrest condominium (discussed below) had a reserve study by Association Reserves (1990), which specializes in this work. Many other condominiums have been increasing their fees to build up reserves, and the resort to special assessments has decreased. In 1991, 98 per cent of income of Fort Ellsworth was derived from the assessments on the units. Slightly over 1 per cent comes from interest income, with a little raised by late charges and rental charges on the community room.

The parties at Fort Ellsworth seem to be, on the surface, a redistribution of income, since typically only a couple of dozen residents out of some 350 attend them. However, the activists such as Board and committee members attend parties more than others, and new members are also more likely to attend, to get acquainted. Since the community depends on volunteers and the parties build sympathy by fostering acquaintanceship, the cost appears to be more than repaid in the value of the volunteer work it helps to foster.

Utilities in 1991, including fuel oil and gas, electricity, and water and sewerage, were about 40 per cent of total expenses. Utilities can be considered for the most part private goods collectively supplied; most of the expense would be paid for by the units if they were separately metered. It is recognized that this joint consumption incurs more usage than separately paid-for usage and, if the system were being built today, separate meters would be installed and only utilities for the common areas would be an Association expense, although buying in bulk does reduce the total outlay, making up for some of the added use due to common pooling.

'Maintenance' mainly involves the physical plant, such as the air conditioning and heating machinery. The Association formerly paid for repairs, and now has a maintenance contract. Each year, the Association may choose to be taxed either on its total income as a corporation or only on its interest income, the calculations as to which is lower being left to the accounting firm which also handles the audit. Most of the expense items are in effect maintenance items. The costs of maintaining the community goods are mostly mandated once the decision has been made to supply them. The Board's choice consists of how much maintenance to provide and by whom it should be carried out. The truly discretionary items are only a small part of the budget. These include recreation, the newsletter and some of the landscaping. Occasionally some facilities are upgraded; an example is new, larger mailboxes installed in 1991.

The Board does make the important decision of choosing the managing company and the method of maintenance, such as obtaining a maintenance contract rather than fixing the equipment *ad hoc*, which involves a great deal of research (Kass, 1991a). Some maintenance also has discretionary features, such as the choice of the color and type of paint when the contractors are hired for the exterior work every six years or so. For the most part, the decisions of the Board concern the quality of maintenance and the size of the reserve fund rather than which public goods to provide.

The Briarcrest Condominium

As a condominium approximately equal in size to Fort Ellsworth, the Briarcrest Condominium in the North Hollywood section of Los Angeles

City offers a comparative case. The Briarcrest Homeowners Association is a non-profit mutual benefit corporation, with 160 units in two buildings. Originally established in 1979, the condominium in 1988 converted from an apartment cooperative to a home owners association (Herbert J. Strickstein Law Corporation, 1986). As in Fort Ellsworth, each unit pays an assessment in proportion to its percentage interest in the common area. The Board may require additional assessments if needed.

The association has a reserve fund, required by California law. The California Civil Code also requires that community associations distribute a 'reserve study' to their members along with the budget, making an analysis of future maintenance an integral part of the budgeting process, but the law does not mandate any specific reserve requirement (Association Reserves, 1990). Companies have been set up that analyze and calculate the needed reserves. Association Reserves, Inc., in California, offered Briarcrest HOA a reserve study bid for about $1000.

The Briarcrest goods include a swimming pool and jacuzzi, a sauna, billiard tables, a gym, recreation room and laundry facilities. The budget of Briarcrest in 1991, with $371 700 in expenses, was just about equal to that of Fort Ellsworth ($371 301). A major difference in the budget items is that the heating and air conditioning are individually metered at Briarcrest and there is a higher-cost physical plant at Fort Ellsworth probably due to the colder weather in Virginia. Briarcrest has more insurance, including earthquake coverage, and obtains more non-assessment income, including a $100 move-in fee for new residents and income from the laundry operation. When the differences in utilities are factored in, the overall goods provided in both and the overall expenses are not far apart. One other difference is of interest. Whereas the entrances of the Fort Ellsworth buildings are utilitarian, the two large buildings at Briarcrest have luxurious front lobbies, with furniture, fountains, art and sculptures. According to former board member Beatrice Pearlstein, the Board maintains a fine appearance because it is thought to create a good impression, which is reflected in the property value (Pearlstein, 1991).

The two condominiums are remarkably similar in their total expenses, bylaws and operations. Having a similar number of units and facilities, the outcomes in terms of the expense level show that the process of generating the rents to pay for the collective goods functions in a similar way in both communities.

Analysis of Fort Ellsworth's finance

The annual assessment of the condominium units is economically the equivalent of the Arden leasehold payment. These are but different vehicles for the payment of site rent. The condominium fee is based on a unit's percentage interest, approximately proportional to its share of the site value. Any improvement value added by an owner to his unit does not affect the fee. The effect is that, if expenditures are made because they are perceived to add value to the condominium as a whole, a fee based on a percentage interest in the whole is a rent paid for the value of being located in the site, similar to the site rent paid at Arden.

Thus the same conclusions as derived from the Arden case apply to the Fort Ellsworth Condominium, rejecting the hypothesis that incentives for personal gain do not induce private agents to provide the collective goods that the people in a service domain effectively demand. Regarding the other hypotheses, as discussed above, the goods are territorial, hence exclusive. The facilities enhance the rental value of the units, and the assessments for the public goods at Fort Ellsworth have a direct relation to the site rents; the separation of the site and improvement values is accomplished by having a fixed percentage interest for each unit. The demand for the goods is revealed by the purchase of units and the willingness to pay the association fees. The need to pay the fee and the closeness and relative seclusion of the facilities eliminate free-riders.

The assessment and lease payments are like charges for a utility. The association or land trust provides a flow of services, like a utility providing a flow of water, gas or electricity. The consumer pays a periodic utility charge. In contrast, governments typically do not charge consumers directly for their governance, but impose arbitrary costs on private transactions, such as exchanging labor for cash and cash for goods, transactions utterly unconnected with the government civic goods. The property tax is partly related to the goods, but the portion that falls on improvements is again a tax on production unrelated to a city's provision of goods, or bads.

Condominiums do not require public-sector support; they are funded internally. There are legal requirements for proper records, access to the accounts and so on, imposed by governments, but it is not evident that these are necessary for the survival of condominiums. There are cases where the unit owners have faced unexpected costs and unresponsive boards but, as these stories become publicized, the bylaws evolve protectionary clauses for the owners. Legal experts are hired to examine the association documents. A 'consumer's guide' to condominiums, rating various communities, could help guide prospective buyers. Finally, such legal provisions will not prevent the wasteful spending of the association funds; vigilance and constitutional constraints are needed in any governance with principles and agents and asset-specific investments.

Some of the laws regarding condominiums are neither interventions nor subsidies but determine the boundaries of property rights, which some level of governance would do in any case. Examples include provisions for liens on unpaid assessments. Other laws do intervene in voluntary contracts. For example, the Virginia Condominium Act (1991) limits the amount of charges for rules violations to 50 dollars for a single offense or ten dollars per diem for continuing offenses.[2] A freely contractual community would be able to determine its own penalties, and its bylaws could set maximums that would safeguard the owners from arbitrary assessments. Another limitation of the provision of goods at a condominium is that expenditures that replace those provided by the local government do not entitle the condominium to tax rebates. Some police protection, for example, such as patrol and surveillance, could be provided at the condominium level. If the cost were rebated up to some upper limit from taxes paid to the city, the lower net cost would induce more private provision of such services. Another imposed cost is the increased property tax that is paid when the community makes any net improvements to its common facilities that result in increased property values.

Fort Ellsworth and Briarcrest are both large apartment buildings, but the condominium form of ownership can be applied to any type of property, including single-family homes and shopping centers. Besides land leasing and condominiums, another common type of contractual community is the home owners' association, which is examined in the next chapter.

Notes

1. City of Alexandria Code section 11–50 (b) (2).
2. Article 3, Section 55–79.90.

12 Garden city of today: the Reston Association

Can there be a city with contractual governance? The two previous case studies were a village and a condominium unit, each with about 500 persons. While these demonstrate the feasibility of the voluntary provision of civic goods, it could be argued that what is feasible for a small community is not workable for a large one. Reston offers a test case for this proposition. It is also an example of market correction: even when an entrepreneur makes an error and produces goods not wanted by the market, the project does not necessarily fail. A third element of the Reston case is the financing of its civic goods by equal assessments rather than according to site values. Does it make any difference?

The hypothesis

The same hypothesis is used as for Fort Ellsworth: *Incentives for personal gain do not induce private agents to provide the public goods that the people in a service domain effectively demand, because there is no way to induce individual users to each pay for a portion of a good so that its total amount is paid for.* Since Reston is the size of a small city, a second hypothesis is that *a contractual community association does not provide as abundant a level of desired civic goods, either in quantity or in quality, as a similar sovereign government would.* As with Arden and Fort Ellsworth, the other hypotheses which will be tested are: (1) the public goods produced by Reston are non-excludable; (2) the public goods do not increase the site values and rents; (3) the funding for the public goods has little relation to the site rents; (4) the demand for the public goods cannot be truthfully revealed; (5) free riders prevent the provision of the goods; (6) the provision of the goods requires public-sector support; and (7) the separation of the site and improvement values is impractical.

General description

Located in Fairfax County, northern Virginia, Reston is a planned community with commercial areas and a home owners' association of 56 000 persons and 7400 acres (11.56 square miles) of land. Unlike a condominium, the common property is owned by the association rather than directly by the owners as percentage interests. The 18 000 residential units (another 2000 are planned) have an assessed valuation of $3.37 billion. About 40 per cent of the land is open space available to the Reston Association members. The capital assets of the community total $15 million, with an annual budget of some $6.5 million (Cleveland, 1989, p. 7; *Report*, 1988; Redding, 1992). Total development costs at completion are expected to be $39 billion (Planned Communities, 1992). Commercial sites, not part of the residential associa-tion, encompass some 2 100 firms with 34 500 jobs. The completion of the development is anticipated to take place during the mid-1990s, with 62 000 residents and 50 000 jobs ('Transportation', 1991).

Founded by Robert E. Simon, Jr., the community features recreational facilities, including 1045 acres of open space, an athletics field, exercise trail, 50 miles of pathways, 17 swimming pools, four lakes, landscaped grounds, 44 tennis courts, a 70-acre nature center and a community center for cultural, civic, educational, social and recreational events. Reston was named after Simon's initials plus the ending 'ton' for 'town', which in Old English meant a group of houses. The residential community is divided among seven 'village' centers: Lake Anne, Hunters Woods, Tall Oaks, South Lakes, Dogwood, North Hills and North Point. Each contains retail stores and the Town Center has offices and other enterprises as well. The US Geological Survey is headquartered at Reston, and there has been a boom in high-technology firms locating at the Town Center, taking advantage both of the workforce and amenities of Reston and the proximity to the Dulles International Airport.

Reston was planned to include a variety of housing styles and types. Single-family houses have a median price of $325 000; those facing a lake are priced at $500 000 and up. Houses are also available in the $150 000 range and a few sell for about $1 million. The median price for townhouses is $150 000, lakeside properties selling for $275 000 or more. Condominium units range from $70 000 to $130 000 or higher. Rental condominium units cost $600 to $750 per month, with townhouses ranging from $750 to $1000 and single-family houses $1200 to $1500 *(Reston Handbook,* 1991). The fact that lakeside lots have a price premium demonstrates the capitalization of this good in site value.

A community with a mission

Like Walt Disney World and Arden, Reston is an intentional community: the entrepreneur had a mission. Simon had a social vision as well, a 'commit-ment to reorder the composition and quality of the living environment'. Before the plan, there was a concept, or what Simon called a 'program' (Grubisich and McCandless, 1985, p. 33). Simon's idea was a place where people could work where they lived and where urban life coexists with

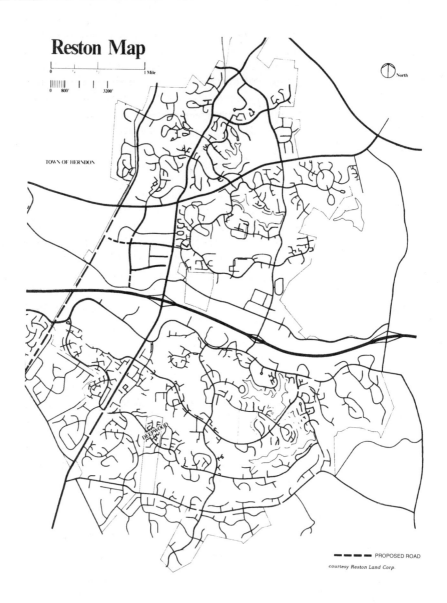

Map of Reston, reproduced from *Reston Handbook*, (1991) pp. 32–33, courtesy of Reston Land Corporation.

countryside, 'trails leading from apartments to glades of trees' (p. 13), just as Ebenezer Howard dreamed of in his 'garden city'.

Simon's mission encompassed seven goals: (1) a wide range of recreational and cultural services; (2) the ability of a resident family to upgrade dwelling quality within Reston, there being a wide range of housing styles and prices, providing a varied community; (3) the individual resident as the focal point of planning, taking precedence over large-scale concepts; (4) the ability to both live and work in Reston; (5) the availability of the non-residential goods and services – commercial, cultural, recreational – when the first residents settle; (6) structural and natural beauty, necessary for a good life; (7) that Reston be a financial success (Grubisich and McCandless, 1985, pp. 38–9).

The history of Reston

Reston's development demonstrates several principles regarding the private production of civic goods. First, market incentives do not necessarily induce a mix of goods that meets the demand. But, second, when it does not, the market can correct the error. Third, a failing enterprise can be replaced without eliminating the civic goods it has produced and planned for. Entrepreneurial failure (which is distinct from market failure) is not necessarily permanent or fatal. In contrast, when government expenditures do not meet the desires of the target population, a means of correction may not exist, even when one set of governing agents is replaced by another.

Simon's father, Robert Simon, Sr., was the head of a company which owned several real estate properties in Manhattan. In 1928, Simon Sr. had participated in financing the 'new town' of Radburn, New Jersey, America's first 'garden city', designed by Clarence Stein. Simon Jr. had witnessed its creation and had even helped name some of the streets. When Robert Sr. died in 1935, his son joined the family real estate firm, the Hercer Corporation, and was soon running it (Grubisich and McCandless, 1985, p. 33). The Simon properties, including Carnegie Hall, were clustered in 57th street, Manhattan, where art galleries coexisted with shops and restaurants and, above them, apartments. In 1945, the Simon family moved to the planned community of Levittown, Long Island. Robert Simon learned that country life had its inconveniences, such as having to join a club for recreation facilities, involving travelling long distances. Social life was restricted to weekends. After a long journey from work, it was late and he was tired. During the 1950s, Simon became involved in shopping centers, which he noticed involved travelling long distances and were poorly integrated into their neighborhoods (Grubisich and McCandless, 1985, p. 34; Netherton, 1989, pp. 47–8).

To put all these concepts together would require building a new community in which residences, work, recreation and shopping would be designed as a new 'program' for urban living, with Radburn as a smaller-scale model (p. 35). Funding became available when New York City bought Carnegie Hall for $5 million to preserve it as a landmark. Simon received an offer to buy the Sunset Hills Farm, 6 750 acres in Fairfax County, which he visited, 'fell in love with' and purchased for $13.15 million from Lefcourt Realty Corporation (Grubisich and McCandless, 1985, pp. 35, 109; Netherton, 1989, p. 48). Additional acreage was purchased later. According to Glenn Saunders (1991), Simon's project engineer, Simon wanted to prove that private enterprise could create and run a new town. A key asset of the site was that it was a large block of undeveloped land within the metropolitan area's 'next growth belt' (p. 1). The Dulles airport was projected to be a major future employer and the expected 'outer circumference highway' was expected to be built just west of Reston.

Reston illustrates another case where government policy was prohibitory to the private provision of civic goods, which could only take place if restrictions were removed. The development of the Reston plan required a change in the zoning ordinances. A plan for 13 neighborhoods was submitted to Fairfax County officials in September 1961 and met with opposition. The plan attempted to create residential clusters in conformity with the existing zoning and building codes; townhouses were fitted into 'arbitrary and awkward cul-de-sacs'. Simon's vision required a less restrictive land-use ordinance. Indeed, to Simon, standard zoning laws were responsible for, as he put it, 'the diffusion of our communities into separate, unrelated hunks without focus, identity or community life' (Grubisich and McCandless, 1985, p. 41). Simon deplored what he felt was a waste of land in typical suburban developments.

Simon hired a New York planning and architectural firm, Whittlesey & Conklin, to help redo the master plan. According to Glenn Saunders, the Simon team decided 'to plan Reston exactly the way we wanted it to be, as if there were no zoning ordinances at all'. After obtaining agreement from the county staff, they would then create the ordinances to permit it (Grubisich and McCandless, 1985, p. 43). The result was a zoning innovation called 'residential planned community' (RPC) (changed to Planned Residential Community (PRC) in 1978), using 'density zoning' that left the overall density the same as with traditional zoning, but with heterogeneous density within the area (Netherton, 1989, p. 52; 'Reston', 1970, p. 7; Yaremchuk, 1968, p. 1).

Simon opposed the establishment of a sovereign town because it would lead to the taxation of businesses, and industry was vital to the mixed-use plan. The fact that Reston does not have a town status has helped to attract enterprises to Reston. However, the commercial areas could have been included in the association without reducing enterprise if the assessments were based on the land rent, in accord with the analysis of Chapter 3. Such funding would have placed the association on a firmer financial basis, avoiding some problems that would develop years later, as discussed below. Columbia, Maryland, a similar development, did include the commercial land in the community association.

According to E.A. Prichard (1992), author of the Reston governing documents, the decision to have one flat fee paid by all owners of residences in Reston was made early, before any residents moved in. It was a unanimous decision by the development team, including Simon. The Simon team was thinking that the county would be providing most public services, with the Reston association supplementing them with parks and recreation. Thus the association fee was regarded not as a type of tax but as admission to the goods. They also wanted to have an assessment limit. There was little analysis done on the option of *ad valorem* assessments. The decision to have a flat fee would eventually lead to a funding controversy when the swimming pools were switched in 1991 from user fees to funding under the assessments.

Fairfax County adopted the RPC ordinance in 18 July 1962, but reduced the land allotted to industry from 1152 to 914 acres and set an overall density limit of 11 persons per acre. The county also rejected the inclusion of industry within the village centers as incompatible with residential usage (Grubisich and McCandless, 1985, pp. 42, 44; Netherton, 1989, pp. 50–2; 'Chronology', 1987, p. 1). Hence the market process was not permitted full effect. The seven villages would have individual characters determined in part by their topography ('Economic Basis', 1962, p. 4). There would be community facilities in the town center and in each neighborhood. Many of the streams and much of the ground cover would be kept in their natural condition (p. 9). The residential areas would be composed of 15 per cent apartments, 70 per cent townhouses, and 15 per cent single-family detached houses (Moore, 1991, p. 20).

The social development of Reston

Reston's allocation of land for churches, schools, libraries and other complementary facilities set it apart from the usual practice of developers then to disregard such facilities, shifting the problem and costs to future residents and governments, which often find it difficult and expensive to obtain the sites (Netherton, 1989, p. 58). Simon also provided initial funds and quarters at low rent to the Lake Anne Nursery School and Kindergarten (LANK) (p. 74).

The Reston community was officially dedicated on 21 May 1966 (Netherton, 1989, p. 78). The first Reston residents were aware that Reston was an experimental new concept, and they liked taking part in the venture. One couple interviewed, the Gradys, said they felt like pioneers and eagerly attended the community meetings (McWhirt, 1990, p. 13). This sentiment is an example of the Smithian sympathy, discussed in Chapter 7, which has been a key element in maintaining private communities such as Reston, Arden and Fort Ellsworth. The anthropologist Margaret Mead visited Reston in 1973 and expressed the view that new towns were valuable for the chance they provided to try out new approaches and accommodate different life-styles; she also noted the value of having housing available for three genera-tions of families (Netherton, 1989, p. 98).

Later, after Simon was replaced, a new organization, the Common Ground Foundation, was started by Embry Rucker, rector of the Episcopelian Con-gregation at Reston. The group built a coffee house, started a local bus service, organized a babysitting referral, provided daycare service and set up a job search service. Community organizations begun by the residents in-cluded the Reston Players, a community newspaper, *The Reston Times*, the Reston Choral and the Greater Reston Arts Center (Grubisich and McCandless, 1985, p. 67; Halligan, 1990, p. 1). The Reston Interfaith Housing Corpora-tion aids low-income tenants.

Developing the physical goods

As Heath and MacCallum noted, much of the profit from real estate develop-ment consists in the creation of land values. The construction often takes place in stages, sales of one set of units providing cash flow for the next set. As Netherton (1989, p. 52) put it, in Reston 'the land itself became a "cash crop"'.

In principal–agent theory, the owner of a project would want those with key responsibility to also have an interest in the value of the project. Simon in fact provided his top executives in the project with the right to an equity participation in the development. Reston was a town financed entirely by an entrepreneur, with no government financing. 'The flexibility of private fi-nancing allowed Reston ultimately to succeed while most of the federally supported new towns elsewhere in the country were dying because of botched strategies or inadequate funding' (Grubisich and McCandless, 1985, p. 45). Each village was to have its own theme, such as boating at Lake Ann, horse riding at Hunters Wood (extending to street names such as Trotter Lane). This is a type of product differentiation, which induces greater demand as a result of the increase in choices, and is an application of the Tiebout theory of 'voting with your feet' in the selection of a community, but in this case it was the developer himself creating the choices within a development.

The Reston civic structure consists of several levels of decentralization: the town is divided into villages, and the villages into condominiums and clusters of townhouses. Single-family houses do not have a cluster organization. Just as the villages had individual identities, so did the clusters. The three clusters at Lake Anne had what Simon called 'vanilla, chocolate and strawberry' flavors of housing styles. Waterview has 90 lakeside townhouses with pastel hues, suggesting a French fishing village. Hickory Cluster's 90 townhouses have bold color-accented panels and had a contemporary look. Chimney House, 47 townhouses with gothic crenelations, makes yet another urban statement.

The average prices were higher than originally proposed because the architects, given a free hand, designed 37 different floor plans requiring non-standard materials. Simon insisted on high quality even when faced with a shortage of funding (Grubisich and McCandless, 1985, p. 49). An acquaintance of Simon's remarked that Reston was Simon's 'try for greatness' (p. 50). The gratification of the entrepreneur's ego is a factor in such private provision of civic goods, in addition to the commercial gain, but it is self-sustaining only if it meets Simon's seventh goal – financial success. Simon hoped that, if he first built quality housing and environments, the concept would create its own market (Netherton, 1989, p. 63); he could build the lower-priced housing later. But in the market place, according to sales manager Chuck Veatch, Reston was a 'hard sell' (Grubisich and McCandless, 1985, pp. 50–51).

A Louis Harris Survey listed as problems that Reston was isolated, too expensive, too contemporary and had a liberal image in a conservative region (Grubisich and McCandless, 1985, p. 51). Veatch felt the problem was not the concept but the timing: by the late 1970s, people wanted the community services offered by Reston. In the second development, Hunters Woods, the single-family homes sold moderately well but, with two developments, Simon's funds were being depleted.

Development by Gulf and Mobil

Needing cash, Simon obtained a $15 million loan in February 1964 from the Morgan Guarantee Trust Company, guaranteed by Gulf Oil, which obtained a first mortgage as collateral. The Gulf chairman then sent controller William L. Henry to Reston in early 1966. Henry concluded that the project could succeed, but that Simon needed help. Henry and a Gulf Comptroller, Glenn Westman, members of Simon's board of directors, came to believe that Simon would not be able to fulfil his goals, with his lack of marketing, poor forecasting and too heavy reliance on the planners and architects (Grubisich and McCandless, 1985, p. 81). On 28 September 1967, Gulf officials assumed operation of the project under the subsidiary Gulf Reston, Inc.

After Gulf took over, the Reston boom began. The population rose from 1291 in 1967 to 11 500 residents in 1970 ('Chronology', 1987, p. 2). Jim Todd, president of Mobil Land Corporation, which later owned the Reston Land Corporation, stated that, 'had it not been for Gulf and Mobil, Reston would have gone down the tubes and been a big subdivision. Corporate money has made Reston the beautiful place that it is' (Netherton, 1981, p. 1). Under Francis Steinbauer, president of Reston Land Corporation, Gulf tried to preserve the basic Simon plan while modifying it to address the 'economic logics' so that it could survive (p. 7). Gulf's takeover was a market correction to that of too-idealistic Simon. Profit and loss signal the success of market processes, whereas political processes, able to use coercion to obtain their funds, can perpetuate projects indefinitely.

Simon had wanted to start the town center even if there were no good market for it, while Gulf instead wanted to meet whatever market was already there (Netherton, 1981, p. 31). Because of their different approaches, Simon was asked to resign. He refused, and was fired on 26 October (Grubisich and McCandless, 1985, p. 82; Netherton, 1989, p. 194). In November 1967, some of the stunned activist residents formed the Reston Community Association (RCA), which had a thousand members within a few months. As theorized in Chapter 7, free-riders are not an obstacle when residents are sufficiently aroused. The RCA became a residents' lobby which sought to preserve the Simon plan and protect the interests of the residents.

In 1963, Simon had created separate home owners' associations for the areas north and south of the Dulles access road. A study by Gulf Reston conducted by consultants Booz-Allen and Hamilton concluded that two associations were more costly than one, and split the town. The two HOAs were consolidated into the Reston Home Owners Association (RHOA) in 1970 (Grubisich and McCandless, 1985, p. 60), which changed its name to the Reston Association (RA) in 1987. Reston would henceforth be governed at the town rather than village level. Perhaps some type of federative system which left much of the decision making at the village level as in Columbia, Maryland, could have preserved the village HOAs, leaving the provision of services with larger economies of scale to the Reston Association.

In 1975, with losses again at Reston during a recession, the Gulf company decided to leave the real estate business and sell Reston's undeveloped land to a buyer committed to the Reston concept. Mobil Oil in 1975 had investigated Reston as a site for a new headquarters, but did not wish to locate on a site owned by a rival. As it turned out, Gulf sold the 3700 acres of undeveloped land to Mobil in July 1978 for $31 million, $8278 per acre. A condition of the sale was that Mobil carry out the master plan (Grubisich and McCandless, 1985, pp. 94, 112).

Mobil formed the subsidiary company, the Reston Land Corporation (RLC). Its managers determined that its best strategy was to concentrate on community-wide development of the 'amenities package', marketing and land sales, leaving the home building and center development to other firms (Netherton, 1989, p. 120). Mobil bought in just when an industrial boom was about to begin at Reston, sparked by the Dulles Toll Road, with ramps for local traffic. Mobil's sale of the land, especially to the Sperry firm, helped start a high-tech rush of business to Reston. Simon's vision of a residential–industrial mix had come true (Cirillo, 1991, pp. 55–6; Grubisich and McCandless, 1985, p. 95).

In 1985, the residents obtained control of the Reston Home Owners Association. The Documents Review Committee, which revised the RHOA charter, avoided broadening the association's scope of authority, remaining more like a land-management organization than a sovereign town (Grubisich and McCandless, 1985, p. 68). During the late 1980s, the Town Center came to fruition as Reston's urban commercial core, with the density of a downtown area – 'a taste of 57th Street in western Fairfax County' (Grubisich and McCandless, 1985, p. 108). As of 1988 there were over 1400 companies in Reston, employing 31 000 persons. Among the attractions that company officials speak of are the amenities of Reston and the 'talented work force' (Cleveland, 1989, p. 9), which itself has been attracted by the Reston civic goods, a compounding of public-good complementarities.

Reston's legal status

The Reston Association is tax-exempt under the 501(c) provision of the US internal revenue code. In contrast to HOAs, condominiums generally cannot file as tax-exempt because their common areas are legally owned by the unit owners, not by the association itself, although their income related to the operation of community property can be tax-exempt.

Reston is a not-for-profit non-stock Virginia corporation. In Virginia, the codes governing home owners associations are the Non-Stock Corporation Act (NSCA) (section 13.1-801) and the Horizontal Property Act (Chapter 4.1 of Title 55).

Under a Fairfax County law passed in 1985, the open space owned by a residential association is assessed at zero, paying no property tax. Fairfax County officials recognize that an 'Individual property owner's tax assessments, on the other hand, should reflect the value of the common area' (*Fairfax County Homeowners Association Manual*, 1990, p. 194). The Fairfax County real estate tax rate in 1990 was $1.11 per $100 of assessed value (which is supposedly based on the market value). Residential real estate in Reston is taxed an additional $0.06 per $100 of assessed value to pay for the Reston Community Center (*Reston Handbook*, 1991, p. 23). Residential associations pay a personal property tax on their equipment, as well as a county utility tax.

A study conducted by Booz-Allen and Hamilton in 1972 found that revenues from Reston to Fairfax County exceeded expenditures on Reston by the county by $1.5 million, with a projection to $16 million in 1980 (Netherton, 1989, p. 98). This suggests that, unless there are substantial economies of scale, some of the services such as police protection and school run by the county could be transferred to and fully funded by Reston residents.

The Reston governing documents

The Deed of Dedication of Reston, also known as the Reston Deed or the 'Protective Covenants', is the legal basis for the community. It is incorporated into the deed of each residential lot. The 'User's Guide to the Governing Documents' (1987) states that 'the Deed is like a constitution' (p. 1). The deed is also the 'enabling document' for the Cluster Associations in Reston.

All residential property owners and residents of Reston are members of Reston Association (RA). The Deed provides a legal contract governing a residential lot at Reston. The Board of Directors has nine members, seven elected to staggered three-year terms. The Reston Land Corporation will be represented on the Board by a director until the year 2000, providing a monitoring function. The owners of apartment buildings also appoint a director. The three main functions of RA are the operation of the open space and facilities, the administration of the covenants, and the preservation of the architecture through its appointed Design Review Board. The members have the right to vote, the right to use the common areas, the responsibility to comply with the covenants and rules, and the obligation to pay assessments.

Since it has no percentage interests, the voting in a HOA is more flexible than in a condominium. In Reston, owners have one vote per lot and unit residents have one vote per unit (owner-occupants thus have two votes). Tenants may vote only for directors ('Protective Covenants', 1987). The members of the Design Review Board (DRB) are appointed equally by the Board of Directors and the Developer. The DRB is endowed with the power to render decisions regarding the design covenants, but the enforcement is left to the Board of Directors.

An owner covenants to pay assessments to the Association regardless of his usage of the common areas. *This contractual obligation, tied to the site, eliminates the free-rider problem in the provision of collective goods by the association.* The Reston constitution sets a maximum assessment for a lot, either one-half per cent of its assessed valuation by Fairfax County or a dollar amount which increases each year by the consumer price index ($315 for 1991), whichever is less, unless the Category A members vote to waive it.

The objectives of the Design Covenants are 'To promote those qualities in the environment which bring value to the Property' and to foster its attractiveness and utility. Among the standards the DRB applies are harmony among the exteriors of buildings and the quality of improvements. Structures require prior approval. A Cluster Association is incorporated as a non-stock membership corporation to own and manage the Cluster Common Area and promote its interests. Its members include the owners of lots and may include others as specified by the articles of incorporation (p. 11). A Cluster may fix its assessments 'on a fair and equitable basis' (p. 12), which does not exclude an *ad valorem* rate.

The Reston Bylaws govern its operation. Because of Reston's size, voting is generally conducted not at the meetings but in referenda, with a quorum of 10 per cent except on non-binding matters, which have no quorum (p. 17). The directors are not to receive any compensation (p. 19). The Bylaws mandate an annual capital and operating budget, an adequate level of reserves, adequate insurance and the prior approval of members for major improvements (p. 20), safeguards for the site-specific investments.

The 'Basis for Assessments' is 'an equal amount for each Apartment Unit or Lot'. Certain owners, such as those qualifying for real estate tax reductions, may be granted a reduction in the Assessment. Robert Simon, in deriving the idea for a garden city in part from Ebenezer Howard and his followers, did not take up one of the foundations of his concept, its financing. Howard (1965 [1902], p. 58) had written, 'Its entire revenue is derived from rents.' The provision for equal payment treats Reston like a club in which members have an equal benefit, but this ignores the capitalization of the civic goods in land value and rent, as evidenced by the greater value of lakeside lots. The disregard of capitalization may not have been significant earlier, when fees were lower, but, with the large recent increase in assessments, the financing of the budget has become contentious, as discussed below. Nevertheless, such an equal assessment is still closer to a payment of site rent than is a payment based on the value of the entire property, since the equal payment is independent of any improvements made by the owner. Hence it amounts to an uneven collection of the site rent generated by the association's territorial public goods.

The covenants

The protective covenants of Reston are a contractual alternative to zoning and land-use laws. The deed covenants also mandate the maintenance of the commonly owned sites. An Architectural Board of Review examines proposed alterations to property to enforce the covenants and preserve the attractive appearance of the community (Netherton, 1989, p. 52). The strictness of the architectural covenants is a recurrent issue in Reston. For example, at the 26 September 1991 Board meeting, members complained about legal actions taken against members, which could have been avoided by issuing advisories. A public hearing was authorized to investigate the covenants enforcement.

The Reston Association publishes a user guide, *Use Covenants and Procedures* (1988), which explains that Restonians 'live together under the terms of an agreement' (p. 1). The Use Covenants govern eight major areas: vegetation, refuse, boats, vehicles, utility lines, restoration of buildings, the maintenance of improvements and the failure to maintain one's property. Another user guide is the *Design Guidelines and Design Review Process* (1990). Owners who wish to change the external appearance of their property must obtain prior approval from the Design Review Board. One reason given for this process is to 'Uphold property values for all residents' (p. v). The design criteria described by the guide include the harmony of the community architecture, impact on neighbors, workmanship, safety and security. The guide specifies detailed instructions regarding various types of improvements. It also has a section on redevelopment, which is subject to DRB review.

The governance of Reston

As is usual for contractual communities, the developer at first had control over the governance, protecting its interest, and gradually let the Reston Home Owners Association (RHOA) assume greater control by expanding its share of the board of directors. In 1980, a referendum on changing the governance to a municipal government rejected the proposal; residents were satisfied with the association governance and were wary of the higher taxes that a sovereign government could impose (Netherton, 1989, p. 142). The idea keeps recurring, however. In November 1987, 150 Reston residents met at the first Reston Forum to consider alternative forms of governance (*Report*, 1988). They established a Governance Task Force to study three alternatives: a tax district, incorporation as a town, and city status. Reston Association would still continue to exist, enforcing some of its covenants with the alternative plans. The study did not lead to any action, since there was little support for any change.

There would be a tax advantage in becoming a sovereign agency. The Reston assessments are not deductible against income taxes. Tax deductions would reduce the costs to home owners by 34 per cent or more. A sovereign government could also tax businesses. A sovereign government would also provide more local control over some services, such as street lighting. However, there would be less local control over park and recreational facilities since, under a sovereign government, the deed restrictions affecting their use, such as public access, could be unenforceable; these amenities would be open to anyone in the county. A tax district would turn over control of the goods and services at Reston to the Fairfax County Board of Supervisors.

The desire of Restonians for more autonomy could be accomplished without a change of the association structure by a Walt Disney World-style autonomous district in which service would be transferred to Reston at its request, and the costs would be deducted from the taxes paid by the Reston property owners. There is little incentive to the county officials to grant such autonomy, since they receive a net gain from Reston's taxpayers.

Reston's civic goods

The Town Center is not part of the residential association but provides community amenities. Aside from the commercial enterprises, the Town Center has become a focus of social life, featuring holiday festivals, weekend and evening concerts, ice skating and merchant promotions. Fountain Square is a popular gathering place; perched at the top of the fountain is a statue of Mercury or Hermes, the god of commerce. A telephone recording provides a schedule of events. (There is an annual Reston festival sponsored by the Reston Community Association.)

The 1045 acres of Reston Association's open space include woodland, trails, a linear park with jogging and horse trails, four lakes, ponds, rental garden plots, two golf courses, football and baseball playing fields, 'tot lots' for infants, tennis courts, 16 swimming pools and two warm-water spas. The lakes provide fishing as well as boating. This richness of recreation and accessible nature preserves exceeds that of typical city governments such as the nearby towns of Herndon or Vienna in Fairfax County. The second hypothesis, that *a contractual community association does not provide as abundant a level of desired civic goods, either in quantity or in quality, as a similar sovereign government would*, is therefore rejected.

The high-density clusters at Reston made the Reston Internal Bus System (RIBS), with an express service to Metro stations, economically feasible. Usually, single-family developments on typical quarter-acre lots are not dense enough to pay for a self-financing transit system (Harris, 1991). At the same time, the Reston plan has reduced external transportation needs; some

9000 persons both live and work in Reston. The mixed-use nature of Reston has reduced the number of trips into and out of the community by 25 per cent. A Reston Town Center transportation management program, LINK, provides telephone information to Reston residents and workers on various transit options, including car pools. The 50 miles of paved walking and bicycle paths also reduce the number of car trips within Reston. Though most of the streets in Reston were constructed privately by the developers, most recently by the Reston Land Corporation, the roads and streets are maintained by the Virginia Department of Transportation. Some of the streets in Reston remain private, for example those within cluster and commercial areas. The residential private roads are maintained by the cluster or condominium associations ('Transportation', 1991).

Some historical and archeological artifacts in the area were preserved by the development. Brown's Chapel, dating from the late 1800s, was moved to the Lake Anne Village Center in 1968. The building is maintained by the Reston Association. Reston has won awards for historical preservation. The preservation effort has been part of the conservation goals of the development, which employed a professional forester to save trees, plant new ones and control soil erosion (Erten, 1991).

The recreational facilities and parks at Reston, with 20 acres per 1000 persons, have a higher standard than the National Recreational Association's standard of 9.7 acres per 1000 persons (Alhosain and Aldeaijy, 1991, p. 69). The association complements the nature preserves with information, such as the *Twin Branches Nature Trail* booklet for a self-guided hike, including a map and illustrations of the wildlife. Motor vehicles other than for Association use are prohibited on the commons. The greenery of Reston is an amenity not only to the members of the residential association but also to the businesses located in the community. This attraction has been a factor in drawing enterprises to Reston, which in turn brings about the urban/rural mix that was desired. George Eckert, of Tandem Computers headquartered in Reston, expressed the appeal to his employees as including 'the general environmental impact' as well as the nearby recreational opportunities, such as jogging paths (Grubisich and McCandless, 1985, p. 14).

The master plan itself is a collective good. In a typical suburban development, the residents have no assurance that the features that make their neighborhood attractive will remain; zoning can be changed at any time or developments can take place that are not anticipated. The Reston master plan removes this uncertainty by making such assurance a constitutional provision which preceded the development. The residents have known where the open space, residences and industry would be located, and residents have indicated an appreciation of this assurance (Grubisich and McCandless, 1985, p. 14).

The artistic qualities that Simon emphasized for Reston are another element of its civic goods. Examples include fountains, sculptures and the street furniture. An example is a large fountain in Washington Plaza whose 'sprays of water are forced out of different openings to create a fascinating design of their own in the sunlight'. This and other artworks in that plaza were designed by well-known artists. Even the light fixtures there are works of art; one type used throughout Lake Anne Village Center uses light bulbs enclosed in a clear covering, a design created by Seymour Evans Association (Netherton, 1989, p. 6). This public good characteristic, the fancy street lights, exceeds that of typical city or county fixtures.

Another element in creating an attractive environment was the decision to put utilities underground (Netherton, 1989, p. 54). Simon also established a cable system with the cables underground; Warner Cable Television purchased the system in 1972 (p. 92). Another threat of visual ugliness was the plan by the Virginia Electric Power Company to bisect Reston with a high voltage overhead transmission line, with 110-foot high towers. The line was relocated to the western edge of Reston with a gift of land by RLC for the transmission and a substation (p. 126).

Volunteer organizations

As at Arden, many Restonians have chosen to be voluntary drivers instead of free-riders and have organized numerous civic organizations as well, as 22 churches. Reston Interfaith, sponsored by religious organizations, offers aid to the poor, including food, clothing, counseling and transportation aid. Interfaith operates the Embry Rucker Shelter for the Homeless and a Transitional Housing Program. The Laurel Learning Center offers low-cost child care ('Community Services', 1991). Reston Interfaith owns five townhouses that are made available to its low-income aid recipients (Keum, 1991, p. 88).

Another charitable group is F.I.S.H. (Friendly Instant Sympathetic Help), which provides emergency aid such as financing, furniture and transportation. It serves the Reston–Herndon area. The Fellowship Square Foundation owns the Fellowship House buildings, which offer apartments for the aged and handicapped. Other facilities for the elderly include Tall Oaks Fellowship House, offering supervised housing; Thorcau Place, a condominium for those aged over 55; and the FASTRAN transportation aid ('Community Services', 1991).

As discussed above, the Reston Community Association (RCA) was formed to ensure that developers subsequent to Simon adhered to the original plan. On 20 January 1992, its directors voted to change the name to the Reston Citizens Association ('RCA changes name', 1992). Now that the membership controls the policy making in RA, the original goal is no longer necessary, but the RCA has found a continuing role to play. Its Planning and Zoning Committee still acts as a watchdog. As a volunteer civic association, it still 'speaks for the principles on which Reston was founded' (*Reston Handbook*, 1991, p. 16). Its membership and board are open to renters as well as owners. RCA revenues are raised mainly from sponsoring the annual Reston Festival (Netherton, 1989, p. 161). The business community has its own organization, the Reston Board of Commerce, which sponsors seminars, fairs and networking, and promotes the economic and social affairs of the community.

The Reston Community Center is a combined government and voluntary facility. In 1975 a Special Service District (Small District Number 5) that encompasses the Reston area was created by Fairfax County. Residents voted in a referendum to issue bonds, funded by a special tax (6¢ per $100 of assessed real estate) within the district for the Center, which opened at Hunters Woods in 1979. The Center has its own Board of Governors (Netherton, 1989, p. 166). The Center was not established by RA because of the large costs involved and the willingness of the County to provide it if the residents were willing to set up the tax district (Grubisich, 1992; Green, 1992). The property tax paying for the district is tax deductible, so if the association fee had also been deductible, then the Reston Association could have constructed and maintained it at the same net cost.

Over 100 community groups use the Reston Community Center for meetings, parties, recreation, performances and workshops. The Center includes a theater, an indoor swimming pool, a social hall, a woodshop and photography darkroom, and classrooms. Its staff organizes over 500 classes and activities and rents rooms to outside groups ('Community Services', 1991). The Reston Community Players and Reston Chorale perform at the Reston Community Center as well as other locations. The Greater Reston Arts Center runs a gallery and a school program. The Reston Institute for the Arts offers classes, and there is a League of Reston Artists. The Reston Association also has its own Outdoor Arts Committee (Netherton, 1989, p. 170).

In 1984, some Restonians organized the Planned Community Archives, Inc., to preserve the archives of Reston and other communities and to facilitate programs in urban studies. These records are located in Fenwick Library at George Mason University.

Budget, operations and controversies

Of the 1991 RA income of $7.4 million, assessments were $5.5 million, 74 per cent, and very close to the budgeted amount, demonstrating the reliability of assessment income. Income from the athletic club was $1 million, 13.5 per cent, and there was also income from operations, services and interest.

Major expenses were open space management (29 per cent), swimming pools (15 per cent), athletic club (17 per cent), and financial services (11 per cent).

In 1990, the standard annual membership assessment in Reston Association was $238. Members paid user fees to use the swimming pools and tennis courts. One could also obtain a 'Gold Plus' membership for one year's use of the recreational facilities, which included the RA Athletic Club. There were also various annual membership fee options for using particular facilities, and different fees for individuals, households and juniors (*How to Enjoy Reston*, 1990). Towards the end of 1990, the RA Board voted to include the swimming and tennis facilities with the association assessment. The athletic club and services such as lessons retained a user fee. For 1991, the RA assessment was raised to $300 and remained at $300 for 1992. Federally subsidized units were assessed $290, and owners exempt from the county property tax (such as the totally disabled) were assessed $150.

The services that a $300 assessment pays for include 'open space, environmental programs, and other amenities' ($114), swimming pools ($55), covenants administration ($32), management services ($29), financial services ($28), tennis courts ($11), 'corporate and nonoperating' ($11), communications ($10), legal services ($6) and community buildings ($4). RA employs a staff of 70, including specialists in administration, education, forestry, parks, water resources, recreation, health and fitness ('Your Reston Association Passport', 1991). The swimming pool 'roll in' amounted to $59 of the increase. As the population had aged, the user fees were not sufficient to pay for all the pool upkeep. This 'roll in', eliminating user fees and instead funding pool operations from the annual assessments, resulted in 100 000 additional pool users during the year, more than double that of the previous year, but it also aroused opposition. RA members had voted 2–1 against the 'roll in' in a non-binding referendum conducted in 1990, and some felt that the will of the majority was being thwarted. It was also pointed out that the increase in usage did not necessarily imply a proportionate increase in pool users, since there was also increased usage by the same users. Only one-third of the Reston households used the pools during the year (*Pools Usage Study – 1991*).

A survey of the membership (*Pool Usage Study – 1991*) had revealed that some 60 per cent of the respondents stated that the pools were a poor or only fair value for the money, but 70 per cent were open to a combination assessment/fee payment (Kalmus, 1991b). Condominium owners tended to feel that the pools did not add to their property values, whereas owners of single-family homes felt that they did contribute to values. They may both be right, since the houses would capitalize more of the value. If the payments were proportional to the land value, then the condominium owners would pay proportionately less for the added costs of the pools. What seems superficially to be a user fee versus assessment problem may be, more deeply, the result of an economically flawed system of assessment, as discussed above.

Some constitutional rules, such as the method of funding, may have consequences that do not manifest themselves until much later. Had Reston begun with a fee based partly on site value, had commercial areas been included in the association land, had RA specified more detailed rules for enforcing the architectural rules, and had there been more decentralization, some controversies may have been reduced in scope and intensity. Political contention may indicate too large a size of governance and an imbalance of fiscal burdens. Clearly, civic-goods provision at Reston is not without flaws, but the economic point to be made in this study is that, despite human failure in the development of the community, the goods are indeed provided, and abundantly so.

Analysis of the hypotheses

As Jim Todd, president of Mobil Land Corporation, stated, 'the financial significance of Reston is that it's been done entirely through private financing' (Netherton, 1981, p. 28.). 'We built the roads,' he added. 'We put in all the sewer lines' (p. 29).

The first two hypotheses, regarding the feasibility of the contractual finance of civic goods and their inferiority to those of government have been rejected above. Of the other hypotheses:

1. The civic goods produced by the Reston Association are mainly excludable, being territorial, and there is a significant amount of benevolent provision goods as well.
2. The association goods do increase the site values and rents, since the property owners willingly pay what is in effect a site fee, which they would not do if the goods had no value.
3. The funding for the goods has a substantial relation to the site rents, although the relation is not as direct as it could be. The flat-fee assessment in Reston is independent of improvements to a unit; the owner can upgrade his residence without incurring an assessment penalty. Though not *ad valorem*, the assessment acts like a rent on the site.
4. The demand for the civic goods is revealed by the purchase of real estate in Reston, which is tied to the goods.

In Chapter 3 it was theorized that the rent generated by territorial public goods could exceed its total cost at the level where the marginal rent equals marginal costs, since the first increments of goods may generate more than proportional rents. To test this theory for Reston, as well as to test whether the level of civic goods is too high (which would reduce property values relative to similar nearby neighborhoods), profile sheets of real estate for sale in Reston (Haefer, 1992) were obtained on 23 January 1992 and compared with similar properties outside Reston. The sample consists of 43 single-family houses with four or five bedrooms, 15 in Reston and 28 in similar areas just outside Reston in Fairfax County. The mean price of the houses in Reston is $293 000 and the mean of the sample outside Reston is $226 000, a difference of $67 000. A regression of price as a function of lot size, age of the building, and location in Reston yields an adjusted R^2 of 0.49 and T-ratios of 0.91, −1.1, and 4.9, respectively, with a partial correlation of the Reston variable of 0.62. A regression of price to lot size and age within both areas yields the result that these are not statistically significant in determining the price. Location is evidently the key difference between the samples. Though this represents one small sample, a hypothesis that Reston real estate suffers from its services is not supported by these data. More comprehensive comparative studies would be needed to test this differential for various locational factors and types of property, but this small sample is at least suggestive. It should also be noted that, because of the townhouses and condominium units available at Reston, housing in general (the total housing median price) is not necessarily more expensive in Reston than in other areas of northern Virginia.

5. As noted above, free riding is prevented by the need to pay the association fee if one purchases a lot or condominium unit. Residents do have a free ride on the volunteer club activities, but this has not prevented the sympathetic services of the volunteers.
6. The provision of the recreation, nature and architectural goods at Reston is funded by the assessments, without public-sector support. The public sector inhibits rather than stimulates the private-sector provision owing to its legal restrictions and the lack of rebates for substitute civic goods.

Reston also demonstrates that a contractual community 100 times larger than the village size of Arden or Fort Ellsworth can provide civic goods.

That community associations offer public goods above the level of other developments was noted in a description of a 'new town' as a mixed-land-use development which seeks 'to produce a range of valuable social, environmental and economic benefits that more conventional, less comprehensively planned developments are not likely to achieve' (Flynn, 1989).

Other home owners' associations

A few other residential associations are examined here to provide some comparison and contrast. These test the hypothesis that Reston has been a unique case and demonstrate different forms of contractual governance and methods of funding the goods.

Columbia, Maryland

Columbia is a community association in Howard County, Maryland, built at the same time that Reston was developed. It contains 15 000 acres, purchased secretly in 1963 from 140 farms and parcels. Like Robert Simon, the developer, James Rouse, Chairman of the Board of Directors of The Rouse Company, envisioned a new city, planned to avoid the urban sprawl and inconveniences of typical developments. Like Reston, Columbia combines work and residency, and urban and rural services. Columbia was developed entirely by private funds (*Columbia, Maryland*, 1990, p. 1).

Unlike the Reston case, at Columbia the commercial land is included in the association jurisdiction, and 37 per cent of the community revenues comes from assessments on office buildings, a mall, shopping centers and industrial parks (*Six Pages*, 1990). 'The Mall' at the Town Center opened in 1971. Columbia's businesses comprise 50 000 jobs (*Columbia, Maryland*, 1990, p. 3).

Columbia too was built around the cluster concept. Similar to the experience at Reston, Columbia also required a change from conventional zoning. In 1965, Howard County passed a 'New Town District' zoning ordinance (*Columbia, Maryland*, 1990). The Columbia Association (CA) was founded in 1965 as a non-stock corporation, like Reston. The population of 70 000 is ethnically diverse; African-Americans make up 20 per cent of the population (Burkhart, 1981, p. 21). At full development, expected in the mid-1990s, there will be 100 000 people and about 34 000 dwelling units, with an assessable base of $1.5 billion and $15 million in annual revenue (*The Columbia Association*, 1990, p. 5).

CA operates parks, playgrounds, pathways, swimming pools, tennis courts, a golf course, lakes, horses, an ice rink and many other services. Columbia too has an athletic club with facilities and classes similar to the RAC. The Community Services Division of CA operates programs for children and teenagers, including daycare and camps. Like Reston, Columbia has an internal bus system, ColumBus, connecting the villages and Town Center. CA has 2000 acres of open space, with a planned increase to 3000.

Columbia is governed by a board made up of one director elected from each village as Columbia Council Representatives. There are currently nine villages, with one last village being developed. The board elects one of its members as president. Each village has a board governing the local education, roads, grounds and social events. Each resident, whether renter or owner, has a vote, and a non-resident owner may also vote. The rules may vary slightly among the villages; for example whether a married couple in one unit has one or two votes (Blimmel, 1992; Parrish, 1992).

The architectural review process is administered by the villages with funds provided by the Columbia Association; this ensures that villages do not shirk funding the covenants enforcement, but leaves them with the flexibility of local control. Though there are nine village associations, these encompass six village community centers and 15 neighborhood centers. The villages are divided into neighborhoods of between 600 and 800 dwelling units. The budgets of the villages are mostly funded by CA (*Newcomers Guide*, 1990, p. 28). As at Reston and Arden, there are numerous volunteer groups at Columbia, with over 200 civic and fraternal organizations listed in its telephone directory in addition to groups for sports, arts and so on.

The assessments are based on property values, the maximum rate being 75¢ per $100 of assessed value (equivalent to $200 of the presumed market value as determined by the State of Maryland). As discussed in Chapter 3, the improvement value of the property has little relationship to the civic goods, but, so long as the fees are a relatively low percentage of the annualized yield of the improvements, the disincentive effect on improvements and distortion of prices may not be severe. The budget is spent on open space (39 per cent), community services (28 per cent), membership facilities (13 per cent), administration (15 per cent) and deficit reduction (5 per cent) (*Six Pages*, 1990).

Players Club at Sawgrass, Florida

Another example of a residential/commercial contractual community is provided by the Players Club at Sawgrass, St. Johns County (with county seat at St. Augustine), Florida, containing 1400 acres. The property includes private roads, a drainage system and security for residences (within the gates). The Sawgrass Players Club Association encompasses sub-associations, and the condominiums and commercial projects maintain their own internal property and governance. The project includes a shopping center, an office park and a hotel, the commercial properties contributing to the Players Club budget as in Columbia. The community obtains its water and sewerage privately from the St. Johns Service Company (Metcalf, 1990).

The 'Declaration of Covenants' specifies that the residential units pay the same fee, with lots paying half the unit fee and commercial properties paying one unit fee per 10 000 square feet. The Articles of Incorporation specify that only property owners, including the developer (the Arvida Corporation), may vote.

An example of a residential sub-association is the Cypress Creek Homeowners Association, which has its own Declaration of Covenants and Restrictions. This association is made up of single-family lots, and has its own common areas, including roadways. The assessments of unimproved lots is half that of improved lots, and the rate is uniform among improved lots.

The Sawgrass Village Office Park is a commercial association with its own Declaration of Covenants and other governing documents. Each lot owner, including the developer, is a member. The Covenants specify a maximum assessment per acre or fraction thereof, and maximum increases. As with residences, assessments are uniform for improved lots, and there is also an Architectural Review Board. Of special interest is a 'golf easement' which the developer reserves (for example to recover golf balls, to allow the usual noise level associated with games), since the Sawgrass development is the home base for PGA Tour, Inc.

Sawgrass thus shows the similarity of the basic structure of a civic association to Columbia and Reston, along with some moderate differences. It has subunits which are larger than those in Reston but which are self-financing, unlike Columbia. At Columbia, the commercial properties do not have their own associations, unlike Sawgrass. Reston and Sawgrass have flat assessments per unit, whereas Columbia's are based on the property value. What is similar among the three is the basic concept of an association collecting assessments from the property owners to finance the spatial collective goods.

Ford's Colony, Virginia

Located near Williamsburg, Virginia, Ford's Colony is a 2500 acre residential community with single-family houses, townhouses and condominiums, which opened in 1985. The main attraction is the golf course, which has its own membership. All buildings must adhere to the protective covenants. The bylaws require a uniform rate of assessment.

A notable feature of the 'Ford's Colony at Williamsburg Homeowners Association' is that it owns the streets and roads within the development, whereas at Reston and Columbia the streets are maintained by the county, except for some private areas in clusters at Reston. According to Mel Overman (1990), a salesman for the developer, the Ford's Colony roads are maintained at a higher standard than those maintained by the public sector. Entrance to the property is through one secured gate with 24-hour guards – another feature different from Reston or Columbia. Residency includes membership of the home owners' Swim & Tennis Club offering exercise facilities, tennis courts, a 25-meter pool, a children's pool and a sundeck ('Ford's Colony Fact Sheet', 1990).

The Woodlands, Texas

The Woodlands, a residential association planned for 49 000 units, opened in 1974. As in Reston and Columbia, the developer sought to create an integrated community offering recreation and culture and the preservation of forests, a place where urban problems such as blight would be alleviated. Influenced by Columbia, the plan was based on villages and included commerce (Morgan and King, 1987, p. 133). The noteworthy feature of this case is that it was built in partnership with the US Department of Housing and Urban Development (HUD) and was the only Title VII new town to survive. Other HUD-backed new towns failed, and in The Woodlands the HUD review process delayed contracting and did not deliver expected supplementary grants (p. 74). HUD severed its relationship with The Woodlands in 1983 (p. 149).

The failure of government-backed new towns and trouble experienced by The Woodlands contrast with the success of private development in Reston and Columbia, providing further evidence that rejects the hypothesis that the contractual provision of civic goods requires government support. These residential and neighborhood associations in many different locations demonstrate that civic associations are reproducible in various forms, rejecting the hypothesis that they are due to special circumstances.

13 They do own the road: the private places of St. Louis

Case studies of contractual communities should not overlook the remarkable private places of St. Louis, which date back to the mid-1800s. These communities are significant because they are integrated within the city of St. Louis and the towns of St. Louis County, demonstrating the feasibility of consensual civic goods in the midst of the government infrastructure. Besides the 'private places' in St. Louis, there are also neighborhoods with non-land-owning residential associations. These are significant as an example of volunteer governance in low-income and middle-class areas, demonstrating that private governance is not an exclusive phenomenon of wealthy areas.

St. Louis was selected as a case study of metropolitan organization by the Advisory Commission on Intergovernmental Relations (Parks and Oakerson, 1988) because of its polycentric governance (called by the authors 'jurisdictional fragmentation').[1] In 1982, it had 151 government units plus at least 427 private street-providing organizations (p. 9). The City of St. Louis itself separated from St. Louis County in 1876 because the residents of the city did not wish to pay, in addition to city taxes, a county tax that primarily benefited the non-city population (p. 15). Many communities in St. Louis County incorporated as municipalities to avoid annexation by other cities and to shift control over local affairs from the county to the local area (p. 17). Many unincorporated communities as well as municipalities are served by autonomous school and fire protection districts. There has thus been a pattern of decentralized governance which can be contrasted with centralized cities.

These jurisdictions provide an example of the way small communities associate to provide goods with large-area economies of scale. Small municipalities have provided for common police services such as dispatch centers. The fire districts have mutual aid and first-response agreements. There are metropolitan area organizations of school districts which offer joint purchasing of supplies and other services such as the cross-district movement of students. A cluster of small municipalities has formed a council providing services as well as a common agency representing them in higher-level governments (Parks and Oakerson, 1988, p. 21). An analysis of economies of scale in the municipalities of St. Louis County found no significant diseconomies due to polycentricity relative to service levels, consistent with other studies of size effects (p. 122).

The polycentric nature of governance in St. Louis, both County and City, include the 'private places', neighborhoods having a consensual ownership of their streets through deed covenants (or 'trust indentures') and residential associations governed by a board of trustees. St. Louis has had an extensive system of privately owned residential streets since the mid-1800s. Many of these are in predominantly Black neighborhoods (Fitzgerald, 1988, p. 48). The use of the term 'place' in St. Louis for the private neighborhood and its streets may have derived from the French colonial legacy, the French term 'place' meaning town square (Savage, 1987, p. 4).

The most common method of raising revenue in the private places is a flat fee per residency. Some base their assessments on acreage or the value of the frontage to the street (Parks and Oakerson, 1988, p. 51). The mean annual assessment for the 39 communities for which data were available is $130, varying from $25 to $800 (p. 85). There can be considerable annual variation due to capital improvements. Since these private places tend to have lots of similar value, the assessments are essentially based on the land rent generated by the locally provided civic goods, more so than the local property taxes, which vary according to the value of improvements.

In two of the municipalities of St. Louis county, over 50 per cent of street mileage is provided by private places and, in another four, they are a major proportion. The total number of private places in the city and county is unknown; the figure of 427 cited above is what has been reported, but is incomplete (Parks and Oakerson, 1988, p. 84). Among the services provided by various private places are street maintenance, sewerage, snow removal, sweeping, mowing, tree trimming, street lighting, traffic control and access restriction, entrance signs and architectural covenants. A few also provide refuse collection, a security patrol and park maintenance. The varied mix of services offers a choice among the places in the level of civic goods provision.

The ability to restrict access is a key advantage of a private place and, in many of them, one end of a street is closed off by gates, chains and barricades. Besides reducing traffic, the barriers provide protection against crime. Some subdivisions also restrict access through a layout of streets that avoids the typical grid pattern. A study by Oscar Newman found that restricted streets had lower crime rates and higher property values than similar housing in government streets, although the precise cause, such as closure or the effect of being a neighborhood association, was not factored out (Parks and Oakerson, 1988, p. 88). The reduction of pollution is another service provided by some of the private places. Some, for example, prohibit the burning of bituminous coal (Beito and Smith, 1990, p. 276).

The demand for private neighborhoods indicated the utility of restrictive covenants, which prevented inferior buildings and uses that decreased property values. The private places were also stimulated by the limits on expenditures placed on St. Louis City by its charter, restricting the funds available for infrastructure. 'Necessity demanded a heavy reliance on private enterprise to fill the gap' (Beito, 1989, p. 12). The history of the private places indicates that the private sector can provide these local public goods when not preempted by government provision. The St. Louis experience also illustrates the possibility of integration between the government and private sectors; not only did the streets connect with the city grid, but the private sewers were able to connect to those of the city. Covenants also exist in government streets but, without residential associations, enforcement is in the hands of the lot owners and, in practice, the restrictions are often not enforced.

Not only the residential streets, but even some boulevards have been privately owned in St. Louis. By 1908, there were seven miles of boulevards under private control. An advantage of such ownership is the ability to control the utilities along the route; the private routes had no utility poles (Beito and Smith, 1990, p. 288). 'Street ownership represented the means to control the "commanding heights" of the local economy' (Beito, 1989, p. 35).

The decline of the St. Louis private places began when city spending increased, while charter amendments enabled the city to override private provisions of the neighborhoods. Besides not having rebates for private provision, the association fees are not deductible from income taxes, unlike property taxes. Despite such handicaps, some streets that were not private have become so since World War II (Savage, 1987, p. xi). Among these is Waterman Place, an integrated lower-class neighborhood which was experiencing crime and physical deterioration. In 1974, the residents formed a residential association and partially closed the street, spending $40 000 to erect a gate. A block watch was started, and crime decreased. The association was able to borrow funds to improve the street and housing. Property values doubled (Fitzgerald, 1988, p. 47; Frazier, 1989 [1988], p. 64).

Even in neighborhoods with government streets, volunteer governance provides some collective goods. In their study of St. Louis non-landed associations, Schoenberg and Rosenbaum (1980) define a 'neighborhood' as a territory which is identified by a name by the residents, which contains at least one local institution, and which has at least one common tie among the residents. A 'viable' neighborhood is then one in which the residents can control the social order, that is set goals and implement programs to accomplish them. As a proposition, supported by evidence, Schoenberg and Rosenbaum state that a viable neighborhood has mechanisms to enforce shared agreements on public behavior: that is, a governance structure to enforce rules. Safe passage is a prime example, enforced by surveillance and the identification of strangers. In areas where there are no enforced rules on public behavior, public space may become dangerous and not be used by the community, an example of the tragedy of the unmanaged commons. Rules also deal with property maintenance, refuse disposal, children and visitors. The social mechanisms include a formal organization that provides communication, neighborhood definition and leadership.

For example, in an ethnically Italian neighborhood called 'The Hill', four organizations form an interlocking network: a church, a neighborhood organization, a business club and a political party. Hill residents have a high degree of social control over their neighborhood. Whereas other urban sections in St. Louis experienced declining property values, valuations have increased in The Hill (Schoenberg and Rosenbaum, 1980, p. 135). Another case, Lafayette Park, is a historic wealthy area, formerly the site of some private places, that had deteriorated but then underwent gentrification. New residents formed the Lafayette Square Restoration Committee. With increased surveillance, crime decreased (p. 72) and the park was restored as usable space. Another organization, the Lafayette Park Neighborhood Association, promotes youth employment and conducts clean-up campaigns. The city had abandoned the neighborhood and intended to replace it with new development, but the restorationists revitalized the old land-use structure and restored it as a viable urban neighborhood, an example of a contractually provided public good.

The case studies by Schoenberg and Rosenbaum demonstrate that lower- and middle-income neighborhood associations can provide or promote local collective goods such as safety, architectural restoration, refuse disposal and youth activities. The private places and neighborhood associations of St. Louis offer a model of the way the provision of civic goods could devolve from unicentric to polycentric governance, from imposed to voluntary provision. If neighborhood residents and site owners may form an association with neither subsidies nor tax penalties, then there could be a spontaneous privatization of civic goods according to the demand for voluntarism by the users. The transition from government to market provision of civic goods will be examined in Chapter 15.

Note

1. The term 'polycentric' was used by Michael Polanyi in *The Logic of Liberty* (1951) to distinguish decentralized from centralized governance.

14 Urban economics and public choice

Two aspects of urban economics examined here are the economies of scale involved in contractual communities (whether decentralism is inefficient) and the role that civic associations can play in urban economics. A comparison of unilateral and multilateral governance is then made, using public choice theory.

Size and centricity

'Centricity' is defined here as the degree of concentration in a set of governing units, similar to concentration in an industry. In the traditional view of urban organization, the decentralization or 'fragmentation' of authority and overlapping of jurisdictions have been considered to be detrimental to the efficient and harmonious provision of civic goods, characterized by wasteful duplication and lack of coordination (Parks and Oakerson, 1988, p. 1). However, there is little empirical support for this view. Local civic goods such as police protection and refuse collection tend to be labor-intensive (p. 121). An analysis of economies of scale among St. Louis jurisdictions, which are among the most polycentric in the USA, has shown no significant evidence of diseconomy effects of size on per capita expenditures, consistent with other findings (p. 122). Evidence that 'fragmentation' limits economic growth is also lacking (p. 136). Moreover, the voters of municipalities have tended to reject consolidation proposals, whereas they often favor the creation of special districts (p. 2).

Jurisdictional separation does not imply functional fragmentation. Although a metropolitan government may have economies of scale in the production of some of its territorial goods, a network of smaller jurisdictions may generate similar economies. Communities do cooperate to provide capital-intensive goods, and individual communities contract with producers which operate on a large scale, provision being distinct from production. With decentralized jurisdictions, economies of large scale can be satisfied while preserving the benefits of smaller-scale community governance. Studies have found that small agencies tend to be more responsive in providing neighborhood police services. Decentralized communities have lower per capita expenditures for given levels of services (Parks and Oakerson, 1988, p. 3).

A more neutral term than 'fragmented', with its pejorative connotation of broken or incomplete pieces, is 'polycentric'. (Note that an industry is not called 'fragmented' when it has a low degree of concentration.) The Herfindahl index H can be used as a measurement of centricity, just as it is used to measure industry concentration. Its inverse serves as a measure of polycentricity, just as it can measure the amount of diversification in a firm or industry. Parks and Oakerson (1988, p. 9) measure 'fragmentation' as the number of governmental units per 10 000 persons, but this measurement does not take into account the relative sizes of the units. For example, a metropolitan area with a city of 999 991 inhabitants plus nine villages of 1000 persons would have the same 'fragmentation' index as ten cities of 100 000 persons, yet, in terms of the total population, the former would be much more unicentric. An index of polycentricity measured by 1/H would yield a measure of almost one in the former case and ten in the latter.

Ostrom, Tiebout and Warren (1961), analyzing the scale of community public-goods packages, identify four scale criteria: control, efficiency, representation and self-determination. Examples of circumstances subject to control are traffic and crime. Though some circumstances, such as air pollution, are metropolitan-wide, others, such as crime, may be controllable on a neighborhood scale. Regarding efficiency, labor-intensive goods, such as police and schooling, generally have small-scale economies relative to capital- or land-intensive goods. Representation involves the inclusion of those affected by some circumstance within the jurisdiction that affects it, and the exclusion of those not affected. Self-determination presumes that those affected by some situation are the appropriate decision makers in applying the other criteria. Differing criteria for different goods suggest overlapping or nested jurisdictions of various sizes. Such is the case in Reston, for example, where cluster associations manage the neighborhood services and the Reston Association manages the parks and recreation. As noted by Ostrom, Tiebout and Warren, the jurisdictions both cooperate and compete, both for jurisdictional provision and goods production.

On the cost side, polycentric governance is subject to greater spillover effects. But communities can and do cooperate to create agencies of larger scale to accommodate such externalities, with unresolved conflicts subject to arbitration and the courts. Changing circumstances may make the previous boundaries and property jurisdictions obsolete, but private boundaries can be flexible, especially when partial jurisdiction in the form of easements is required.

Decentralism has been proposed for Washington, DC, by William Niskanen (1991), who has noted that the expenditures of the city are about twice those of state and local averages. He proposes that individual communities in the District of Columbia be granted the authority to form separate cities and select their services and property tax rates. Niskanen also proposes that the property tax be gradually shifted to the taxation of land values rather than buildings by exempting the future increases in the value of improvements. This would make land rent increasingly a basis for funding civic goods. There would also be congestion fees on vehicles crossing the District boundaries during peak hours. Other taxes could then be reduced or eliminated. This principle, allowing local districts, whether contractual or governmental, to become established and the funding of their civic goods from the generated rents, is flexible enough to have application in many types of governing structures.

Urban economics: the theories of Jane Jacobs

What role can proprietary communities and residential associations play in urban economics, both as a science and as ways to stimulate urban economies? Contractual communities can facilitate decentralized governance and, as indicated above, polycentric communities may offer efficient economies of scale, but is civic self-governance necessarily a net benefit?

Jane Jacobs (1969, 1984) presents the theory that cities, rather than countries, are the key entities of economic growth and development. According to Jacobs (1969, p. 38), rural economies are built upon those of cities: 'city economies invent the things that are to become city imports from the rural world, and then they reinvent the rural world so it can supply these imports'. New work – new goods and services – is added to old work, multiplying the division of labor. Jacobs believes that Adam Smith gave the division of labor unwarranted credit for economic advances. Stagnant economies also have a division of labor. It is as a source of *new* work that the division of labor becomes significant for development (p. 81). Many of the evils of urban life – congestion, pollution, noise – are blamed on progress, but are actually evils of stagnation (p. 102). These are opportunities for new services.

In Jacobs' view, a city constitutes a natural economic unit, whereas, from an economic perspective, the boundaries of countries and their subdivisions are often arbitrary. Cities grow by replacing imports and adding export work to the local work, which multiplies jobs. Exports are facilitated by more autonomy, by the control of variables such as currency and taxation: 'national or imperial currencies give faulty and destructive feedback to city economies' (Jacobs, 1984, p. 158). To this one should add national policies that impose uniform banking and credit policies. Regarding the value-added tax, Jacobs (1984, p. 226), states:

> no neater little tax contrivance could be imagined for favoring large, relatively self-sufficient enterprises such as multinational corporations with their many subsidiaries and many internal transactions, while penalizing symbiotic production. VAT heedlessly twists the knife in the very vitals of city economies. Any other form of sales tax on producers' goods or services does the same.

This insight can be generalized to all taxation on production, which penalizes small, local firms more than large ones. The distinction between taxes on incomes and those on expenditures is administrative rather than economic, other than the timing of the taxes (a tax on expenditure penalizes borrowing, while that on income penalizes saving, but overall borrowings equal savings). Workers sell their labor, and the taxation of labor is a tax on the sale of labor. A tax directly related to profits and the return on capital goods also acts upon sales, the essential difference being the stage of the production process at which the costs are imposed.

The taxation of products is tantamount to a tax on production. Property taxes on buildings and other improvements are a drag on urban growth, penalizing the very process of growth. As Gaffney (1989, p. 4) puts it, urban blight is a failure to maintain urban capital goods. The taxation of the value of improvements skews the market towards the retention of older buildings and the avoidance of maintenance. The construction and renewal of buildings draws tenants from the older ones and stimulates other construction and thus can produce synergistic increasing returns (p. 6). Hence Jacobs' statement on sales taxes applies also to the taxation of all urban production and products. An alternative is fiscal equivalence, paying for what you get. As discussed in Chapter 6, user fees, congestion fees and site rents are the main media for fiscal equivalence. Just as condominiums and home owner associations fund their public goods from the generated site rents, the theory in Chapter 3 implies that cities too would stimulate growth and renewal by funding their public services from rents and user fees,[1] rather than taxing improvements and productive effort.

National product standards and mandated production methods also harm cities, hindering differentiation for local markets and then for exports (Jacobs, 1984, p. 226). A policy implication of Jacobs' theory is decentralized governance, with autonomy for regions and cities. Contractual communities offer a way to decentralize, not according to some top-down plan, but by letting market processes determine the extent of polycentricity. Gordon Tullock (1993) also theorizes that many services can be devolved to the neighborhood level, which could become a predominant level of government if policy permits. He notes that small-scale government is more in accord with individual preferences, and that the Fairfield company, a developer in Arizona, has designed its communities to attract different types of residents in each. Robert Nelson (1989) suggests that a neighborhood association could have the option of selling part or all the neighborhood, retaining flexible responses to changes in the real estate market and enabling the neighborhood to profit from new development. The example of the St. Louis private places, described in Chapter 13, demonstrates the feasibility of local neighborhood control.

Aside from decentralized governance, contractual communities offer a different model of governance, which could restore community vitality. The problems of modern urban life in the USA and elsewhere are familiar – economic stagnation, crime, pollution, congestion, poverty and ugliness. As MacCallum argues, there is a counter-trend in the development of real estate. Proprietary governance offers different, more market-oriented, incentives than sovereign governance. Proprietary and associative governance can reduce the rent-seeking conflicts common in sovereign governance by the combined effects of exit (mobility facilitated by small governance size), voice (voting and personal influence enhanced by small size and property-based voting), sympathy (volunteerism) and capitalization (of rent from civic goods, including governance).

There is an increasing trend towards the volunteer provision of services such as neighborhood protection. Judge Richard Neely (1990) has described how neighborhood associations are being set up for protection against crime, supplementing rather than substituting for government policing. The private provision of police services would in many instances be more concerned with the protection of property and personal safety and less with the enforcement of cultural standards such as what people read, or the protection of state monopolies such as gambling.

Reston and other 'new town' developments of the 1960s and 1970s helped change the pattern of developments, which had previously isolated residential areas from both employment and cultural centers. According to Francis Steinbauer, former president of Reston Land Corporation, Reston has had a 'monumental and pervasive impact on urban and suburban development in the United States'. Reston proved that the traditional integrated patterns of urban life could be applied to modern development (Steinbauer, 1985, p. 9). A study by Gulf Reston found that the Reston example had helped to improve development in Fairfax County. In 1969, the county adopted Planned Unit Development (PUD) zoning, based on Reston's 1962 RPC zoning code. PUD allowed for Reston-style mixed land use, and developers found that community planning could be profitable. Developments throughout Northern Virginia have been built with clusters, open space, pathways and other amenities (Netherton, 1989, p. 98).

Contractual communities thus contribute to urban economies by substituting for more centralized governance, by offering a different model of governance and by improving urban development.

Public choice analysis of public goods

The two methods of providing civic goods, the economic means and the political means, can be compared using public choice theory. In a democracy, the political means is subject to a 'market for legislation', creating dysfunctional incentives to provide goods to groups that can exert influence rather than to the public at large. Another problem is that governments typically provide these benefits by the restriction and taxation of private transactions. Not only do the citizens receive fewer of the goods they desire, but their ability to provide their own goods is sharply reduced. These problems are illustrated by the example of the dam in Chapter 1; the dam does get built, but it is larger and more expensive than warranted by the benefits, and resources are wasted in the process.

The banking and savings and loan fiasco of the early 1990s in the US demonstrates these principles at work. The public good of deposit insurance combined with fiscal policies that induce real-estate speculation led to malinvested capital and an increase in the public debt. The beneficiaries were concentrated among those with large deposits, borrowers who failed to repay loans, and banking interests, among others. The increase in taxation and the public debt (to pay off depositors and handle the failed banks) is spread among the population. In the alternative of a purely private banking system, safety would be an outcome of competition for deposits and bank notes (cf. Selgin, 1988), it being in the mutual interest of banks to ensure the safety of banking as a whole. But government agents would then lose their ability to pursue monetary policy, with its bias towards inflation and induced booms and busts (Wagner, 1980; Frey 1978), so this avenue is closed off.

A rationale for government expenditures is the provision of collective goods. But the democratic political process, which in the USA and most other countries has few constitutional fiscal constraints, results in a tragedy of the commons. The wealth and income of the population becomes a common pool to be exploited by those who can pass legislation. Brennan and Buchanan (1977) posit a model of a 'Leviathan' state whose agents seek to maximize government revenues within the constraints of the constitution. In contrast, contractual governance is restrained by the very need for contractual consent. A proprietor in competition with other communities earns revenue by charging market rents and fees rather than by imposing arbitrary costs. A civic association is constrained not only by its size and constitution, but by the fact that assessments are visible and capitalized in property values.

Ways that interest groups can direct funds to their benefits include setting agendas, restructuring proposals in their favor, increasing the size of the losing side and by log-rolling, trading votes and exchanging benefits with other groups. A related political pathology is that transfer or rent seekers will spend funds to obtain the benefits up to the amount of the benefits, dissipating resources in negative-sum games. In a democracy, when there are various alternative choices and different preferences, the outcomes can be arbitrary; public choice theorists have referred to this as 'cycling'. Where log-rolling is possible, members of a losing coalition have an incentive to join the winning group and alter the outcome. This too generates a cycle. Agenda setting thus results in an effective dictatorship.

Under a non-democratic proprietary governance, a single agent makes the choice, which eliminates these pathologies of democracy, in addition to reducing the tendency towards budget maximization by bureaucrats, since the owner is a residual claimant. With civic associations, the feasibility of rent or transfer seeking is dampened by the smaller size of the membership, by voting rules tied more to the ownership of property, by the limited options allowed by a constitution and by the need to raise funds from assessments, limiting the fiscal illusion of the payers, as discussed in Chapter 3.

The payment for civic goods by the rents generated accomplishes Wicksell's prescription of tying the payment to the benefit. A test for an expenditure is the question, will this measure increase the rent or property value? With rent capitalized into property values, the voter-owners have an incentive to monitor their agents, and the opportunity is provided even in a community the size of Reston. Members attend board meetings and voice their opinions, and the meetings are shown on the local cable television. With unicentric governance, those civic goods that do benefit the public at large tend to be geared to the interests of the median voter, since politicians compete for this vote. Polycentric governance provides a greater range of civic goods, leaving more choice for those persons at the tails of preference distributions.

Multilateral governance differs from unilateral governance in several ways. Primarily, multilateral communities have an explicit contractual relationship among the membership or with their customers, whereas, with an imposed government, the citizens are born into it or automatically come under its jurisdiction when they reside in or visit its geographical area. As contractors, the members or customers of a contractual community have an equal legal relationship with one another and with the organization, whereas sovereign governments typically claim some immunity from lawsuits.

Second, the power of a consensual community is limited to the organization's constitutional provisions or to contractual obligations, whereas the power of a sovereign government to impose costs is broad, formal constitutions often containing vague constraints that have been interpreted broadly. On the other hand, local or special-purpose contractual organizations have a greater scope for the provision of collective goods because they are not constrained by the interests of the broader community.

Third, the government in a majoritarian democracy typically carries out redistributional activities, with tax payments often having little relationship to services rendered. 'Government becomes an arena in which contending factions try to form winning coalitions in a competition to be net recipients of transfers' (Wagner, 1989, p. 138). The result is a larger civic expenditure than that warranted by non-redistributive goods. In contrast, consensual communities are financed through a rough fiscal equivalence, much as private goods are paid for.

Fourth, contractual communities are typically governed by those owning the community property, often in proportion to the property owned, and to a lesser extent by residency, whereas, in sovereign governments, property owners usually have no more voting power than other residents. Property owners have a greater incentive to be informed about governance, since their property values are at stake.

Government agents do not own the property they direct, and the productivity of the property is not 'choice influencing', in the terminology of Buchanan (1978 [1969]). As Mason Gaffney (1976, p. 115) states, government is real estate-extensive, holding much land tax-free and unmortgaged. The forgone gains from underused land are often unreported and do not impose costs on government agents. An example given by Gaffney is military bases; their annual rental value does not appear in the budget as an input cost. Other aspects of the production or provision of collective goods by government that have been analyzed by the industrial organization literature include the difficulty of defining the output, the monopolization of production, the uncertainty of the technology of production, and the difficulty of measuring the efficiency of the production (Wolf, 1988, p. 51).

Studies have shown that the private sector produces civic goods at a lower cost than governments (Poole, 1976), which is consistent with the differing incentives faced by agents in an imposed governance, where resources can be commanded, and in a consensual governance, where resources are exchanged or donated. A study by Borcherding, Pommerehne and Schneider (1982) (summarized in Appendix B of Wolf (1988)) compared the technical efficiency of private and government production in five countries and found that, in 40 of the 50 cases studied, private production was less costly, with only three cases of more efficient non-market production (one being refuse collection, which in other cases (cf. Chapter 11) is more expensively provided by governments).

A premise of public choice theory is that agents in a political process are subject to the same economic principles that apply to agents in a market process. A social pathology follows in which, as Wagner (1988b, p. 1) puts it, 'Political interventions into the economy will follow an economic logic that is orthogonal to the dictates of welfare economics.' Rent seeking, the expenditure of resources to obtain favorable policies, privileges or subsidies from the government, is often accomplished when the benefits are concentrated in an interest group and the costs are spread among a large public, so that individual payers lack the incentive to monitor it and initiate legislation against it. Costs and restrictions can also, of course, be imposed on minorities who have less clout. It occurs because government agents are able to impose the costs. A government agency can also be an interest group, pursuing its own private goals in addition to its government function. Owing to its need for standards of performance, an agency creates rules that lead to what Wolf (1988, p. 66) calls 'internalities', internal goals that are a counterpart to externalities.

Residential associations are also subject to privilege seeking, since democracy itself poses principal–agent problems. Many residents in RCAs are apathetic about their governance, unless policy directly affects them negatively, and rational ignorance can provide some scope for the appropriation of funds for the private benefit of members of a board. The smaller scale of RCAs, both in size and in scope, combined with the visible form of the assessment, make such rent seeking less feasible in the RCAs than in the larger and more complex tax structures of local governments.

In a multilateral governance, the members or customers can obtain an estimate of the costs and their future expansion from the explicit contract which they sign. An association may impose special assessments, but the type and amount of cost are constiutionally constrained, and the incentive to impose them are reduced because they become capitalized into lower property values. In territorial clubs, rent seeking is literally 'ground rent' seeking and is therefore more difficult to hide. Mobility is another constraint upon rent seeking. The ability of the proprietor to appropriate the rents can be limited by contractual restraints as well as by provisions, as in the example of Shannon, to guarantee the value of the investments of the residents in their real estate.

The same constitutional structures that lead to transfer seeking also prevent a fundamental reform of the system that would 'transform government from an infringer on the rights of person and property to a participant within the framework of those rights' (Wagner, 1989, p. 17). But there are ways to achieve contractual governance. Some possibilities will be explored in the next chapter.

Note

1. User fees are paid in direct exchange for receiving a service rather than imposed as an excise tax on the purchase of goods or on an activity. On the recent tendency of governments to call excise taxes 'user fees', see Wagner, ed., *Charging for Government* (1991).

15 Towards consensual governance

We shall first consider some voluntary methods of funding collective goods that have been proposed and contrast them with the fees and rents discussed above. The second part of this chapter then explores how we can move towards consensual governance.

Other voluntary methods

Three broad approaches to funding collective goods are arbitrary taxation, fiscal equivalence and donation. One vehicle for fiscal equivalence not explored above is a fee for the enforcement of contracts, proposed by Tibor Machan (1982). Collective goods can be financed without coercion by tying them to the severable good of the protection of contracts. Those who wish to have a government enforce their contracts would pay a fee, and civic goods would be paid for from these fees.

Contract fees raise many questions, such as implied contracts. Is it presumed that the purchase of a product implies some type of contract, for example that the product is not dangerous? If no such contract is implied, then one would seek assurances each time one bought something, and then the question of the scope of contracts is left open. Can one sign one contract good for all transactions for a lengthy time period and large scope of operations? Clearly, a fee, especially a large one, would induce the broadest possible contracts. Either contracting would be inhibited or the fee would only be paid once for such a large number of transactions that few funds would be collected. Unlike land, which has a market value, a contract has no natural exchange value. Having no fixed bounds, it may become indefinitely elastic. Ultimately, people could arrange affairs so that there only needs to be one umbrella contract for all possible future transactions by all persons in one jurisdiction.

Other writers such as David Friedman (1989, p. 136) propose the old idea that an entrepreneur, say one building the famous dam, could require an agreement by all those affected. Although Friedman recognizes the gaming problem this involves, he thinks that some may find it in their interest to pay, but it is not clear why any individual would, unless he has Smithian sympathy for the project, which Friedman does not include in the utility. (Friedman then suggests that the entrepreneur could purchase the land.)

Another method proposed is a user fee with a surcharge, but then an alternative firm without the surcharge would have an advantage. Voluntary donations again fall victim to the free-rider problem unless sympathy is added. These free-market schemes have in common with much of the public-goods literature the absence of space and capitalization, which offer a solution to the problem for territorial goods.

Voluntary means for funding collective goods boil down to user fees and donations. Donations can fund some collective goods, as discussed in Chapter 7, but, as indicated there, sympathy is a scarce resource and will be spent for the cases with the greatest sympathy, which implies those felt to be deserving, that cannot get funds by other means. Hence sympathy may not be a reliable source for a service such as national defense, which may get volunteers at times of peril, but not necessarily during other times. User fees are a direct payment for a service, whether it be dues for a club, entrance to a park, or rent for periodic civic goods. Add-ons, such as fee surcharges, are not likely to be marketable, and fees not directly paid for a service, such as to enforce contracts, are likely to be evaded. But why search under the bed and in the closet for the key when it is already on the kitchen table? Since most civic goods are territorial, rent as a user fee is available, and the case studies show that it has worked well.

Towards constitutional reform

As indicated in the literature on constitutional economics (Buchanan, 1990), changes below the constitutional level, whether they consist of electing better politicians or changing the laws, will tend to be thwarted by the incentives that led to the dysfunctional outcomes. To change outcomes, the fundamental rules of the game need to be changed. Such constitutional rules include: (1) those which prescribe the governance structure, (2) those which prescribe the behavior of the members, and (3) those which prescribe the powers of the organization.

Constitutional reform begins with an awareness of the meta-constitution, the ethical framework in which the constitution itself is created. This ethical basis cannot itself be an agreement, since it sets the foundation for agreements. This ethic was derived in Chapter 5 as what Locke called a 'law of nature', based on the premises of human independence and equality. A recognition of our independence and equality is the foundation of a constitution that does not hinder self-governance. Such a fundamental change is not impossible. Historical examples abound, including the American revolution and movements such as the abolition of slavery and equal rights for women. The incentives against change in the normal political process can be overcome by a large movement focused on some fundamental but specific reform, to which office seekers would have to cater. An aroused citizenry can overcome ignorance and apathy. But such movement would most likely require a crisis and a political entrepreneur who could arouse the people.

This fundamental change could take the form of three amendments to a constitution. The first, regarding the behavior of the citizenry, could be the codification of the Lockeian universal ethic: *Any act which does not coercively harm others shall not be restricted, any state interest notwithstanding.* Any peaceful and honest act would be constitutionally permitted. This measure would in one fell swoop eliminate all laws and regulations on enterprise not involving force or fraud, including forming self-governing contractual communities. The second fundamental amendment regards the power of the state. It would eliminate the taxation of individuals and firms by all levels of government, eliminating the mining of private wealth. A federal government would obtain its funds either from its constituent states or else from true user fees and rent on the use of natural resources such as offshore oil or charges for using the oceans and the atmosphere as pollution dumps. States, provinces and counties, not being able to tax transactions or wealth, would need to resort to collecting site rents and user fees for revenue. The third amendment concerns the government structure, or the ability to change it. Exit options from government jurisdictions allow contractual communities to become established in equal competition with sovereign governance.

The structure provided for in the US Constitution is that of a division of powers (the three branches of government) and federalism (parallel state and federal sovereignty), which amounts to an oligopoly of governance. This division of government has preserved a level of liberty that seems high relative to much of the world, but it has not prevented the transfer-seeking pathology described in the previous chapter. This pathology has now gone beyond normal taxation to arbitrary confiscation under 'civil asset forfeiture' laws that enable federal and state governments to seize property, including cash, cars and real estate, as 'civil' actions without having to be charged or convicted of a crime (Schrama, 1992). Some 80 per cent of seizure victims are never charged with a crime (Wollstein, 1992). The seizures are considered a civil rather than a criminal action, so criminal due process protection does not apply. Since government agencies keep the property (or sell it and keep the proceeds), there is a strong incentive for governments increasingly to use confiscation as a source of revenue, in effect imposing a random tax.

The fundamental problem is that, as noted in Chapter 5, there is no free entry into the sovereign government business, and the states or provinces can use the federal government as a monopoly cartel, for example riding on top of the federal income tax to collect state income taxes. Mandatory expenditures that appear to be imposed on the states by the federal government may in effect be a cartel agreement by the states to prevent tax competition among them. The three branches of government are in broad agreement on the fundamental principle of taxation and restriction, though they may disagree on the types and levels. Moreover, in the USA the two major political parties form a cartel for power sharing (restricting ballot access by other parties) and fight over the ability to exploit it – but not over the system itself. Hence there is broad cooperation over the fundamental *de facto* constitutional provision for rent seeking, with competition only for the spoils. In oligopolies producing severable goods, there is an incentive for one producer to cheat on the cartel, selling its goods slightly below the cartel price, but, in the government oligopoly, collusion is less likely to break down, because the cooperation of all the agencies is required to provide the output, transfers of wealth.

A different structural reform is one that would permit entry and exit into the government business itself, underpricing the cartel. It would permit any person or organization having a title to land to withdraw the site from any government jurisdiction and create its own governance. Buchanan and Faith (1987) and Allen Buchanan (1991) have theorized on secession from a government as a constraint on the potential opportunism of a ruling coalition. As also noted by Anton Lowenberg (1992), an exit option helps maintain the post-constitutional enforcement of constitutional rules. 'Voice' or voting alone may not be sufficient. An individual has little control over the political process, but legalized geographical exit (what Buchanan and Faith, 1987, call 'internal exit') would enable him to withdraw from a dysfunctional process as an alternative to an infeasible reform of the system. As analyzed by Buchanan (1991), a constitution could set forth only procedural requirements for withdrawal, not requiring any substantive grounds to justify the secession. The procedure would include the payment of mutual obligations, like a fair-property settlement in a divorce (p. 133), including an exit fee as described below.

Michael Marlow (1992) notes that government monopolies are favored by those who perceive government to be too small (for example, to handle externalities) and competitive governments are favored by those who perceive government as being too big, overexpanded as the result of perverse incentives. But the primary issue is not the size of government *per se*, but whether the expenditures are those chosen by the citizens. Size becomes a problem precisely because there are expenditures not freely chosen by the taxpayers and citizens. The purpose of secession is to widen choice, rather than necessarily to decrease the proportion of expenditures provided by governance.

The ability to secede would be a powerful check on transfer seeking. Besides the mobility of the Tiebout model, there would be geographic exit, secession, from large-area jurisdictions. Personal exit would be a more feasible option for small associations, such as a condominium, and geographic exit for large jurisdictions. Let the site owner that is seceding be called the 'seceder', the seceding area the 'new realm', and the government or association being seceded from be called the 'old realm'. If legalized secession is implemented by countries or their states and provinces, the old realms could still retain 'residual sovereignty'. For example, if a person withdrew his land from the jurisdiction of both Virginia and the USA, both could still claim to have nominal jurisdiction regarding their federal or international boundaries, but they would exercise no power within the new realm other than defensive measures as set forth in the constitution. Geographical exit could also be a constitutional provision of large contractual communities, and there could be some residual ownership rights held by the old realm, so that secession need not be a complete break from the old realm.

Secession would create free-riders on large-area territorial services unless it was accompanied by some payment agreement. If a secession amendment is linked to the passage of the tax amendment indicated above, or the payment of civic goods from site rents, then the free-rider problem could be overcome. With all taxes eliminated except those tapping site rents, the withdrawal of a lot from a jurisdiction would be permitted providing the seceder paid an exit fee that in effect purchases the land from the old realm, or more specifically, purchases that amount of land value generated by the services rendered by the old realm.

The exit fee would compensate the old realm for the future services rendered. The question then becomes whether the compensation is best based on the entire land rent tax or assessment or some fraction of it. A 100 per cent payment would be too high, for several reasons. First, it may be difficult to estimate the rent generated by a service such as defense. Second, the cost of an inefficient or unwanted service may be higher than the generated rents and, hence, an assessment of rent may tap rent not generated by the services. Third, even if the marginal induced rent can be estimated, if most of the territory of the old realm seceded, then the small territory remaining would end up with much of the land value and control of the large-area civic goods. Fourth, secession would not accomplish the goal of withdrawing a new realm from the dysfunctional governance of the old realm, since the old realm would be compensated for its continuing governance.

On the other hand, a zero payment would be too low since, if only a few sites secede, then they have a financial free ride. As a simple compromise, the constitution could specify an exit fee equal to the present value of *half* the assessment or tax of land rent, the 50 per cent figure leaving also a margin for error in case some of the assessments do not generate much rent. The amendment could be specified as follows:

Any person or organization holding title to land may withdraw it from the jurisdiction of the government (or association), provided that the title holder pay 50 per cent of the present value of the annual land-value taxes or land-rent fees payable at the time of secession. This amount equals half the current payments divided by the average real long-term interest rate for lowest-risk bonds during the preceding ten years. The seceder shall then not be subject to any legislation of the government, but no adult person shall be forced to remain in the seceding territory against his will, nor may the seceding territory enact any law violating the natural or contractual rights of the residents or visitors. If such rights are negated, then the secession becomes null and void.

Alternatively, the new realm could choose to continue to pay rent to the old realm rather than the exit fee. If the new and old realms later mutually agreed to merge, then the old realm would rebate the exit fee, less some amount for the transaction costs, in effect buying the land value back.

If both secession and the elimination of all restrictions and taxation are infeasible, lesser reforms could facilitate consensual governance. First, contractual communities would have a constitutionally guaranteed right of free association. Adults could have any kind of internal agreement they wished. Aside from fiscal equality, private communities often do not have legal equality vis-à-vis the sovereign governments. Local and state governments do not endow the private associations with governance autonomy. The case of Arden demonstrates the state alteration of contractual agreements, and the case of Fort Ellsworth is an example of city government imposing rules on the condominium, such as on the use of the private swimming pool. In addition, disgruntled association members have appealed to local government for aid in their disputes with the RCA boards (Dean, 1989a, p. 5). Government regulations induce a standardization of RCA governing documents, whereby developers often use the language of government forms (Winokur, 1989 [1988]).

Second, governments would permit 'tax substitution', a rebate or credit for civic goods that take the place of those provided by government. Tax substitution amounts to a limited secession. Such a proposal has been advocated for education; tuition for alternative schools, up to some level, would be credited against tax liabilities. The elimination of tax advantages for land ownership (such as the ability to deduct interest payments of mortgages but not of personal loans) and the abolition of taxes on civic association property would also stimulate contractual governance. The case studies of Walt Disney World, Arden and Reston demonstrate that the contractual provision of collective goods is enhanced by the removal of restrictions and non-reimbursed taxes imposed by higher levels of government. Neighborhoods and residential associations could then substitute their own police, street maintenance, parks and other services for those provided by governments.

Entrepreneurs would be able to buy easements and rights to neighborhoods and corridors, create civic goods and then charge for passage or use of the goods, which would be credited against taxes for government substitutes.

'Hold-outs' – those who refuse to sell land rights or easements to these entrepreneurs – could be dealt with in several ways. First, they would be excluded from the civic association, losing some severable benefits such as police protection or access from the dwelling's driveway to the street. Second, they would suffer a loss of sympathy or the goodwill of their neighbors. Third, they would seldom be autonomous agents, but already be in some community, such as under a sovereign government and tax regime, so the choice would be which agency to affiliate with, rather than that of affiliation in itself. Finally, 'hold-outs' are not without social benefits, since the ability to refuse to join an association prevents the association from becoming exploitative.

Rather than requiring sovereign intervention and finance, the case studies show that private provision has been hindered by government policy. Many of the problems facing these communities stem from sovereign interventions. In the case of WDW and Reston, the elimination of restricting zoning was necessary for the development of the communities. The failure of government to protect the original contract law was a key factor in moving Arden towards a less proprietary governance.

Tax policy pushed Arden towards a municipal government, and the status of governance has been a continuing question at Reston. In Connecticut, Oronoque Village switched from an RCA to a tax district to obtain tax deductions (Dean, 1989a, p. 19). Local government profits from the tax revenues of residential association property, which are greater than the expenditures of local government for those areas since the infrastructure is maintained privately. RCAs seldom obtain reduced tax liabilities for services which take the place of those of local government. Dean (p. 5) also notes that RCA owners pay property taxes on the higher values which are due to their own private services and that, in some states, the amenities of the home owner associations are taxed as well.

In some jurisdictions, RCAs have obtained more autonomy and tax substitution. In Connecticut, some 20 condominium associations have formed special taxing districts, the taxes being in lieu of association fees, and such taxes are deductible from income taxes (Dean, 1989b, p. 11). Refuse collection is one service that often receives tax credits or rebates. An equal treatment of RCA assessments with property taxes and the ability of RCA owners to take tax credits for RCA expenses which substitute for local government services would enable the private communities to provide those services desired by their members.

Wagner (1988b, p. 21) suggests that constitutional provisions limited to constraints do not address the impetus of political entrepreneurship to accomplish goals; a constitutional framework can also allow for active governors 'limited only by the natural forces of competition, rightly constructed'. Communities would have fluid boundaries, with both secession and annexation (p. 25). The three amendments proposed above would give full scope for political entrepreneurs to form contractual communities in which they could promote whatever goals they wished, so long as the community permitted exit and pursued their goals peacefully. As noted by MacCallum (1970), private governance avoids the dilemma of taking property in order to protect property, and gives both the developers and the residential associations the ability to provide public goods, limited only by the forces of competition.

A devolution from unicentric to polycentric governance would not eliminate civic goods with large economies of scale. As discussed in Chapter 14, civic associations do cooperate to provide larger-area services. They form associations of associations. Local groups would form regional associations, which would then join in continental associations providing services such as national defense and the determination of property rights such as airline routes. National defense has been considered an example of a public good unable to be provided by voluntary means. But the model usually presented is one of millions of atomistic households hopelessly stuck in a giant prisoner's dilemma: everybody wants to benefit at the expense of others, so no one benefits. But since human beings are always, already, in community, this model is an economic myth. In a free society, households would be members of one or more civic associations or proprietary communities, which would federate into ever higher levels, reaching a continental level that could indeed provide defense services, if that were regarded as useful. It would be a market provision of large-area defense because each household would be in a contractual relationship with a proprietor or association, free to leave the relationship when the contract expired. The argument against the market provision of large-area defense is based on one particular form of market organization (defense agencies contracting with atomistic households), whereas the market would more likely consist of multi-level federations.

There are three types of federation: bottom-up, parallel and top-down. Bottom-up federation consists of an umbrella organization formed by the smaller entities, from which any member may leave. The governance is controlled by the constituent members. Trade associations are an example. Parallel federation is a union in which the federal agency and its provinces or states have an equal governance status; the USA is an example, where the federal and state governments are equally sovereign. Top-down federation consists of sub-units controlled by the central organization, as are the counties of states. When private communities federate, they usually form bottom-up federations, which achieves economies of scale without giving up independence. Condominium leagues that have formed in some cities are an example. The union may still have strong bonds, providing a package of services that the members find difficult to do without, but, if need be, they could secede from an ineffective federation and refederate. Bottom-up federation thus provides for flexibility and reduces the potential for opportunism by the federal governance. Successive levels of bottom-up federation could extend to a continental or global area, as Heath (1957, p. 96) envisioned, so that even world-wide territorial services such as the coordination of satellite routes could be provided, as they now are among countries.

Conclusion

The theory presented in Chapters 1 to 8 presents the proposition that territorial public goods generate rents and, if an organization has ownership rights to the sites on which the rents arise, the rents reveal the demand for the goods and provide the means to pay for them. Volunteer efforts and tie-ins between private and public goods provide other ways that private communities finance collective goods.

The primary hypothesis – that incentives for personal gain do not in general induce private agents to provide the public goods that the people in the service domain effectively demand, because there is no way to induce individual users to each pay for a portion of the good – has been rejected for territorial as well as other collective goods in the five major case studies. The case studies demonstrate that decentralized private communities are providing public goods abundantly. Since the issue is the *feasibility* of private provision, the existence of the case study communities is sufficient to reject the hypothesis of market failure. Contractual communities can provide such goods, although the provision in any specific time and place is not automatic but depends on institutional factors permitting such provision and entrepreneurial efforts to implement the provision.

The existence of empirical examples in whole communities of various sorts therefore implies that statements about public goods, such as that the decentralized price system cannot be used or that market mechanisms will not provide them 'optimally', are not universally true and, in particular, not valid for territorial public goods, the category into which most civic goods fit. The market-failure proposition is rejected in general for excludable goods, and also does not necessarily hold for non-excludable goods, since it is possible for Smithian sympathy to induce its provision.

Besides not taking space into account, much of the literature on public goods overlooks the fact of private governance, with RCAs as a prime example. As MacCallum (1986, p. 3) states, hundreds of proprietary communities around the world are creating environments in which people bid rents that finance the community services. Theory needs to acknowledge and understand this, so that it does not foreclose available options. Consensual communities eliminate the false alternatives of governance and markets in the provision of public goods. Private firms and associations operate under governance, yet in a market setting in which firms compete in a spontaneous order. Private communities unite governance with market competition in the provision of public goods.

Bibliography

General

SEE ALSO SPECIFIC REFERENCES FOR CHAPTERS 9–13.

Alchian, Armen R. and Demsetz, Harold (1972), 'Production, Information Costs, and Economic Organization', *American Economic Review,* **62** (5) December, 777–95.

Allen, James B. (1966), *The Company Town in the American West*, Norman: University of Oklahoma Press.

Arrow, Kenneth J. (1969), 'The Organization of Economic Activity: Issues Pertinent to the Choice of Market versus Nonmarket Allocation', in *The Analysis and Evaluation of Public Expenditures: The PPB System*, vol. 1, Washington, DC: Government Printing Office (Joint Economic Committee, US Congress).

Atkinson, Anthony B. and Stiglitz, Joseph E. (1987) [1980], *Lectures on Public Economics*, international edition, Singapore: McGraw-Hill.

Auerbach, A.J. and Feldstein, M. (1987), *Handbook of Public Economics*, Vol. II, Amsterdam: North-Holland.

Auld, D.A.L. and Eden Lorraine (1990), 'Public Characteristics of non-public Goods', *Public Finance*, **45** (3), 378–91.

Auster, Richard D. (1977), 'Private Markets in Public Goods (or Qualities)', *Quarterly Journal of Economics*, **91** (3), August, 419–30.

Barnett, Randy E. (ed.) (1989), *The Rights Retained by the People*, Fairfax, VA: George Mason University Press.

Barton, Stephen E. and Silverman, Carol J. (1989), 'The Political Life of Mandatory Homeowners' Associations', in Debra Dean (ed.), *Residential Community Associations: private governments in the intergovernmental system?*, Washington, DC: ACIR (Advisory Commission on Intergovernmental Relations), 31–7.

Barzell, Yoram and Sass, Tim R. (1990), 'The Allocation of Resources by Voting', *Quarterly Journal of Economics*, **90** (3), August, 745–71.

Bator, Francis M. (1958), 'The Anatomy of Market Failure', *Quarterly Journal of Economics*, **72** (3), August, 351–79, reprinted in Tyler Cowen (ed.) (1988), *Theory of Market Failure*, 35–68.

Becker, Gary S. (1965), 'A Theory of the Allocation of Time', *The Economic Journal*, September, 493–517.

Beito, David T. (1988), 'Voluntary Association and the Life of the City', *Humane Studies Review*, **6** (1), Fall, 1–2, 17–22.

Beito, David T. (1989), 'Owning the "Commanding Heights": Historical Perspectives on Private Streets', in *Essays in Public Works History*, **16**, December, 1–47.

Benson, Bruce L. (1990), *The Enterprise of Law: Justice Without the State*, San Francisco: Pacific Research Institute for Public Policy.

Berglass, Etian (1976), 'Distribution of Tasks and Skills and the Provision of Local Public Goods', *Journal of Public Economics*, **6** (4), November, 409–23.

Berglass, Etian (1984), 'Quantities, Qualities, and Multiple Public Services in the Tiebout Model', *Journal of Public Economics*, **25** (3), December, 299–321.

Berman, H.J. (1983), *Law and Revolution: the Foundation of the Western Legal Tradition*, Cambridge, Mass.: Harvard University Press.

Boadway, Robin and Flatters, Frank R. (1982), 'Efficiency and Equalization Payments in a Federal System of Government: A Synthesis and Extension of Recent Results', *Canadian Journal of Economics*, **15** (4), November, 613–33.

Board of Governors of the Federal Reserve System (1991), *Balance Sheets for the U.S. Economy*, Washington, DC: Federal Reserve Board.

Borcherding, Thomas E., Pommerehne, Werner W. and Schneider, Friedrich (1982), *Comparing the Efficiency of Private and Public Production: The Evidence from Five Countries*, Institute for Empirical Research in Economics, University of Zurich.

Boudreaux, Donald J. and Holcombe, Randall G. (1989), 'Government by Contract', *Public Finance Quarterly*, **17** (3), July, 264–80.

Boudreaux, Donald J. and Holcombe, Randall G. (1993), 'Contractual Governments in Theory and Practice', forthcoming in David T. Beito, (ed.), *The Voluntary City*.

Bowen, H.R. (1943), 'The Interpretation of Voting in the Allocation of Economic Resources', *Quarterly Journal of Economics*, **58** (1), November, 27–48.

Bowen, H.R. (1948), *Toward Social Economy*, New York: Rinehart.

Bradford, D.F. and Hilderbrandt, G.G. (1977), 'Observable Preferences for Public Goods', *Journal of Public Economics*, **8** (2), October, 111–31.

Brennan, Geoffrey and Buchanan, James M. (1977), 'Towards a Tax Constitution for Leviathan', *Journal of Public Economics*, **8**, 255–73.

Brown, Harry Gunnison (1936), *Economic Science and the Common Welfare*, Columbia, Mo.: Lucas Brothers.

Brown, Harry Gunnison (1979) [1924], *The Economics of Taxation*, Chicago: University of Chicago Press.

Brubaker, Earl R. (1975), 'Free Ride, Free Revelation, or Golden Rule?', *Journal of Law and Economics*, **18**, April, 147–61, reprinted in Tyler Cowen (ed.) (1988), *Theory of Market Failure*, 93–110.

Buchanan, Allen (1991), *Secession*, Boulder: Westview Press.

Buchanan, James M. (1949), 'The Pure Theory of Public Finance: A Suggested Approach', *Journal of Political Economy*, **57** (6), December, 496–505.

Buchanan, James M. (1958), 'Ceteris Paribus: Some Notes on Methodology', *Southern Economic Journal*, **24** (3), January, 259–70.

Buchanan, James M. (1962), 'Politics, Policy, and the Pigovian Margins', *Economica*, **29**, February, 17–28.

Buchanan, James M. (1965), 'An Economic Theory of Clubs', *Economica*, **32**, February, 1–14.

Buchanan, James M. (1967), 'Public Goods in Theory and Practice', *Journal of Law and Economics*, **10**, October, 193–7, reprinted in *Explorations into Constitutional Economics* (1989), pp. 213–17.

Buchanan, James M. (1968), *The Demand and Supply of Public Goods*, Chicago: Rand McNally.

Buchanan, James M. (1977), *Freedom in Constitutional Contract*, College Station: Texas A&M University Press.

Buchanan, James M. (1978) [1969], *Cost and Choice*, Chicago: University of Chicago Press.

Buchanan, James M. (1981) [1973], 'Introduction: L.S.E. cost theory in retrospect', in J.M. Buchanan and G.F. Thirlby (eds), *L.S.E. Essays on Cost*, New York: New York University Press, 1–16.

Buchanan, James M. (1987a), 'Constitutional Economics', *The New Palgrave*, London: Macmillan, 585–8.

Buchanan, James M. (1987b), *Economics: Between Predictive Science and Moral Philosophy*, ed. Robert D. Tollison and Viktor J. Vanberg, College Station: Texas A&M University Press.

Buchanan, James M. (1987c), *Public Finance in Democratic Process*, Chapel Hill: University of North Carolina Press.

Buchanan, James M. (1989), *Explorations into Constitutional Economics*, ed. Robert D. Tollison and Viktor J. Vanberg, College Station: Texas A&M University Press.

Buchanan, James M. (1990), 'The Domain of Constitutional Economics', *Constitutional Political Economy*, **1** (1), Winter, 1–18.

Buchanan, James M. and Faith, Roger L. (1987), 'Secession and the Limits of Taxation: Toward a Theory of Internal Exit', *American Economic Review*, **77** (5), December, 1023–31.

Buchanan, James M. and Goetz, Charles J. (1972), 'Efficiency Limits of Fiscal Mobility', *Journal of Public Economics*, 1, 25–43.

Buchanan, James M. and Stubblebine, William Craig (1962), 'Externality', *Economica*, **29**, November, 371–84.

Buchanan, James M. and Tullock, Gordon (1965) [1962], *The Calculus of Consent*, Ann Arbor: University of Michigan Press.

Buchanan, James M. and Wagner, Richard E. (1977), *Democracy in Deficit: The Political Legacy of Lord Keynes*, New York: Academic Press.

Burstein, M.L. (1960), 'The Economics of Tie-in Sales', *Review of Economics and Statistics*, **42** (1) February, 68–73.

Cheung, Steven N.S. (1983), 'The Contractual Nature of the Firm', *Journal of Law and Economics*, **26**, April, 1–21.

Christensen, Carol Ann (1978), 'The American Garden City: Concepts and Assumptions', dissertation, Urban and Regional Planning, University of Minnesota.

Clarke, Edward (1971), 'Multi-part Pricing of Public Goods', *Public Choice*, **11**, Fall, 17–33.

Coase, Ronald H. (1937), 'The Nature of the Firm', *Economica*, **4**, 386–405.

Coase, Ronald H. (1960), 'The Problem of Social Cost', *Journal of Law and Economics*, **3**, October, 1–44.

Coase, Ronald H. (1974), 'The Lighthouse in Economics', *Journal of Law and Economics*, **17**, October, 357–76.

Coleman, James S. (1988), 'Social Capital in the Creation of Human Capital', *American Journal of Sociology*, supplement, S95–S120.

Coleman, Jules (1988), 'Constitutional Contractarianism', *Constitutional Political Economy*, **1** (2), Spring/Summer, 135–48.

Community Associations Factbook (1988), Alexandria: Community Associations Institute.

Congleton, Roger D. (1991), 'Rational Ignorance, Rational Expectations and Fiscal Illusion', manuscript, paper presented at a seminar of the Center for the Study of Market Processes, George Mason University, 17 September 1991.

Cord, Steven (1985), 'How Much Revenue Would a Full Land Value Tax Yield? Analysis of Census and Federal Reserve Data', *American Journal of Economics and Sociology*, **44** (3), July, 279–93.

Cord, Steven (1991), 'Land Rent is 20% of U.S. National Income for 1986', *Incentive Taxation*, July/August.

Cornes, Richard and Sandler, Todd (1984), 'Easy Riders, Joint Production, and Public Goods', *Economic Journal*, **94**, 580–98.

Cornes, Richard and Sandler, Todd (1986), *The Theory of externalities, public goods and club goods*, Cambridge: Cambridge University Press.

Cowen, Tyler (1985), 'Public Goods and Their Institutional Context: A Critique of Public Goods Theory', *Review of Social Economy*, **43**, 53–63 .

Cowen, Tyler (1988), 'Public Goods and Externalities: Old and New Perspectives', in T. Cowen (ed.), *Theory of Market Failure*, Fairfax, VA: George Mason University Press, 1–26.

Cowen, Tyler (1990), 'Law as a Public Good: The Economics of Anarchy', manuscript, George Mason University.

Cremer, Jacques and Riordan, Michael H. (1985), 'A Sequential Solution to the Public Goods Problem', *Econometrica*, **53** (1), January, 77–84.

Dahlman, Carl J. (1979), 'The Problem of Externality', *Journal of Law and Economics*, **22**, April, 141–62 .

Davis, J. Ronnie and Hewlett, Joe R. (1977), *An Analysis of Market Failure: Externalities, Public Goods, and Mixed Goods*, Gainesville: The University Presses of Florida.

Dean, Debra, ed., (1989a), *Residential Community Associations: Private Governments in the Intergovernmental System?*, Washington, DC: ACIR (Advisory Commission on Intergovernmental Relations).

Dean, Debra (1989b), *Residential Community Associations: Questions and Answers for Public Officials*, Washington, DC: ACIR (Advisory Commission on Intergovernmental Relations).

Demsetz, Harold (1964), 'The Exchange and Enforcement of Property Rights', *Journal of Law and Economics*, **7**, October, 11–26, reprinted in Tyler Cowen (ed.) (1988), *Theory of Market Failure*, 127–46.

Demsetz, Harold (1970), 'The Private Production of Public Goods', *Journal of Law and Economics*, **13**, October, 293–306, reprinted in Tyler Cowen (ed.) (1988), *Theory of Market Failure*, 111–26.

Demsetz, Harold (1982), *Economic, Legal, and Political Dimensions of Competition*, Amsterdam: North-Holland Publishing Co.

Demsetz, Harold (1988), 'The Theory of the Firm Revisited', in *Ownership, Control, and the Firm*, Oxford: Basil Blackwell, 144–65.

Den Uyl, Douglas J. (1985), *Studia Spinoza: Spinoza's Philosophy of Society*, n.p.

De Tocqueville, Alexis (1946) [1835], *Democracy in America*, Volume I, New York: Alfred A. Knopf.

Dicey, A.V. (1982) [1885], *Introduction to the Study of The Law of the Constitution*, Indianapolis: Liberty Classics.

Doernberg, Richard L. and McChesney, Fred S. (1987), 'On the Accelerating Rate and Decreasing Durability of Tax Reform', *Minnesota Law Review*, **71**, 913–62.

Dudey, Marc (1990), 'Competition by Choice: The Effect of Consumer Search on Firm Location Decisions', *American Economic Review*, **80** (5), December, 1092–1104.

Dunbar, Peter M. (1988), *The Homeowners Association Manual*, 2nd edn,

Clearwater, Florida: Suncoast Professional Publishing Corporation, and Alexandria, Virginia: Community Associations Institute.

Ellickson, B. (1973), 'A Generalization of the Pure Theory of Public Goods', *American Economic Review*, **63** (3), June, 417–32.

Enke, Stephen (1955), 'More on the Misuse of Mathematics in Economics: A Rejoinder', *Review of Economics and Statistics*, **37** (2), May, 131–3.

Epple, Dennis and Zelenitz, Allan (1981), 'The Implications of Competition among Jurisdictions: Does Tiebout Need Politics?' *Journal of Political Economy*, **89** (6), December, 1197–1217.

Feldstein, Martin (1977), 'The Surprising Incidence of a Tax on Pure Rent: A New Answer to an Old Question', *Journal of Political Economy*, **85** (2), April, 349–60.

Feldstein, M.S. and Inman, R.P. (eds) (1977), *Economics of Public Services*, London: Macmillan.

Fishman, Robert (1982), *Urban Utopias in the Twentieth Century*, Cambridge, Mass.: MIT Press.

Fitzgerald, Randall (1988), *When Government Goes Private*, New York: Universe Books.

Flatters, Frank, Henderson, Vernon and Mieszkowski, Peter (1974), 'Public Goods, Efficiency, and Regional Fiscal Equalization', *Journal of Public Economics*, **3** (2), May, 99–112.

Foldvary, Fred E. (1980), *The Soul of Liberty*, San Francisco: The Gutenberg Press.

Foldvary, Fred E. (1989), 'Rental Income in the USA: the Mystery of the Missing Billions', in Ronald Banks (ed.), *Costing the Earth*, London: Shepheard-Walwyn, 177–81.

Frazier, Marc (1980), 'Privatizing the City', *Policy Review*, **12**, Spring, 91–108.

Frazier, Marc (1989) [1988], 'Seeding Grass Roots Recovery: New Catalysts for Community Associations', in Debra Dean (ed.), *Residential Community Associations: private governments in the intergovernmental system?*, Washington, DC: ACIR (Advisory Commission on Intergovernmental Relations), 63–74.

Frey, Bruno S. (1978), 'Politico-Economic Models and Cycles', *Journal of Public Economics*, **9**, April, 203–20.

Friedman, David (1989), *The Machinery of Freedom*, La Salle: Open Court.

Friedman, Lawrence (1967), 'Psychological Pricing in the Food Industry', *Prices: Issues in Theory, Practice, and Public Policy*, Philadelphia: University of Pennsylvania Press.

Friedman, Milton (1962), *Price Theory: A Provisional Text*, Chicago: Aldine Publishing.

Gaffney, Mason (1968), 'The Valuation of Public Goods', in Morris Garnsey and James Hibbs (eds), *Social Sciences and the Environment*, Boulder: University of Colorado Press, 154–60.

Gaffney, Mason (1970), 'Adequacy of Land as a Tax Base', in Daniel Holland (ed.), *The Assessment of Land Value*, Madison: University of Wisconsin Press.

Gaffney, Mason (1976), 'Toward Full Employment with Limited Land and Capital', in Arthur D. Lynn, Jr. (ed.), *Property Taxation, Land Use, and Public Policy*, Madison: University of Wisconsin Press.

Gaffney, Mason (1982), 'Two Centuries of Economic Thought on Taxation of Land Rents', in *Land Value Taxation: The* Progress and Poverty *Centenary*, Madison: University of Wisconsin Press, 151–95.

Gaffney, Mason (1989), 'The Role of Ground Rent in Urban Decay and Revival', *Distinguished Papers*, 89F-1, Business Research Institute, St. Johns University.

Galantay, Ervin Y. (1975), *New Towns: Antiquity to Present*, New York: George Braziller.

Garner, John S. (1984), *The Model Company Town*, Amherst: University of Massachusetts Press.

Geiger, George R. (1933), *The Philosophy of Henry George*, New York: The Macmillan Company.

George, Henry (1890), 'The Single Tax: What it Is and Why We Urge It', *The Christian Advocate*, reprinted by the Robert Schalkenbach Foundation, New York.

George Henry (1975) [1879], *Progress and Poverty*, New York: Robert Schalkenbach.

Glazer, Amihai and Niskanen, Esko (1991), 'Why Voters May Prefer Congested Public Clubs', manuscript, paper presented at the conference of the American Economic Association, New Orleans, 4 January 1992.

Goldin, Kenneth (1977), 'Equal Access vs. Selective Access: A Critique of Public Goods Theory', *Public Choice*, **29**, Spring, 53–72, reprinted in Tyler Cowen (ed.) (1988), *Theory of Market Failure*, 69–92.

Gonzales, R.A. and Mehay, S.L. (1987), 'Municipal Annexation and Local Monopoly Power', *Public Choice*, **52** (3), 245–55.

Gorman, W.M. (1980), 'A Possible Procedure for Analyzing Quality Differentials in the Egg Market', *Review of Economic Studies*, **47**, 843–56.

Groves, T. and Ledyard, J. (1977), 'Optimal Allocation of Public Goods: A Solution to the Free Rider Problem', *Econometrica*, **45**, 783–810.

Gwartney, James D. and Wagner, Richard E. (eds) (1988), *Public Choice and Constitutional Economics*, Greenwich, CT: Jain Press.

Hamilton, Bruce W. (1975), 'Zoning and Property Taxation in a System of Local Governments', *Urban Studies*, **12** (2), June, 205–11.

Hamilton, Bruce W. (1991) [1987], 'Tiebout Hypothesis', in John Eatwell, Murray Milgate and Peter Newman (eds), *The World of Economics*, New York: W.W. Norton, 672–7, first published in *The New Palgrave: A Dictionary of Economics*, London: Macmillan.

Hawkins, Robert B. (1988), Preface, *Metropolitan Organization: The St. Louis Case*, M-158, Washington, DC: ACIR (Advisory Commission on Intergovernmental Relations).

Hayek, Friedrich A. (1941), *The Pure Theory of Capital*, Chicago: University of Chicago Press.

Hayek, Friedrich A. (1945), 'The Use of Knowledge in Society', *American Economic Review*, **35** (4), September, 519–30.

Hayek, Friedrich A. (1960), *The Constitution of Liberty*, Chicago: University of Chicago Press.

Hayek, Friedrich A. (1967), 'The Results of Human Action but not of Human Design', in *Studies in Philosophy, Politics and Economics*, Chicago: University of Chicago Press, 96–105.

Hayek, Friedrich A. (1976), *Law, Legislation and Liberty*, vol. 2, *The Mirage of Social Justice*, Chicago: University of Chicago Press.

Hayek, Friedrich A. (1979) [1952], *The Counter-Revolution of Science*, Indianapolis: Liberty Press.

Hayek, Friedrich A. (1985) [1978], 'Competition as a Discovery Procedure', in *New Studies in Philosophy, Politics, Economics and the History of Ideas*, Chicago: University of Chicago Press, 179–90.

Hayek, Friedrich A. (1988), *The Fatal Conceit: The Errors of Socialism*, London: Routledge.

Head, John G. and Shoup, Carl S. (1969), 'Public Goods, Private Goods, and Ambiguous Goods', *The Economic Journal*, **79**, September, 567–72.

Heath, Spencer (1936), 'Politics Versus Proprietorship', manuscript.

Heath, Spencer (1957), *Citadel, Market and Altar*, Baltimore: Science of Society Foundation.

Heilbroner, Robert L. and Thurow, Lester C. (1987), *Economics Explained*, New York: Simon & Schuster.

Heiner, R.A. (1988), 'The Necessity of Imperfect Decisions', *Journal of Economic Behavior and Organization*, **10** (1), July, 29–56.

Henderson, J. Vernon (1985), 'The Tiebout Model: Bring Back the Entrepreneurs', *Journal of Political Economy*, **93** (2), April, 248–64.

High, Jack (1985), 'Is Economics Independent of Ethics?', *Reason Papers*, **10**, Spring, 3–16.

High, Jack and Ellig, Jerome (1988), 'The Private Supply of Education: Some Historical Evidence', in Tyler Cowen (ed.) (1988), *Theory of Market Failure*, 361–82.

Hirschman, Albert O. (1970), *Exit, Voice, and Loyalty*, Cambridge, Mass.: Harvard University Press.

Hochman, Oded (1981), 'Land Rents, Optimal Taxation and Local Fiscal Independence in an Economy with Local Public Goods', *Journal of Public Economics*, **15** (1), February, 59–85.

Holcombe, Randall G. (1988) *Public Sector Economics*, Belmont, CA: Wadsworth Publishing.

Holcombe, Randall G. (1989), 'The Distinction Between Clubs and Governments', manuscript, Florida State University.

Holländer, Heinz (1990), 'A Social Exchange Approach to Voluntary Cooperation', *American Economic Review*, **80** (5), December, 1157–67.

Holtermann, S.E. (1972), 'Externalities and Public Goods', *Economica*, **39** (153), February, 78–87.

Hotelling, H. (1938), 'The General Welfare in Relation to Problems of Taxation and of Railway and Utility Rates', *Econometrica*, **6**, 242–69.

Howard, Ebenezer (1965) [1902], *Garden Cities of To-Morrow*, Cambridge, Mass.: MIT Press.

Hume, David (1978) [1739], *A Treatise of Human Nature*, 2nd edn, Oxford: Clarendon Press.

Hutchison, Terence (1988), *Before Adam Smith*, New York: Basil Blackwell.

Institute for Community Economics (1982), *The Community Land Trust Handbook*, Emmaus: Rodale Press.

Jacobs, Jane (1969), *The Economy of Cities*, New York: Random House.

Jacobs, Jane (1984), *Cities and the Wealth of Nations*, New York: Random House.

'King Street Gardens Park' (n.d.), Alexandria, Virginia: Alexandria Commission for the Arts.

Klein, Daniel B. (1990), 'The Voluntary Provision of Public Goods? The Turnpike Companies of Early America', *Economic Inquiry*, **28** (4), October, 788–812.

Kropotkin, Petr (1974) [1914], *Mutual Aid*, Boston: Extending Horizon Books.

Lachmann, Ludwig (1978) [1956], *Capital and its Structure*, Kansas City: Sheed Andrews and McMeel.

Lancaster, Kelvin J. (1966), 'A New Approach to Consumer Theory', *Journal of Political Economy*, **74** (2), April, 132–57.

Lancaster, Kelvin J. (1971), *Consumer Demand: A New Approach*, New York: Columbia University Press.

Lavine, T.Z. (1989), 'The Interpretive Turn from Kant to Derrida: A Critique', in T.Z. Lavine and V. Tejera (eds), *History and Anti-History in Philosophy*, n.p.: Kluwer Academic Publishers.

Lee, Dwight R. (1982), 'On the Pricing of Public Goods', *Southern Economic Journal*, **49** (1), July, 99–105.

Lee, Dwight R. (1985), 'Rent-Seeking and its Implications for Pollution Taxation', *Southern Economic Journal*, **51**, January, 731–44.

Lindahl, Erik (1958) [1919], 'Just Taxation – A Positive Solution', in R.A. Musgrave and Alan T. Peacock (eds), *Classics in the Theory of Public Finance*, 168–76.

Locke, John (1947) [1690], *Two Treatises of Government*, ed. Thomas I. Cook, New York: Hafner Press.

Lowenberg, Anton D. (1992), 'Efficient Constitution Formation and Maintenance: The Role of Exit', *Constitutional Political Economy*, **3** (1), Winter, 51–72.

MacCallum, Spencer (1965), 'The Social Nature of Ownership', *Modern Age*, **9** (1), Winter 1964/5, 49–61.

MacCallum, Spencer (1970), *The Art of Community*, Menlo Park: Institute for Humane Studies.

MacCallum, Spencer (1971), 'Jural Behavior in American Shopping Centers: Initial Views on the Proprietary Community', *Human Organization*, **30** (1), Spring, 3–10.

MacCallum, Spencer (1972), 'Associated Individualism: a Victorian dream of freedom', *Reason*, **4** (1) April, 17–24.

MacCallum, Spencer (1977), 'Drafting a Constitution for ORBIS', *Rampart Individualist*, **1** (1&2), 35–52.

MacCallum, Spencer (1986), 'Outgrowing Government as We Know It', from a lecture, San Pedro, CA: The Heather Foundation.

Machan, Tibor (1982), 'Dissolving the Problem of Public Goods: Financing Government without Coercive Measures', in *The Libertarian Reader*, Totowa: Rowman and Littlefield, 201–8.

Maine, Henry Sumner (1986) [1861], *Ancient Law*, London: Dorset Press.

Manne, H. (1965), 'Mergers and the Market for Corporate Control', *Journal of Political Economy*, **73**, 110–20.

Mansfield, Edwin and Behravesh, Nariman (1989), *Economics U\$A*, 2nd edn, New York: W.W. Norton.

Margolis, Julius (1955), 'A Comment on the Pure Theory of Public Expenditure', *Review of Economics and Statistics*, **37** (4), November, 347–9.

Marlow, Michael L. (1992), 'Intergovernmental Competition, Voice and Exit Options and the Design of Fiscal Structure', *Constitutional Political Economy*, **3** (1), Winter, 73–88.

Marshall, Alfred (1961) [1920], *Principles of Economics*, New York: Macmillan Company.

Martin, D. and Wagner, R. (1978), 'The Institutional Framework for Municipal Incorporation', *Journal of Law and Economics*, **21**, 409–25.

Mazzola, U. (1958) [1890], 'The Formation of the Prices of Public Goods', in R.A. Musgrave and Alan T. Peacock (eds), *Classics in the Theory of Public Finance*, 37–47.

Menger, Carl (1976) [1871], *Principles of Economics*, trans. James Dingwall and Bert Hoselitz, New York: New York University Press.

Mieszkowski, Peter and Zodrow, George R. (1989), 'Taxation and the Tiebout Model', *Journal of Economic Literature*, **27** (3), September, 1098–1146.

Miles, Mike (1990), 'What is the Value of All U.S. Real Estate?', *Real Estate Review*, **20** (2), Summer, 69–75.

Miller, Dean J. (1989), 'Life Cycle of an RCA', in Debra Dean (ed.), *Residential Community Associations: private governments in the intergovernmental system?*, Washington, DC: ACIR (Advisory Commission on Intergovernmental Relations), 39–44.

Minasian, Jora R. (1964), 'Television Pricing and the Theory of Public Goods', *Journal of Law and Economics*, **7**, October, 71–80.

Mishan, E.J. (1969), 'The Relationship between Joint Products, Collective Goods, and External Effects', *Journal of Political Economy*, **77** (3), May/June, 329–48.

MIT Dictionary of Modern Economics (1986), ed. David W. Pearce, 3rd edn, Cambridge, Mass.: MIT Press.

Mueller, Dennis C. (1977), 'The Effects of Conglomerate Mergers: A Survey of the Empirical Evidence', *Journal of Banking and Finance*, **1**, 339.

Mueller, Dennis C. (1979), *Public Choice*, Cambridge: Cambridge University Press.

Munzer, Martha E. and Vogel, John Jr. (1974), *New Towns: Building Cities from Scratch*, New York: Alfred A. Knopf.

Musgrave, Richard A. (1939), 'The Voluntary Exchange Theory of Public Economy', *Quarterly Journal of Economics*, **53** (2), February, 213–37.

Musgrave, Richard A. (1959), *The Theory of Public Finance*, New York: McGraw-Hill Book Company.

Musgrave, Richard A. (1969), 'Provision for Social Goods', in J. Margolis and H. Guitton (eds), *Public Economics: An Analysis of Public Production and Consumption and their Relations to the Private Sectors: Proceedings of a Conference held by the International Economic Association*, London: Macmillan, 124–44.

Musgrave, Richard A. (1983), 'Public Goods', in E. Cary Brown and Robert M. Solow (eds), *Paul Samuelson and Modern Economic Theory*, New York: McGraw-Hill, 141–56.

Musgrave, Richard A. and Musgrave, Peggy B. (1989), *Public Finance in Theory and Practice*, New York: McGraw Hill.

Musgrave, R.A. and Peacock, Alan T. (eds) (1958), *Classics in the Theory of Public Finance*, London: Macmillan & Co.

Neely, Richard (1990), *Take Back Your Neighborhood*, New York: Donald I. Fine.

Nelson, Robert H. (1989), 'The Privatization of Local Government: From Zoning to RCAs', in Debra Dean (ed.), *Residential Community Associations: private governments in the intergovernmental system?*, Washington, DC: ACIR (Advisory Commission on Intergovernmental Relations), 45–52.

Netherton, Nan (1989), *Reston: A New Town in the Old Dominion*, Norfolk, VA: The Donning Company.

The New Palgrave: A Dictionary of Economics (1987), ed. John Eatwell, Murray Milgate, Peter Newman, London: The Macmillan Press (4 volumes).

Ng, Yew-Kwang (1973), 'The Economic Theory of Clubs: Pareto Optimality Conditions', *Economica*, **40**, August, 291–8.

Ng, Yew-Kwang (1974), 'The Economic Theory of Clubs: Optimal Tax/Subsidy', *Economica*, **41**, August, 308–21.

Niskanen, William A. (1991), 'The District of Columbia: America's Worst Government?', *Policy Analysis*, **165** (CATO Institute), 18 November.

Noyes, Charles Reinold (1936), *The Institution of Property*, New York: Longmans, Green.

Oakland, William H. (1972), 'Congestion, Public Goods and Welfare', *Journal of Public Economics*, **1** (3/4), November, 339–57.

Oates, Wallace E. (1969), 'The Effects of Property Taxes and Local Public Spending on Property Values: An Empirical Study of Tax Capitalization and the Tiebout Hypothesis', *Journal of Political Economy*, **77** (6), November/December, 957–71.

Olson, Mancur (1971), *The Logic of Collective Action*, Cambridge, Mass.: Harvard University Press.

Olson, Mancur (1989) [1987], 'Collective Action', in John Eatwell, Murray Milgate and Peter Newman (eds), *The Invisible Hand (The New Palgrave)*, New York: W.W. Norton, 61–9.

Ostrom, Vincent, Tiebout, Charles M. and Warren, Robert (1961), 'The Organization of Government in Metropolitan Areas: A Theoretical Inquiry', *American Political Science Review*, **55**, December, 831–42.

Pantaleoni, Maffeo (1958), 'Contribution to the Theory of the Distribution of Public Expenditure', in R.A. Musgrave and Alan T. Peacock (eds), *Classics in the Theory of Public Finance*, London: Macmillan and Co.

Patinkin, Don (1965), *Money, Interest, and Prices*, 2nd edn, New York: Harper & Row.

Polanyi, Michael (1951), *The Logic of Liberty*, Chicago: University of Chicago Press.

Pommerehne, Werner W. and Schneider, Friedrich (1978), 'Fiscal Illusion,

Political Institutions, and Local Public Spending', *Kyklos*, **31**, fasc. 3, 381–408.

Poole, Nancy W. (1991), 'Fire-Fighting for Profit', *The Freeman*, **41**, (8), August, 309–313.

Poole, Robert W., Jr. (1976), *Cut Local Taxes*, Santa Barbara: Reason Press.

Poole, Robert W., Jr. (1980), *Cutting Back City Hall*, New York: Universe Books.

Rand, Ayn (1964), *The Virtue of Selfishness*, New York: New American Library.

Rand, Ayn (1973), 'Government Financing in a Free Society', in E. S. Phelps (ed.), *Economic Justice*, Baltimore: Penguin Books, 363–7.

Rosenberry, Katharine (1989) [1985], 'Condominium and Homeowner Associations: Should They Be Treated Like "Mini-Governments?"' in Debra Dean (ed.), *Residential Community Associations: private governments in the intergovernmental system?*, Washington, DC: ACIR (Advisory Commission on Intergovernmental Relations), 69–74.

Samuelson, Paul A. (1954), 'The Pure Theory of Public Expenditure', *Review of Economics and Statistics*, **36** (4), November, 387–9.

Samuelson, Paul A. (1955), 'Diagrammatic Exposition of a Theory of Public Expenditure', *Review of Economics and Statistics*, **37** (4), November, 350–56.

Samuelson, Paul A. (1958), 'Aspects of Public Expenditure Theories', *Review of Economics and Statistics*, **40** (4), November, 332–8.

Samuelson, Paul A. (1964), 'Public Goods and Subscription TV: Corrections of the Record', *Journal of Law and Economics*, October, 81–3, reprinted in *The Collected Scientific Papers of Paul. A. Samuelson,* vol. III, 518–20.

Samuelson, Paul A. (1967), 'Indeterminacy of Governmental Role in Public-Good Theory', *Papers on Non-Market Decision Making,* vol. III, reprinted in *The Collected Scientific Papers of Paul. A. Samuelson,* vol. III, 521.

Samuelson, Paul A. (1968), 'Pitfalls in the Analysis of Public Goods', *Journal of Law and Economics*, January.

Samuelson, Paul A. (1969), 'Pure Theory of Public Expenditure and Taxation', in J. Margolis and H. Guitton (eds), *Public Economics: An Analysis of Public Production and Consumption and their Relations to the Private Sectors: Proceedings of a Conference held by the International Economic Association*, London: Macmillan, 98–123.

Samuelson, Paul A. (1972), *The Collected Scientific Papers of Paul. A. Samuelson*, vol. III, ed. Robert C. Merton, Cambridge, Mass.: MIT Press.

Samuelson, Paul A. (1983) [1947], *Foundations of Economic Analysis*, Cambridge, Mass.: Harvard University Press.

Sandmo, Agnar (1973), 'Public Goods and the Technology of Consumption', *Review of Economic Studies*, **40** (4), October, 517–28.

Sandmo, Agnar (1989), 'Public Goods', in John Eatwell, Murray Milgate, and Peter Newman (eds), *Allocation, Information, and Markets (The New Palgrave*, New York: W.W. Norton, 254–65.

Sax, Emil (1958) [1924], 'The Valuation Theory of Taxation', in R.A. Musgrave and Alan T. Peacock (eds), *Classics in the Theory of Public Finance*, 177–89.

Schmidtz, David (1991), *The Limits of Government: An Essay on the Public Goods Argument*, Boulder: Westview Press.

Schrama, Kathleen A. (1992), 'Greed Gone Mad', *F.E.A.R. Chronicles*, **1** (2), June, 2.

Selgin, George A. (1988), *The Theory of Free Banking*, Totowa: Rowman & Littlefield.

Sidney, Algernon (1990) [1698], *Discourses Concerning Government*, ed. Thomas G. West, Indianapolis: Liberty Classics.

Smith, Adam (1976a) [1776], *The Wealth of Nations,* vol. 1. ed. Edwin Canaan, Chicago: University of Chicago Press.

Smith, Adam (1976b) [1776], *The Wealth of Nations*, vol. 2, ed. Edwin Canaan, Chicago: University of Chicago Press.

Smith, Adam (1982) [1790], *The Theory of Moral Sentiments*, Indianapolis: Liberty Classics.

Smith, Adam (1982) [1978], *Lectures on Jurisprudence*, Indianapolis: Liberty Classics.

Spiers, M. (1976), *Victoria Park: A Nineteenth-Century Suburb in its Social and Administrative Context*, Manchester: Cletham Society.

Spooner, Lysander (n.d.) [1852], *An Essay on the Trial by Jury*, Mesa, AZ: Arizona Caucus Club, originally published Boston: John P. Jewett and Company.

Steinbauer, Francis C. (1985), Foreword, in *RESTON: The First Twenty Years*, Reston, VA: Reston Publishing Company, 9–10.

Stigler, George and Becker, Gary (1977), 'De Gustibus Non Est Disputandum', *American Economic Review*, **67**, March, 76–90.

Stiglitz, Joseph E. (1977), 'The Theory of Local Public Goods', in *Economics of Public Services*, 274–333.

Stiglitz, Joseph E. (1983), 'The Theory of Local Public Goods Twenty-Five Years after Tiebout: A Perspective', in George R. Zodrow (ed.), *Local Provision of Public Services: The Tiebout Model after Twenty-Five Years*, New York: Academic Press, 17–54.

Stiglitz, Joseph E. (1986), *Economics of the Public Sector*, New York: W.W. Norton.

Strauss, Erwin (1984), *How to Start Your Own Country*, 2nd ed., Port Townsend, WA: Loompanies Unlimited.

Sutter, Daniel (1991), 'Public Goods, Indivisible Goods, and Market Failure', Manuscript, George Mason University.

Thompson, Earl (1968), 'The Perfectly Competitive Provision of Collective Goods', *Review of Economics and Statistics*, **44** (1), February, 1–12.

Tideman, T. Nicolaus (1985), 'Efficient Local Public Goods Without Compulsory Taxes', in *Perspectives on Local Public Finance and Public Policy*, vol. 2, Greenwich, Conn.: JAI Press, 181–202.

Tideman, T. Nicolaus (1990), 'Integrating Land-Value Taxation with the Internalization of Spatial Externalities', *Land Economics*, **66** (3), August, 341–55.

Tideman, T. Nicolaus and Tullock, Gordon (1976), 'A New and Superior Process for Making Social Choices', *Journal of Political Economy*, **84** (6), December, 1145–59.

Tiebout, Charles M. (1956), 'A Pure Theory of Local Expenditure', *Journal of Political Economy*, **64**, 416–24.

Tucker, Gilbert M. (1958), *The Self-Supporting City*, New York: Robert Schalkenbach Foundation.

Tullock, Gordon (1971), *The Logic of the Law*, New York: Basic Books.

Tullock, Gordon (1985), 'A New Proposal for Decentralizing Government Activity', in *Rationale Wirtschaftspolitik in komplexen Gesellschaften*, Stuttgart: Verlag W. Kohlhammer, 139–148.

Tullock, Gordon (1993), *The New Federalist*, Vancouver: The Fraser Institute.

Twomey, Steve (1993), 'Home(owner) Rule Reaches the Senate', *The Washington Post*, 6 May 1993, C1.

Vaggi, Gianni (1987), *The Economics of François Quesnay*, Durham: Duke University Press.

Varian, Hal (1984), *Microeconomic Analysis*, 2nd edn. New York: W.W. Norton.

Vickrey, William (1961), 'Counterspeculation, Auctions and Competitive Sealed Tenders', *Journal of Finance*, **16**, 8–37.

Vickrey, William (1977), 'The City as a Firm', in Martin S. Feldstein and Robert P. Inman (eds), *Economics of Public Services*, Hampshire: Macmillan, 334–43.

Vickrey, William (1990), 'Rent and the Provision of Public Services', manuscript, paper presented for the conference on 'Concepts and Procedures for the Social Collection of Rent in the Soviet Union', New York, August 1990.

Viti de Marco, Antonio de (1936), *First Principles of Public Finance*, trans. Edith Pavlo Marget, New York: Harcourt, Brace, & Co.

Wagner, Richard E. (1979), 'Optimality in Local Debt Limitation', *National Tax Journal*, **23** (3), September, 297–3

Wagner, Richard E. (1980), 'Boom and Bust: The Political Economy of Economic Disorder', *Journal of Libertarian Studies*, **4** (l), Winter, 1–37.

Wagner, Richard E. (1986), 'Liability Rules, Fiscal Institutions and the Debt', in *Deficits*, New York: Basil Blackwell, 199–217.

Wagner, Richard E. (1988a), 'The Calculus of Consent: A Wicksellian Retrospective', *Public Choice*, **56**, 153.

Wagner, Richard E. (1988b), *Parchment, Guns and Constitutional Order*, Aldershot, UK: Edward Elgar Publishing, 1993.

Wagner, Richard E. (1989), *To Promote the General Welfare*, San Francisco: Pacific Research Institute for Public Policy.

Wagner, Richard E. (1991a), 'Economic Efficiency, Rent Seeking, and Democracy: Zenoistic Variations on Coasian Themes', paper presented at the Fifth Hayek Symposium on Knowledge, Evolution, and Competition, Freiburg, 25–8 May 1991.

Wagner, Richard E. (1991b), 'Tax Norms, fiscal reality, and the democratic state: user charges and earmarked taxes in principle and practice', in Richard E. Wagner (ed.), *Charging for Government*, London: Routledge.

Walras, Léon (1896), *Studies in Social Economics*, Lausanne: F. Rouge and Co., unpublished trans. by Mason Gaffney, 1967.

Warner, Sam Bass, Jr. (1968), *The Private City: Philadelphia in Three Periods of Its Growth*, Philadelphia: University of Pennsylvania Press.

Weisbrod, B.A. (1964), 'Collective-Consumption Services of Individual-Consumption Goods', *Quarterly Journal of Economics*, **78** (3), August, 471–7.

Wicksell, Knut (1958) [1896], 'A New Principle of Just Taxation', in R.A. Musgrave and Alan T. Peacock (eds), *Classics in the Theory of Public Finance*, 72–116.

Wieser, Friedrich von (1967) [1927], *Social Economics*, trans. A. Ford Hinrichs, New York: Augustus M. Kelley Publishers.

Williamson, Oliver E. (1967), 'Hierarchical Control and Optimum Firm Size', *Journal of Political Economy*, April, 123–38 .

Williamson, Oliver E. (1975), *Markets and Hierarchies: Analysis and Antitrust Implications*, New York: The Free Press.

Williamson, Oliver E. (1979), 'Transaction-Cost Economics: The Governance of Contractual Relations', *Journal of Law and Economics*, **22**, October, 3–61 .

Williamson, Oliver E. (1985), *The Economic Institutions of Capitalism*, New York: The Free Press.

Williamson, Oliver E. (1991), 'Economic Institutions: Spontaneous and

Intentional Governance', *The Journal of Law, Economics, and Organization*, **7**, special issue, 159–87.

Winokur, James L. (1989) [1988], 'Association-Administered Servitude Regimes: A Private Property Perspective', in Debra Dean (ed.), *Residential Community Associations: private governments in the intergovernmental system?*, Washington, DC: ACIR (Advisory Commission on Intergovernmental Relations), 85–93.

Wiseman, Jack (1990), 'Principles of Political Economy', *Constitutional Political Economy* **1** (1), Winter, 101–24.

Wolf, Charles Jr. (1988), *Markets or Governments*, Cambridge, Mass.: MIT Press.

Wolfe, David B. (1978), *Condominium and Homeowner Associations That Work*, Washington, DC: Urban Land Institute, and Arlington, VA: Community Associations Institute.

Wollstein, Jarret (1992), 'The Looting of America: Civil Asset Forfeiture', ISIL Educational Pamphlet Series, San Francisco: International Society for Individual Liberty.

Wuthnow, Robert J. (1991), *Acts of Compassion: Caring for Others and Helping Ourselves*, Princeton: Princeton University Press.

Ye, Meng-Hua and Yezer, Anthony M. (1991), 'Inefficiency in a Homogenous Tiebout Community: Local Government as a Spatial Club', manuscript, paper delivered at the meetings of the American Economic Association, New Orleans, 5 January 1992.

Yinger, John (1982), 'Capitalization and the Theory of Local Public Finance', *Journal of Political Economy*, **90** (5), October, 917–43.

Young, Douglas J. (1989), 'A "Fair Share" Model of Public Good Provision', *Journal of Economic Behavior and Organization*, **11**, 137–47.

Chapter 9 (Walt Disney World)

Allen, Charlotte Low (1989), 'The Mouse that Roared in Orlando's Economy', *Insight* **5** (44), 30 October, 8–17.

Andersen, Kurt (1991), 'Look, Micky, No Kitsch!', *Time*, **138**, 66–9.

Berliner, Harold A. (1978), *The Real Magic in the Magic Kingdom: Disney's World's own Local Government*, n.p.

Bloch, Jeff (1991), *Disney World: 20 Years of Magic*, ed. Christine E. Miles, n.p.: Newsweek Inc.

Clark, Thomas (1973), 'The business behind Walt Disney World', *Sky*, **2**, March, 16–19, 37–9.

De George, Gail (1988), 'A Sweet Deal for Disney is Souring the Neighbors', *Business Week*, August, 48–9.

De Michael, Don (1973), 'Engineered Communities: Inside Walt Disney World', *Actual Specifying Engineer*, **29**, February, 53–64.

'Digest', *The Washington Post*, 13 December 1991, D2.

'Disney World is cited for polluting creek', *The New York Times*, **138**, 10 October 1988, A16.

'Disney World: putting money where the mouse is', (1991), *Chain Store Executive with Shopping Center Age*, **67**, May, 202+.

Facts and Figures (1990), ('Information from Walt Disney World'), Lake Buena Vista: The Walt Disney Company.

Form 10-K: Annual Report Pursuant to Section 13 or 15(d) of the Securities Exchange Act of 1934 (1990), Burbank: The Walt Disney Company.

Garfield, Bob 'How I Spent (and Spent and Spent) My Disney Vacation', *The Washington Post*, **114**, 7 July 1991, B5.

Greene, Katherine and Greene, Richard (1991), 'In the Beginning' in Christine E. Miles (ed.), *Disney World: 20 Years of Magic*, n.p.: Newsweek Inc., 10.

Grover, Ron (1991), *The Disney Touch: How a Daring Management Team Revived an Entertainment Empire*, Homewood, IL: Business One Irwin.

Kerwin, Kathleen and Fins, Antonio N., 'Disney is looking just a little fragilistic', *Business Week*, 25 June 1990, 52–4.

Kobliner, Beth. (1990), 'Disney World on $500 a Day', *Money*, **19** (5), May, 150–60.

Levy, David (1975), 'Learning Economics from Walt Disney World', *Reason*, **7** (6) October, 28–31.

Moore, Alexander (1990), 'Walt Disney World: Bounded Ritual Space and the Playful Pilgrimage', *Anthropological Quarterly*, **53** (3), July, 207–18.

Prototype Systems and Advanced Technologies in Use at the Walt Disney World Vacation Kingdom (1987), ('Information from Walt Disney World'), Lake Buena Vista: The Walt Disney Company.

Ross, Margaret, 'Kid Stuff', Letter, *The Washington Post Magazine*, 8 December 1991, 4.

Sehlinger, Bob (1991), *The Unofficial Guide to Walt Disney World and EPCOT*, New York: Prentice Hall.

Stern, Robert A.M. (1986), *Pride of Place*, New York: Houghton Mifflin.

Taylor, John (1987), *Storming the Magic Kingdom*, New York: Alfred A. Knopf.

Tuchman, Janice L. (1990), 'Construction turns ears to Disney', *ENR*, **224** (4), 25 January, 35–6.

Walt Disney Company Annual Report (1989), Burbank: The Walt Disney Co.

Walt Disney Company Annual Report (1990), Burbank: The Walt Disney Co.

Zehnder, Leonard E. (1975), *Florida's Disney World: Promises and Problems*, Tallahassee, FL: The Peninsula Publishing Co.

Zukin, Sharon (1991), *Landscapes of Power: From Detroit to Disney World*, Berkeley: University of California Press.

Chapter 10 (Arden)

Alyea, Paul E. and Alyea, Blanche R. (1956), *Fairhope: 1894–1954*, Tuscaloosa: University of Alabama Press.

Board of Assessors (1989), 'Report to Town Meeting', 26 June 1989, Village of Arden.

Board of Assessors (1991), 'Report to Town Assembly', 24 June 1991, Village of Arden.

'Chapter 125: An Act to Reincorporate the Village of Arden' (1967), General Assembly, State of Delaware, 510–23.

Court of Chancery, State of Delaware (1935), *Edwin S. Ross, Hamilton D. Ware, William Worthington, Trustees of Arden*, vs. *Samuel Freeman, Louis W. Marmonstein, Harry J. Pressman, Fred Whiteside, Frank Harrison*.

Curtis, Michael (1991), telephone interview, 2 November 1991.

E.F. Schumacher Society (1990), *Handbook of Documents for Use in Establishing a Community Land Trust*, Great Barrington.

Geiger, George R. (1933) – see General Bibliography.

George, Henry (1890) – see General Bibliography.

Hamburger, Aaron (1991), telephone interview, 2 November 1991.

Huntington, Charles White (1922), *Enclaves of Single Tax or Economic Rent*, vol. 2, Harvard, Mass.: Fiske Warren.

Huntington, Charles White (1929), *Enclaves of Economic Rent*, vol. 9, Harvard, Mass.: Fiske Warren.

The Institute for Community Economics (1982), *The Community Land Trust Handbook*, Emmanus, Pennsylvania: Rodale Press.

Intentional Communities (1990), Evansville, Indiana: Fellowship for Intentional Community, and Stelle, Illinois: Communities Publications Cooperative.

Liberman, Carolyn (1974), *The Arden Book*, Arden: Community Planning Committee, Arden Town Assembly.

Liberman, Carolyn and Liberman, Cy (1992), *The Arden Book*, Arden: Community Planning Committee, Arden Town Assembly.

Naureckas, Jim (1990), 'Land Trusts Offer American Land Reform', in *Intentional Communities*, 114–15.

Poole, William (1992), 'In Land We Trust', *Sierra*, **77** (2), March/April, 52–58.

Questenberry, Dan (1990), 'Residential Land Trust Organizing', in *Intentional Communities*, 116–21.

Reinke, Barbara (1975), 'Utopian Communities in America: Potentials, Promises, and Perils', manuscript, Arden Archives.

Ringrose, Isis and Brown, Benjamin (1990), 'Regional Organizing: InterCommunities of Virginia', in *Intentional Communities*, 132–5.

Robinson, Peter (1990), 'A Mixed Economy Model for Intentional Community', in *Intentional Communities*, 85–9.

Sayles, Tim (1988), 'Arden, Delaware', *Mid-Atlantic Country*, February, 24–9.

Stewart, G.T. (1970), 'Economic and Legal Aspects of the Single Tax Colony', *Journal of the Alabama Academy of Science*, 9–16.

Stucki, Jubal and Yeatman, Artie (1990), 'Community Land Trusts', in *Intentional Communities*, 104–8.

Wiencek, Henry (1992), 'Laying out the idyllic life in a latter-day Arden', *Smithsonian*, **23**, (2), May, 124–42.

Wynn, Robert W. (1965), 'The Full Rental Value: A Study of the Tax Rate in Arden Using Single Tax Theory', thesis, Master of Business Administration, University of Delaware.

Young, Arthur Nichols (1916), *The Single Tax Movement in the United States*, Princeton: Princeton University Press.

Chapter 11 (Condominiums)

Fort Ellsworth, Alexandria, Virginia

Alexandria, City of (1991), *Assessments of Real Estate*, Alexandria, Virginia.

Cheney, James R. (1992), 'New Trash Removal Service', Silver Spring: Condominium Management Incorporated.

Condominium Management, Incorporated (1981), letter to George Berls, 15 October, Silver Springs, Maryland.

Condominium Management, Incorporated (1990), 'Summary of Receipts and Disbursements, December 28, 1989', Fort Ellsworth.

Cunningham, Nat (1991), *Fort Ellsworth Cannonball*, ed. Nat Cunningham, various issues.

Fort Ellsworth Condominium Apartments (1973), 'By-Laws of the Fort Ellsworth Condominium Apartments', recorded in Deed Book 1052, Page 442, City of Alexandria, Virginia.

Fort Ellsworth Condominium Association (1989a), 'Amended Parking Regulations'.

Fort Ellsworth Condominium Association (1989b), 'Quick Reference Guide'.

Fort Ward Museum (1990), 'Col. Elmer Ellsworth: "The First to Fall"', Alexandria, VA: City of Alexandria.

Morehouse, Dean (1992), telephone interview, 20 April.

Rader, James (1991a), 'Letter from the Treasurer', Fort Ellsworth Condominium Apartments 1992 Budget (15 November).

Rader, James (1991b), conversation, Fort Ellsworth Condominium, 16 November.

Savage/Fogarty Companies (1973), 'Master Deed Establishing a Plan for Condominium Ownership of Premises Located in Alexandria, Virginia, Pursuant to the Horizontal Property Act of the State of Virginia', Recorded in Deed Book 771, Page 111, City of Alexandria, Virginia.

Strickland, Libby (1991), 'Memorandum' (Protocol for Meetings of Board of Directors, Fort Ellsworth Council of Unit Owners), 10 May.

Virginia Condominium Act (1991), Richmond, Virginia: Department of Commerce, Virginia Real Estate Board.

Virginia Condominium Regulations (1988), Richmond, Virginia: Department of Commerce, Virginia Real Estate Board.

Briarcrest, Los Angeles, California

Association Reserves (1990), 'California Community Associations Legal Requirement for an Annual Reserve Analysis', Calabasas, California.

Briarcrest Homeowners' Association (1988), 'Rules and Regulations', North Hollywood, Los Angeles, California.

'Briarcrest Proposed Budget' (1991), Briarcrest Homeowners' Association, Los Angeles.

Foldvary, Tina (1991), conversation, 26 January, Briarcrest Condominium.

Herbert J. Strickstein Law Corporation (1986), 'Declaration of Covenants, Conditions and Restrictions Establishing a Plan of Condominium Ownership for Briarcrest', Los Angeles, California.

Pearlstein, Beatrice (1991), conversation, 26 January, Briarcrest Condominium.

Other references

Bates, Steve, 'Va. Condo Owners Raise Roof Over Contract', *The Washington Post*, 17 October 1991, Dl, D5.

Hooten, Katie, 'Alexandria House: Best view in town', *Alexandria Port Gazette Packet*, 31 October 1991, 36–7.

Jacobson, Abbe, 'Condo group protests proposed billing change', *Alexandria Gazette Packet*, 31 October 1991, 1.

Kass, Benny L. 'The Tough Job of Selecting a Condo Management Firm', *The Washington Post*, 5 October 1991, F8.

Kass, Benny L. 'Confronting Apathy in Condo Associations', *The Washington Post*, 9 November 1991, E14.

Kirk, Nancye J. (1978), *The Condominium Community*, Chicago: Institute of Real Estate Management.

'Maintaining Real Estate Values in Your Community' (1992), Workshop sponsored by the Washington Metropolitan Chapter, Community Associations Institute, Tysons Corner, Fairfax County, Virginia 4 February.

Thompson, Marc, 'Life in the Condos', *The Washington Post*, 2 November 1991, A22.

Chapter 12 (Reston, etc.)

A Place Called Reston: 1990 Reston Directory (1990), Reston: New Town Publications.

Alhosain, Fahad and Aldeaijy, Emad (1991), 'Land Use, Land Distribution, and Proposed Geographic Information System Solution', in *Case Study of Reston: Planned Community*, 62–78.

Arthur D. Little, Inc. (1962), 'Planning Memoranda on Reston: Report to Simon Enterprises' (January), Folder 1, Box 1, Series 1, Planned Community Archives.

'Articles of Incorporation of Reston Association' (1987), in *Governing Documents of the Reston Association*, 15–21.

Board of Directors, Reston Association (1991a), Meeting, 26 September.

Board of Directors, Reston Association (1991b), Meeting, 24 October.

Board of Directors, Reston Association (1992), Meeting, 23 January.

Case Study of Reston: Planned Community (1991), Planned Community and Urban Systems Engineering, Urban Systems Engineering 659, Professor Terry Ryan, Spring 1991, George Mason University, Planned Community Archives.

Cauthers, Richard (1991), 'Reston Water System, Past and Present', in *Case Study of Reston: Planned Community*, 28–35.

Chamlee, Emily and Wright, Bryan (1992), interview, 23 January.

Changery, Christopher, 'Reston pools show big change under new plan', *The Connection* (Reston), 7 August 1991, 3.

Changery, Christopher, 'Everybody Pays, Not Everybody Plays: Debate Continues Over the Fairness of Reston Association Fees', *The Connection* (Reston), 29 September 1991, 8–9.

'Chronology' (1987), in *Planned Community Association, Inc., Archives*, Fenwick Library, George Mason University, 1–2.

Cirillo, Anne (1991), 'Commuting Trends of Reston Community', in *Case Study of Reston: Planned Community*, 53–61.

Cleveland, James (1989), Foreword, in Nan Netherton, *Reston: A New Town in the Old Dominion*, Norfolk, VA: The Donning Company, 7–9.

'Cluster Exchange' (1991a), newsletter sponsored by the Reston Association and Cluster volunteers, **2** (1), July/August.

'Cluster Exchange' (1991b), newsletter sponsored by the Reston Association and Cluster volunteers, **2** (2), November/December.

'Community Services' (1991), Reston: Reston Land Corporation.

Crellin, Glenn, 'Candidates committed to Reston', letters, *The Connection* (Reston), 1 April 1992, 23.

Cunningham, Carrington, 'Athletic Club garners support', *The Reston Times*, 1 April 1992, A1, A16.

Day, Bill, 'Directors eye fee change', *Reston Times*, 19 December 1990, A1.

Design Guidelines and Design Review Process (1990), 2nd edn, Reston: Reston Association.

'Design Review Board: Request for Approval' (n.d.), Reston Association.

'Economic Basis for Reston' (1962), Simon Enterprises *et al.*, Box 1, Folder 2, Series 1, Planned Community Archives.

Erten, Orhan (1991), 'Impact of Historical [*sic*] and Archeological Site Preservation on the Reston Master Plan', in *Case Study of Reston: Planned Community*, 1–12.

Fairfax County Homeowners Association Manual (1990), 3rd edn, Fairfax County, Virginia: Department of Consumer Affairs.

Ferris, Rich (1991), 'Clusters Work Together to Reduce Trash Cost', *Cluster Exchange*, **2** (2), November/December, 3–5 (Reston Association).

Flynn, Mark (1989), *Planned Community Archives*, Special Collections and Archives, Fenwick Library, George Mason University.

Governing Documents of the Reston Association (1987), rpt. 1989, Reston: Reston Association.

Graham, Patrick, 'Reston home values drop for second straight year', *Reston Times*, 15 April 1992, 1, 13.

Green, Martha (1992), telephone interview, 29 January.

Grubisich, Tom (1992), telephone interview, 27 January.

Grubisich, Tom and McCandless, Peter (1985), *RESTON: The First Twenty Years*, Reston, VA: Reston Publishing Company.

'Guidelines for the Care and Use of Reston Association's Common Lands', (n.d.), Reston: Reston Association.

Haefer, Sylvia (1992), 'Real estate profile sheets', 23 January, Long & Foster Realtors®, Reston, Virginia.

Halligan, Bettina (1990), 'Vision to Reality: Reston, Virginia', manuscript, Planned Community Archives.

Harris, Mike (1991), 'The Existing Transportation System', in *Case Study of Reston: Planned Community*, 44–52.

Hartnett, Tom (1992a), '1991 Year end report', 17 January, Reston: Reston Association.

Hartnett, Tom (1992b), telephone interview, 29 January.

Homeowners' Association Manual (1990), Prince William County, Virginia, Office of Consumer Affairs.

How To Enjoy Reston (1990), Reston: Reston Association.

Jordan, Mary, 'Fighting the Drug War: From Arizona to Fairfax', *The Washington Post*, 6 November 1988, A1, A22–A23.

Kalmus, Stacy, 'RA assessments stir controversy', *Reston Times*, 30 January 1991, A1.

Kalmus, Stacy, 'Reston divided over RA rollover', *Reston Times*, 25 September 1991, A1.

Keum, Peter (1991), 'Housing Development in Reston, Virginia: Lower Income Housing', in *Case Study of Reston: Planned Community*, 79–90.

Kekhia, Fares (1991), 'Existing Conditions at Reston', in *Case Study of Reston: Planned Community*, 12–15.

Leighton, Joe, 'Leighton outlines positions', letters, *The Connection* (Reston), 1 April 1992, 22.

Lowry, Rich, 'RA election spills into last meeting', *The Connection* (Reston), 1 April 1992, 3, 17.

Lowry, Rich, 'Insurgents pick up RA seats', *The Connection* (Reston), 15 April 1992, 1, 21.

Matthews, Allan (1992), interview, 23 January.

McWhirt, Vicki (1990), 'Reston: New Town, Boom Town', manuscript, Planned Community Archives.

Moore, Patrick (1991), 'Reston: Rezoning for Cluster Developments', in *Case Study of Reston: Planned Community*, 16–27.

Netherton, Nan (1981), 'Reston History: Interviews', 14 April, Reston Land Corporation, Box 16, Folder 1, Planned Community Archives.

Netherton, Nan (1982), 'Interview with Fran Steinbauer' in 'Reston History: Interviews', 28 January, Reston Land Corporation, Box 16, Folder 1, Planned Community Archives.

Netherton, Nan (1989) – see General Bibliography.

Planned Communities, New Towns, and Resort Communities in the U.S. and Canada' (1992), *ULI Project Directory*, #501, Washington, DC: Urban Land Institute.

Planned Community Archives – see listing in 'Organizations'.

Policies and Procedures Manual (1990), Reston: Reston Association.

Pools Usage Study – 1991 (1991), Reston: Reston Association.

Prichard, E.A. (1967), letter to George A. Simpson, 28 June, Gulf-Reston Residential Planned Community Ordinance, File 1, Box 2, Folder 4, Series 2, Planned Community Archives.

Prichard, E.A. (1992), telephone interview, 27 January.

'Protective Covenants (Deed of Dedication of Reston)' (1987), in *Governing Documents of the Reston Association*, 5–14.

'RA candidates answer', *The Connection* (Reston), 25 March 1992, 12–14.

'RCA changes name', *Reston Times*, 22 January 1992, A1.

'Realtor Alert' (1991), Reston: Reston Land Corporation (October).

Redding, Whitney, 'Reston Association Head Quits', *The Washington Post: Fairfax Weekly*, 9 January 1992, Va. 1, 5.

Report to the Reston Community on Governance Options (1988), 29 June, Reston: Reston Governance Task Force, Reston Association.

'Reston' (1991), Reston Land Corporation.

'Reston Athletic Club Marketing Survey Research Results' (1991), 20 June, Goldberg, Marchesano, Kohlman, Inc.

'Reston: Density control under the Residential Planned Community (RPC) Chapter of the Fairfax County Zoning Ordinance' (1970), October, Planning and Engineering Staff, Gulf Reston, Inc., Planned Community Archives.

Reston Handbook (1991), Reston, VA: The Handbook Group.

Saunders, Glenn (1991), 25 February, Lecture, Urban Systems Engineering Class (Syst. 659), Professor Terry Ryan, George Mason University.

Steinbauer, Francis C. (1985) – see General Bibliography.

Strickland, Dave (1991), 'Trash Survey Results', *Cluster Exchange*, **2** (2), November/December, 3–5 (Reston Association).

Summer Planner (1991), Reston: Reston Association.

The New Towns (1987), WETA-TV, Washington, DC, ed. Anthony Black and Bill Coyle, Greater Washington Educational Telecommunications Assn.

'Transportation' (1991), Reston: Reston Land Corporation.

'Twin Branches Nature Trail' (1988), Reston Association Natural Areas Advisory Committee.

Use Covenants and Procedures (1988), Reston: Reston Association.

'User's Guide to the Governing Documents' (1987), in *Governing Documents of the Reston Association*, 1–3.

Vitiello, Daniel J. 'Restonians United four endorsed', letters, *The Connection* (Reston), 1 April 1992, 23.

Yaremchuk, John (1968), 'Types of Plan Approval Required for RPC Districts', 21 May, Memorandum to Planning Commission, Fairfax County, from John Yaremchuk, Director of Planning, Gulf Oil Corporation Records, Gulf-Reston Residential Planned Community Ordinance, File 1, Box 2, Folder 4, Series 2, *Planned Community Archives*.

Your Reston Association Passport (1991), Reston: Reston Association.

Columbia, Maryland

Blimmel, Ann (1992), telephone interview, 27 January, Columbia, MD.
Burkhart, Lynne C. (1981), *Old Values in a New Town: The Politics of Race and Class in Columbia, Maryland*, New York: Praeger Publishers.
Columbia Association: The Purposes, Organization and Financing of a Community Institution (n.d.).
Columbia, Maryland (1990), Columbia, MD: Columbia Marketing Department, The Rouse Company.
Newcomers Guide to Columbia, Maryland (1990), Columbia, MD: Patuxent Publishing.
Parrish, Jane (1992), telephone interview, 27 January.
Six Pages (1990), Columbia, MD: Columbia Association.
The Columbia Association (1990), Columbia, MD: Columbia Association.

Ford's Colony, Virginia

'Bylaws of Ford's Colony at Williamsburg Homeowners Association' (1986).
'Declaration of Protective Covenants' (1985), Ford's Colony at Williamsburg.
'Ford's Colony Fact Sheet' (1990), Ford's Colony, VA: Realtec, Inc.
Homeowners Association Handbook (n.d.), Ford's Colony, Williamsburg, VA.
Overman, Mel (1990), conversation at Ford's Colony, 20 September.

Sawgrass, Florida

'Articles of Incorporation of The Sawgrass Players Club Association, Inc.' (1981), Sawgrass, Florida.
'Declaration of Covenants and Restrictions for Cypress Creek' (1981), Sawgrass, Florida.
'Declaration of Covenants and Restrictions for Sawgrass Village Office Park' (1981), Sawgrass, Florida.
'Declaration of Covenants for The Players Club at Sawgrass' (1981), Sawgrass, Florida.
Metcalf, John G. (1990), letter to Fred Foldvary.

The Woodlands, Texas

Morgan, George T., Jr. and King, John O. (1987), *The Woodlands*, College Station: Texas A & M.

Chapter 13 (St. Louis)

Beito, David T. (1989) – see General Bibliography

Beito, David T. and Smith, Bruce (1990), 'The Formation of Urban Infrastructure Through Nongovernmental Planning: The Private Places of St. Louis, 1869–1920', *Journal of Urban History*, **16** (3), May, 263–303.

Frazier, Marc (1989) [1988] – see General Bibliography

Oakerson, Ronald J. (1989), 'Private Street Associations in St. Louis County: Subdivisions as Service Providers', in Debra Dean (ed.) *Residential Community Associations: private governments in the intergovernmental system?*, Washington, DC: ACIR (Advisory Commission on Intergovernmental Relations), 55–61.

Parks, Roger B. and Oakerson, Ronald J. (1988), *Metropolitan Organization: The St. Louis Case*, M-158. Washington, DC: ACIR (Advisory Commission on Intergovernmental Relations).

Polanyi, Michael (1951) – see General Bibliography.

Savage, Charles C. (1987), *Architecture of the Private Streets of St. Louis*, Columbia: University of Missouri Press.

Schoenberg, Sandra P. and Rosenbaum, Patricia L. (1980), *Neighborhoods That Work*, New Brunswick, NJ: Rutgers University Press.

Organizations

Arden Village, The Highway, Arden, Delaware, 19810.

Columbia Association, 9861 Broken Land Parkway, Suite 300, Columbia, MD 21046.

Community Associations Institute, 1630 Duke Street, Alexandria, VA 22314.

E.F. Schumacher Society, Box 76, RD 3, Great Barrington, MA 01230.

Fort Ellsworth Condominium Association, c/o Condominium Management, 8270 Georgia Ave., Silver Spring, MD 20910.

National Association of Housing Cooperatives, 1614 King Street, Alexandria, VA 22314.

Planned Community Archives: The Reston Collection, Department of Special Collections and Archives, Fenwick Library, George Mason University, Fairfax, Virginia.

Reston Association, 1930 Isaac Newton Square, Reston, VA 22090.

Walt Disney Archives, 500 South Buena Vista Street, Burbank, CA 91521.

Walt Disney World, P.O. Box 10,040, Lake Buena Vista, FL 32830.

Index

access restriction 191, 209
admission 17, 42, 108, 130, 132
  fee a rental charge 132
African-Americans 147, 186, 191
Alaska 33, 39
Alchian, Armen 48
Alexandria 85*n*, 102, 152–6, 159–61
altruism 82–3, 85*n*
anti-historical 5
architecture 98, 101–2, 124, 129–31,
  137, 139, 154, 173–4, 181, 187–8,
  191, 193
Arden village 19, 101, 113–49, 151–2,
  163–4, 166–7, 172, 181, 185, 187,
  208–9
  architecture unrestricted 139
  Ardentown and Ardencroft 147
  clubs 145–6
  committees 141–2
  democracy in 137–8, 141–2, 157
  experiment in contractual community
    134
  a garden city 134, 139–40
  governance 140–41
  hypotheses 134, 136, 139, 144, 146–
    9
  leaseholds 137, 140–41
  and rent 142–4
  sense of community 146
  tests explicit rental funding 134, 139,
    144, 148–9
  see also Fairhope; land trusts; Price,
    Will; Stephens, Frank
assessments
  in capacious clubs 64
  constraints on 202
  to fund associations 6, 100, 143–4,
    154, 158–9, 163–4, 171, 176–7,
    182–4, 187–8, 191
  part of price system 44, 164
  same fee versus *ad valorem* 166, 171,
    177, 183–4, 187–8, 191
  techniques 143–4, 159
asset specificity 45–8, 142, 149, 159, 164

requires board of directors 157
  see also site specificity
associations
  of associations 5, 49–50, 72, 89, 102,
    109, 149, 173, 186–7, 190, 210
  and budgets 29, 142–4, 161–3, 182–
    4, 187
  can be sued 106
  commercial 186, 188
  community 6, 29, 47–8
  contractual *see* associations, civic
  defined 55
  exclusion from 209
  and exit 57, 198
  as firms 45, 48
  goods provision by 5, 25–6, 48, 64,
    87, 103, 198
  and governance *see* governance,
    consensual
  history 101–2
  involve politics 99
  and legal autonomy 208
  of merchants 93
  neighborhood *see* neighborhoods
  non-landed 190
  political 14 .
  and privilege seeking 202
  resolve atomism 109
  taxation of *see* taxes: on associations
  see also associations, civic; club;
    communities, contractual;
    private community; residential
    community associations
associations, civic
  assessments not tax-deductible 104
  based on land administration 91
  and communities 6, 55, 57, 60, 187
  and consensual governance 19, 44–
    51, 57–8, 62, 73, 85, 176–7, 182
  constraints on 199, 202
  dampens transfer seeking 200
  and fractionated titles 91, 97
  funding of 6, 197–8
  a government of governments 60